NAKAGAMI, JAPAN

Nakagami, Japan

. . . .

Buraku and the Writing of Ethnicity

Anne McKnight

University of Minnesota Press
Minneapolis
London

The University of Minnesota Press gratefully acknowledges financial assistance provided for the publication of this book from the Association for Asian Studies First Book Subvention Program and from the College of Letters, Arts, and Sciences, University of Southern California.

Part of the Introduction and chapter 3 previously appeared as "Imperial Syntax: Nakagami Kenji's 'Monogatari' and Modern Japanese Literature as Ethnography," *Discourse: Journal for Theoretical Studies in Media and Culture* 28, no. 1 (Winter 2006): 142–65.

Published by the University of Minnesota Press
111 Third Avenue South, Suite 290
Minneapolis, MN 55401-2520
http://www.upress.umn.edu

Library of Congress Cataloging-in-Publication Data
McKnight, Anne, 1966-
  Nakagami, Japan : *Buraku* and the writing of ethnicity / Anne McKnight.
    p. cm.
  Includes bibliographical references and index.
  ISBN 978-0-8166-7285-1 (hc : alk. paper) — ISBN 978-0-8166-7286-8 (pb : alk. paper)
  1. Nakagami Kenji—Criticism and interpretation. 2. *Buraku* people in literature.
3. Other (Philosophy) in literature. I. Title.

PL857.A3683Z75 2011
895.6'35—dc22   2010032639

Contents

Acknowledgments

This book could not have been signed, sealed, and delivered without the kind dispatches of many friends and colleagues.

Most of this research was conducted under a Japan Foundation grant and further study under Komori Yōichi's direction at Komaba, Tokyo University. Very little of the infrastructure of the project could have been done without the inroads through scholarship and bureaucracy and the camaraderie that Professor Komori made possible.

I thank Brian Bergstrom, Trane Devore, Jonathan Hall, Sharon Hayashi, Chika Kinoshita, Wakako Miyakuni, and Yumna Siddiqi for care, feeding, collaboration, and materials as the manuscript grew into its shape. For feedback at key junctures, I am grateful to William H. Bridges IV, Sunyoung Park, and Christophe Thouny. Two reviewers for the *Journal of Japanese Studies* gave astute and useful suggestions. Kitahara Megumi filled in many contexts between library and life when I lived in Tokyo. Ono Masatsugu enlivened Nakagami's works with his tutorials and kept them in tune with current fiction from all over. Jonathan Sterne, Carolina González, and Ramzi Rouighi provided sources and concepts that would have never occurred to me but were exactly right. Nakagawa Shigemi and his community of students facilitated a year of research at Ritsumeikan, under the auspices of a postdoctoral fellowship from the Japan Society for the Promotion of Science. At McGill, my colleagues made it possible to think generatively and on all cylinders. Since coming to the University of Southern California, David Bialock and Akira Lippit have been unflappably supportive colleagues in word and deed. Alan Tansman has been a model advisor, even after the official fact; he, along with David Roman and Katō Yūji, provided venues for circulating these ideas. Nate Heneghan and Rika Hiro helped make the prose and translations far more hospitable. John Tallmadge deserves many thanks for guidance with the editorial architecture of it all. Rositsa Mutafchieva generously shared her own work and introductions.

Finally, I thank my mother, Lola, and brother Gregory for their support and sustenance, both literal and figural, for all this time.

I Is an Other

Parallax

How do you write yourself into a literature that doesn't seem to know you exist? In 1990, shortly before his death, Nakagami Kenji gave a speech at the Frankfurt Book Fair on precisely that subject. His talk was titled "Am I Japanese?"—a question that may have seemed odd to his listeners, most of whom had come to hear the musings of an "insider" of Japanese literature.[1] Instead, Nakagami presented a parallax view of Japanese literary history and his own place in that world.

In his Frankfurt lecture, Nakagami describes the experience of living between a world of vernacular oral language and the world of written language, a distance that sets him apart from organic and traditional Japanese-ness:

> From the day when my mother brought me to the schoolyard, cherry trees in full bloom, I've been in a fissure between the world of my mother's that I love, the alienated world with no relation to writing (*moji*), and the world of writing. I've felt this reasonless anger stretched across my body and it just made me shake and I am aware it will continue. Since I was eighteen, I have used writing to depict my mother, elder brother, sister, and the actions and speech of the people around. However, sometimes still this anger spouts up. In the world of writing, the world of literature, sometimes I short-circuit this anger and it becomes a full-on critique of modern Japanese literature. To put it in an extreme way, it's because the world of literature, in the rich array of this country's writing systems (*hyōki*), does not include us. And yet we're not outside of it either.[2]

This "fissure" between two worlds is alienation, but it also becomes a privileged point of view, inside neither but looking on both.

Parallax is a concept drawn from the rhetoric of visual art and one that is central to this study. It describes a perspective according to which an object viewed along two different lines of sight is seen through two different but simultaneous interpretations. This book focuses on a key viewing position in modern Japanese literature that is sustained by parallax viewing. These two images are mainstream or canonical Japanese literature and *buraku* literary arts. *Buraku* neighborhoods are the modern spaces where historically outcast residents in Japan live. Their residents, people referred to as *buraku-min*, are Japan's largest minority and make up roughly 2 to 5 percent of Japan's population. For most of the twentieth century, *buraku-min* have been defined as a modern underclass with higher unemployment, lower literacy, poorer housing, and shorter lives than mainstream residents of Japan. The two images of *buraku* and mainstream exist side by side, unresolved; but, like vision, they compose a conceptual interface through which we "see" a material world. I choose this metaphor for three reasons: it resonates with two discourses that shaped Nakagami's use of language; it encompasses his relationship with mixed-media forms; and it revises an important metaphor for modernity, the camera obscura.

Yanase Keisuke's 1901 sociological essay "The Society Outside of Society" offers the first discourse in which we find parallax. Its culturalist argument that *buraku* residents live under social rules distinct from mainstream society would set the pattern for understanding the relation between *buraku* and mainstream culture for the next hundred years.[3] W. E. B. Du Bois's 1897 collection *The Souls of Black Folk* describes double consciousness as the way an African American "is gifted in second-sight in this American world."[4] If the American world in 1897 produced double consciousness as both self-consciousness and the "sense of always looking at one's self through the eyes of others" named by Du Bois, Nakagami's question "Am I Japanese?" suggests that although Japanese fiction has been around for a "hundred years since the Meiji restoration," it has not acknowledged how literature has drawn from *buraku* cultural forms.[5]

A second reason for using a visual metaphor such as parallax in relation to Nakagami's writing is that, late in his life, Nakagami used mixed media forms like manga and photo-prose works to tell stories that situate Japan both domestically and in the context of a global South. Finally, the field of vision shaped by parallax presents a model of identity different from the modernist metaphor of the camera obscura. The camera obscura has been used by philosophers to describe how reality is inverted—and misunderstood—when it is seen through a medium of representation and has a specular relationship to the real.[6] For Marx, for instance, the camera obscura isolates consciousness and separates it from reality. Parallax, in contrast, is not resolved by merely inverting the representation to make the image correspond with the actual object. Rather, the two representations are adjacent to each other, and the field of vision is shaped precisely because there is a difference and an oscillation between the two. This difference, the weight placed on movement and exteriority, places Nakagami in broader conversations about Japanese postmodernity. Carl Cassegard reminds us that Nakagami's long time interlocutor Karatani Kōjin, for instance, argued "that even notions designed to pinpoint the purely 'other' of discourse—such as exteriority or cogito—turn into traps as soon as they are regarded as standpoints."[7] The idea of a standpoint is one Nakagami rejected in his fiction, opting instead for the parallax of his sociologized *buraku* neighborhood and the fictional neologism of the *roji* neighborhood that is a major setting for his works, stressing the distance also between author and text.

In modern Japanese letters, Nakagami was the first and, so far, the only canonical writer to self-identify as a *buraku-min* (person from a *buraku* background). *Nakagami, Japan* explores ways in which Nakagami saw representation in language intimately tied to representation in politics and saw understanding ethnography—literally, the writing of ethnicity—as a way not only to understand modern Japanese literature but to transform it. Nakagami's life and work stand at the intersection of debates over national history, identity, and canon formation that have roiled in Japan since the 1960s. Chief among these is what political philosopher Étienne Balibar calls *differential identity*. To many readers of *Nakagami, Japan*, the most fundamental and constitutive kind of differential identity that anchors us in the world is race.[8] I adapt this concept slightly to refer to the ways that *buraku* identity has been differential with respect to concepts of Japaneseness in the postwar era to deny or advance ideas, narratives, and practices about Japanese multiculturalism that include, but go beyond, race.

Certainly concepts of race, along with ethnicity, have been used to articulate *buraku* collectivity and to refer to processes that are like racism and like racialization. At the same time, at the 2001 United Nations–sponsored Third World Conference Against Racism, Racial Discrimination, Xenophobia, and Related Intolerance, *buraku* activists and other human rights advocates argued that racism alone does not account for all discrimination; moreover, the emphasis on race reproduces Eurocentric ways of knowing by negating

indigenous forms of difference and discrimination.[9] They have argued that
the particularities of their experience may be felt, documented, or combated
like racism but needed to be called by their proper names. This book is an
attempt to map how that differential identity manifested by *buraku* residents
of modern Japan has been written into modern literature and how conventions, insights, and critiques of ethnography—writing ethnicity—have
shaped a modern but non-Western body of prose fiction.

For Nakagami, the institutional name of *kokubungaku,* national literature, crystallizes the formal academic structures that place *buraku* cultural
production outside of Japanese literature. In my reading, *kokubungaku* is
shorthand for elements of authority that have made up the study of literature since academic departments of Japanese literary studies were
founded and anthologies compiled in the 1890s.[10] Nakagami's literary
formation and popularity took shape largely outside of formal academic
institutions, but *kokubungaku* encompasses the books, journals, curricula,
publishing, and professionalized ways that writers, critics, and readers
understand Japanese literature and adjudicate what belongs in it. This category, more than the restricted field of prose fiction or even the novel, provides Nakagami a frame within which he can identify how representation
of mainstream and peripheral identities, differential identities, have been
excluded but still underwrite fiction in modern Japan.

In the postwar era, *buraku* activists have published anthologies and
polemics to lay out their stances on culture's role in politics—in other
words, to create a literary criticism on their own terms emerging out of
the postwar *buraku* liberation movement. They used the word *bungei,* or
literary arts, rather than *bungaku,* the formal institution of literature. This
phrasing still refers to the written word. But as I explore in chapter 1, *bungei*
accommodates genres like oration and screenplays, ones that traverse
both oral and written registers and also allow a parallax reading between
fictional and nonfictional materials. My reason for focus on *bungei,* rhetoric, and allusion in this book on *kokubungaku* is that these more expansive
terms better register the ethnographic conventions from both oral and
written realms that cross literary and extraliterary realms to inform the
semantics, narratives, and intertextual constants of literature.

Ethnography has been understood by anthropologists of Japan as gathering information on site, from and about human informants.[11] Recent critiques of the rhetorical workings of ethnography by anthropologists have
focused on how ethnographic authority is created and how subjectivity

and objectivity are intimately mingled even in the most archscholarly writings.[12] Insofar as academics with experience in fieldwork tell us that ethnography is writing that places "the researcher's role and interactions methodologically and rhetorically as a centerpiece and touchstone for the analysis," it is self-reflexive.[13] Most meditations on fieldwork, however, are offered by writers who are professionally employed as researchers in fields such as anthropology and sociology. The ethnographic dimensions I underscore in Nakagami's work are slightly different.

Certainly he is aware of the classical anthropological conversations on participant observation. His most overtly fieldwork-oriented writings feature authoritative references to fieldwork and its founders such as Bronislaw Malinowski.[14] But although he draws on concepts from scholarly writings, Nakagami is an autodidact fiction writer working in an era when studies of myth, folklore, anthropology, and structuralism were popularized and made available in cheap editions in Japan to an extent unparalleled in Euro-American contexts. Works like anthropologist Yamaguchi Masao's studies of kingship in Nigeria and Japan or Claude Lévi-Strauss's elegies on disappearing "primitive" civilizations were widely read in the flush economy of 1970s print culture in Tokyo. Nakagami happened to be interested in how narrative worked in fields other than literature at the very time when popularizers of structuralism looked for universal cultural rules, ones whose articulation had the effect of deterritorializing disciplines and fields.

Unlike many professional ethnographers, Nakagami never completely steps away from being a participant in either the literary field or the field of *buraku* representation by opting into a purely clinical "observer" position on either side. His nonfiction works freely employ the word *buraku* as a real historic referent with cultural associations, but as we will see in later chapters, his fiction works draw on cultural forms that describe or come from *buraku* contexts without ever using the word *buraku*. Instead, he invents a fictional topos, a neighborhood called the *roji*. This is considered by most critics to be the most compelling—or, to activists, the most disappointing—element of his work. According to Hirano Hidehisa, author of the most far-ranging history of *buraku* representations in literature, Nakagami never attached the actual word *buraku* to any of the euphemisms of "that" or "there"; nor did he do so in any of his reportage, essays, writings, or lectures that clearly have the *roji* as their subject.

Hirano finds the omission of "*buraku*" to be "one of the *raisons d'être* for Nakagami's way of representing the literature of the *buraku*."[15] But a later critic, Suiheisha Museum Director Moriyasu Toshiji, argues to the contrary. He contrasts Nakagami's work to *The Broken Commandment* (*Hakai*), a 1906 work by Shimazaki Tōson, which functions as the foundational work about *buraku* characters and themes in both *kokubungaku* and *buraku* literary criticism. "Even before people knew about his origin, without a doubt the *roji* that appears in his works was interpreted as a *buraku* . . . His works had 'meat' on their bones. Many other works, beginning with Shimazaki's character Ushimatsu in *The Broken Commandment,* have contained *buraku* characters, but they had no meat on their bones."[16] By noting that some readers knew how to interpret the *roji* as a *buraku*, Moriyasu suggests the role played by a discursive reader, someone familiar with both the ways Nakagami works with received traditions of Japanese literature *and* familiar with *buraku* rhetorical conventions, who can thus see what is at stake in the discourse in connection with wider social conversations. I argue that such a parallax writing for two audiences is achieved because it draws on an archive of themes and figural language I will call "*buraku* rhetorical activism."

In my view, as I develop over the course of the book, the "lack" that many see in the missing link between *roji* and *buraku* has a function that neither activists nor literary critics have accounted for. Indeed, it is the very function of resisting a function or standpoint that would also fix the relation between author and text. *Buraku* characters in fiction have often been slandered, abjected, and confined, as literary critic Watanabe Naomi says, in a system of signifiers that are interchangeable and whose lock on the signified has changed very little since the late Meiji period.[17] While the reformist impulse to counter pathological pictures (criminality, excessive wealth, physical deformity, and illness) has motivated writers such as Shimazaki, it has resulted in characters so hyperredemptive; beautiful; or, as I explore in chapter 1, self-disciplined that they can literally no longer live in Japan and be "themselves." *The Broken Commandment*'s hero, for example, flees to Texas after confessing his identity in a Meiji-era elementary school. The price for assimilation in the canon of *kokubungaku* is another kind of exile. So, on one hand, I read the "failure" to assimilate as a deliberate gesture. In my opinion, the opaque nature of the *roji* forces readers to narrate the blur, as it were. Nakagami wants readers to make the connection between text and world, rather than giving it to them. In that process of narration, they too become written as collaborative coproducers into the kinds of knowledge making that have composed the text. The archival nature of Nakagami's texts is apparent in his plundering from folklore and myths of nation building, his emphasis on dialect, and his characters' consciousness of their legacies of property, both material and intellectual.

Beginning with *The Cape* (*Misaki*; 1975), Nakagami started to rewrite an entire system of national literature through rewriting the narrative operations of its foundational myths. The name for this assemblage is the *Kishū saga*, named after the area in southwest Japan where it is set. Three central works of the saga center on the story of a construction worker in his twenties, Akiyuki, and are called by critics the Kishū trilogy. The first of these, *The Cape*, is set during the postwar building boom. The saga traces Akiyuki's attempts to come to terms with staying in the same place, the hemmed-in, claustrophobic but familiar *roji*, as all around him things change, people move, and money flows. One of his most significant relationships is with Hamamura Ryūzō, the nouveau riche father who abandoned him as a child. "That man," as Akiyuki calls Hamamura, is an interloper to the town, came on the scene, and started to build a real estate empire "from the bone of who knows what horse."[18] He creates and monumentalizes a half-fake resistance hero from the Tokugawa era, Mago-ichi, giving tribute to his ancestor and marking the inspiration for his plan. The Mago-ichi statue recalls battles where Buddhist monks and outcast members of their sect rioted against centralizing state authority in the 1570s. Where the riots against Oda Nobunaga (who first brought the warring factions of the sixteenth century into a quasi-national formation) ended in mass slaughter and defeat, Hamamura taunts the town by revisiting history and turning the tables to win. Hamamura's drive to control the real estate market and legitimate his empire with a mythical hero literally redraws the map of social mobility in the town. The trilogy conveys an antifoundational message against fetishizing modern "origins" by making Hamamura despondent and ultimately suicidal. The message is that profound economic developments are transforming capitalism and that Hamamura's nostalgia for modern origins cannot survive.

These transformations occur through Akiyuki. He digs blissfully in nature and worksites for what seems to be hundreds of pages but never builds anything taller than a foundation. His stubborn digging is the narrative countermovement to his father's towering monument. He is less a vessel than a force. We have little access to his consciousness, which seems never to transform. In fact, the interlude that should be his time of deepest reflection is kept off screen. At the end of *The Sea of Withered Trees* (*Karekinada*; 1977), he kills his half brother in a fit of rage. Sent away to jail for three years, that interval is a mere ellipsis between two books, not a catalyst of any sort and certainly no prompt to self-knowledge. His story excavates and links laterally to other texts rather than moving upward to a transcendental myth. Akiyuki claims his identity owes to the collective space of the *roji*, not to his parents: to a place of exchange, not descent. In the second and third volumes of the Kishū trilogy, *The Sea of Withered Trees* and *The Ends of the Earth, Supreme Time* (*Chi no hate, shijō no toki*; 1983), the *roji* begins to accumulate a great conceptual weight. It starts to mean something like a community—a set of relationships, experiences, stories, and cultural rules. In Nakagami's late works, it becomes detachable from Shingū altogether. It begins to refer to neighborhoods that are analogized to the Japanese *roji* but are located in far-flung Asian locales and places in the global South, or even in trailers filled with *roji* residents as they tour the Cotton Road of rural industrialization in *The Wings of the Sun* (*Nichirin no tsubasa*; 1984) on the way to visit the imperial palace.[19]

The *roji* is a point of crossing with different waves of characters and stories, many of which are maintained in memory and transmitted by elderly women. Many of the characters who are sent away to work, who pass through, who narrate their personal monocular histories of the *roji*, recur from book to book. With each new appearance, they add new information, new family connections, and new grudges that reorient the reader's overall understanding of the world of the *roji* and the histories it narrates. Each addition not only provides new "content," or information, but changes the differential relations between the respective parts of the preexisting story. For example, Akiyuki's oedipal grudge fuels how we understand his father Hamamura's amoral rise as a black market entrepreneur in the 1976–77 works, early parts of the *Kishū saga*. In contrast, *Forget-Me-Not* (*Hōsenka*; 1980), the work told through Akiyuki's mother Fusa's experiences, associates Hamamura's betrayal of Fusa with his drive for upward mobility. The novel contrasts her own work as a peddler dealing face-to-face with people with Hamamura's investment in a larger economy and sentimentalizes Fusa's direct, unmediated relationships between people. The angles of parallax through which readers understand characters, track the development of the *roji*, and attribute agency and motivation are, in turn, realigned with each work.

Midway through the saga, Nakagami begins to publish nonfictional essays. In *Kumano Stories* (*Kumano-shū*; 1978), short fictions about the *roji* alternate with diary-like essays about redevelopment of the *buraku* he grew up in. The landscape had been considerably changed by construction that used *dōwa* (assimilation, a name that indicates national government funding) money from the 1969 allocation of national funds for improving living conditions in *buraku* nationwide, the Special Measures Law for Assimilation Projects. The nonfictional essays describe a state of stuckness and longing. This is conveyed through Nakagami's ambivalence about growing up in the *buraku*, where he longed to be an aesthete, listening to classical music and growing flowers, pastimes his family had no patience with, as their upward mobility took different forms like building a house outside of the *buraku*. The fictional chapters are full of time travel, as modern characters slip into premodern textual spaces and styles, and the narrative voice assumes the floating quality of classical *monogatari* tales, stories written beginning in the eighth century that retain oral elements and may be made from multiple narrative sources. Fiction and biography, *roji* and *buraku* are juxtaposed in *Kumano Stories,* but Nakagami never synthesizes the two.

Further distinguishing him from scholarly traditions of ethnography is the fact that Nakagami steered clear of formal *buraku* protest movements, even when they successfully mobilized in the 1960s to create influential legislation for social welfare programs. As a social movement, *buraku* efforts at self-determination began after World War I. Dissatisfied with government outreach efforts at harmonization (*yūwa*) after World War I that linked social welfare funding to mechanisms of social control, *buraku-min* started organizing nationally. The name of that first national association, organized in 1922, was the Suiheisha, or Levelers' Association.

In its heyday of the 1920s, the Suiheisha mandate worked to effect social and economic leveling so that the *buraku-min* it represented did not experience the negative effects of socioeconomic parallax—in other words, that their access to rights of citizenship was not qualitatively different from other citizens' access. The Suiheisha *did* advocate a parallax view, however, when placed in an international field of vision. Its program of ethnic self-determination asserted a right to be both *buraku* and Japanese—and, beyond that, to be both human and internationalist. The postwar reformulation of the Suiheisha, the *Buraku* Liberation League (*Buraku kaihō dōmei*, hereafter BLL), led a successful grassroots movement in the 1960s to legislate and fund substantial social welfare projects.

By the mid-1970s, when Nakagami's career took off, Japan had entered the socioeconomic phase many cultural critics refer to as neoliberalism. Geographer David Harvey calls this phase "above all a project to restore class dominance to sectors that saw their fortunes threatened by the ascent of social democratic endeavors in the aftermath of the Second World War."[20] But like most treatises of neoliberalism, with their clear subtext of women's and civil rights and postcolonial demands, Harvey's does not account for the full complexity of how those "social endeavors" might occur in a place whose point of reference is not the United States or the United Kingdom. Japan is the world's third largest economy (at this writing) and the world's largest overseas investor.[21] The postwar *buraku* activist movement is arguably the most successful grassroots social movement in postwar Japan.

By the late 1970s, the *buraku* activist movement decided that economic and legal success needed to be supplemented by culture to counter the negative and heavily freighted images of *buraku* residents and neighborhoods. These flared in places ranging from avant-garde poetry journals to new rules on discriminatory language at newspapers and TV stations. Activists and movement critics placed a new emphasis on culture, specifically on language as a field of power. This heightened attention to language was added to the issue of literacy that was already a concern.[22] Activists and writers affiliated with the BLL developed a philosophy of a liberation literature that expressed their autonomy and will to self-determination. The new emphasis on culture occurred just as Nakagami became the first canonical writer in Japanese literature to self-identify as a *buraku-min* at the height of his career as he lived in the limelight of Tokyo's literary star system.

As he became more publicly engaged with *buraku* issues, Nakagami changed gears. During his most productive period of writing, in the late 1970s and early 1980s, he altered the themes and even the media that composed his fictional works. Until the 1977 publication of the work regarded as his triumph, *The Sea of Withered Trees*, he had set many works in the region of Kumano and had indeed narrated many as *boku*, or I. After *The Sea of Withered Trees*, he began to emphasize the critical and social elements of his writing and to bring in extraliterary contexts to frame characters in forgotten, oral, or foreign contexts. He also traveled widely and lived in Seoul, Iowa City, and Los Angeles. He conducted a wide variety of experiments in genre, voice, and comparison. Most of these contexts are ethnographic, concerned with writing ethnicity into mainstream accounts of literature, often in comparative contexts that look at Japanese literature and the flaws of *kokubungaku* in light of other national literatures, especially fiction and performing arts from Korea and the United States. In 1979, he began rewriting a critical history of Japanese literature by writing about five writers who emphasized orality, myth, and elements of "otherness" that introduce new narrative forms and kinds of storytelling: novelists Satō Haruo, Enchi Fumiko, and Tanizaki Jun'ichirō; folklorist Orikuchi Shinobu; and Edo-period writer Ueda Akinari. These essays were published in the prestigious literary journal *National Literature (Kokubungaku)*. At the same time, he undertook a number of trips bankrolled by popular magazines to places from Peshawar to Davao, doing site visits ranging from Alex Haley's Culver City office near Los Angeles to Korean mask drama performances. Closer to home, he wrote a series of reportage articles on *buraku* in the Kishū region of the country that he visited on a six-month road trip around his home region.

Nakagami came into direct conflict with the BLL in 1978, shortly after he finished his reportage tour of Kishū. Breaking away from the Shingū BLL, he started an organization in his old neighborhood of Kasuga. While the BLL was primarily interested in getting rid of substandard housing and building better facilities, Nakagami opted to organize youth under the umbrella of culture. He invited a series of lecturers, writers from Tokyo, to give talks in a *buraku* neighborhood in Shingū, which he introduced with remarks on Japanese literature and discrimination.[23] The talks were cancelled after eight sessions when a garbage workers' strike broke out in Shingū; since four members of the youth group were involved in the strike, the group fizzled. Nakagami published a statement in the *Mainichi shinbun*, the most populist of Japan's major newspapers. He protested that BLL members had misunderstood the relation between culture and politics that his program represented. BLL members had argued that hosting Ishihara Shintarō, the present mayor of Tokyo and biggest draw of the eight lecturers, revealed the right wing leanings of the lecture series. Moreover, they said that the youth culture group had nothing to do with liberation and was only concerned with literature.[24]

The fifty-volume anthology of *buraku* literature, *Collection of Bungei Works on Buraku Issues (Buraku mondai bungei sakuhin senshū)* was published between 1973 and 1980, as Nakagami's career was at its peak and he took his first steps into the activist realm. The minimal presence of

Nakagami himself in the ongoing composition of *buraku* literary criticism is striking. In the two-volume chronology of *Images of the Buraku in Modern Japanese Literature* (*Bungaku no naka no hisabetsu buraku-zō*, 1980–82), his name appears at the very back, just before an overview of historical novels. Nakagami's own contributions to movement publications are similarly slim. His 1983 essay "Children, As They Are" ("*Ki no mama no kora*") was the only work explicitly published in a *buraku* publication, *Liberation Education* (*Kaihō kyōiku*).[25] Like the Frankfurt speech, it describes a bittersweet relation to being a second generation *buraku* resident living in the fissure between oral and written cultures with access to both but fully present in neither. The relations were tepid between Nakagami and *buraku* cultural activists, but the archival impulse is the same: to excavate and contextualize texts and tropes in the broad arena of *bungei* to establish the terms of *buraku* cultural forms and literary criticism and transform the definition of mainstream Japanese literature.

Since Nakagami's death, treatment of *buraku*-related issues in his collected works is also slight, amounting to a few items including his 1976 reportage, *Kishū: Stories of Country of Trees, Country of Roots* (*Kishū: ki no kuni, ne no kuni monogatari*), from a six-month road trip around *buraku* neighborhoods near his hometown; the announcement of his lecture series in the Shingū *buraku*; and *Kumano Stories*, a collection that alternates first-person reportage about Shingū *buraku* with fictional stories in the worlds of oral folklore that are set in the same place but called by the premodern name of Kumano, the reference that occurs in folklore and connects the same space to a different set of intertexts. What are most missing are writings that construct a literary criticism that links *buraku* issues to *kokubungaku* by assuming a discursive reader. The lectures Nakagami gave to preface the lectures of visiting writers only appeared in a separate volume in 2000. The visiting writers' texts do not appear at all. The roundtables held by the three organizers of the lecture series from the *buraku* were collected and published in 1994 as "Roundtable: The Culture Association and Young Nakagami Kenji." But these materials were not compiled in media that registered on the national radar.

Buraku movement activities are often intensely local, owing to the highly specific nature of incidents of discrimination grounded in struggles that precipitate from local occupational, religious, and social histories. By and large, the critics who blasted Nakagami for "throwing off the quotation marks" of being a *buraku* writer (*kako o furiharatta*) were not local

critics but critics who saw *buraku* issues on a national scale.[26] *Buraku* critics' frustration was heightened because Nakagami was a formidable interlocutor in postwar Japanese print culture. Two volumes of roundtables
were anthologized while he lived, and seven were published by 2009 and
included everyone from writers like Ōe Kenzaburō, Enchi Fumiko, Kim
Chi-ha, and John Irving to performers like filmmaker Kitano Takeshi and
enka singer Miyako Harumi, not to mention scholars like Jacques Derrida
and Asada Akira. His access to national frameworks could have publicly
linked the many local struggles that clustered under the national banner of
a highly diverse group of constituents and made him a powerful ally connecting culture to politics.

Nakagami, Japan argues that Nakagami did indeed write the *buraku* into
national cultural forms and was profoundly concerned with writing ethnography into mainstream literary venues but that he refused to take on the
mantle of representation that activists desired. Throughout his career, and
with maddening frequency, Nakagami would sidestep the role of representative or spokesperson and make statements like "from the time of the Akutagawa
Prize, you could say that all my works were about the *buraku*. Then again,
you could say that they weren't."[27] The metaphor of parallax allows us to
engage a doubled reading of his work both as high literature (*jun bungaku*)
and as a part of a systematic cultural engagement with the representation of
buraku-min, their neighborhoods, and the forms their representation took in
literary history. The term of parallax also allows us to understand how Nakagami can be in conflict with the literary mandate of the activist movement
yet understand its desire to represent politically through representing in cultural forms that most certainly had a life in the public eye. While Nakagami
and the activist movement departed on their approaches to philosophy and
literary genre, they both understood clearly that living and writing in modern Japan and engaging with the critical idiom of *buraku* identity meant seeing yourself as both a subject *and* as an object.

Nakagami approached the ability to see one's self as both subject and
object as something written into the very structure of language itself—
and, by extension, written into the very structure that organized, archived,
and authorized Japanese literature, *kokubungaku*. Nakagami often quoted
poet Arthur Rimbaud's statement that "the self is not a sightseer (*kensha*),
I is an other."[28] That line flaunts a grammatical glitch that demonstrates
this possibility. Grammatically, while this Japanese sentence makes sense
as a pure declarative ("*watashi wa tasha de aru*" ["I am an other"]), the

speaker in the French original (*"Je est un autre"*) refers to something that can actually only be spoken with authority by someone else. To be defined as a subject is also to be defined as an object. This otherness is not possible to speak directly by using Japanese syntax. The fact that the disconnect between grammatical subject and object can only be brought in elliptically in translation is an ironic illustration of the problem that confronts this writer. The relationality that is needed for the epigraph to be meaningful in that clause takes us from the intimate to the institutional, linking Nakagami's personal and singular story to broader intellectual maps.

Nakagami, Japan is an effort to see how Nakagami did this in two phases and worked to transform how Japanese literature saw itself both in domestic and international contexts. The first cluster of works I treat were published in the 1960s through the early 1980s and situate parallax in terms of being both a *buraku* writer *and* a Japanese writer. The second, later cluster provides a bridge to understanding parts of Japan in comparative context with other places of the global South. In the 1980s until his 1992 death, Nakagami wrote as a *buraku* Japanese writer *and* as someone in search of broader solidarities outside Japan, in an unevenly developed world, a primarily southern and Asian world. In these later works set in Korea and elsewhere in Asia, his status as both a subject and an object is very different than it is in the local and national scales of Japan. If parallax makes us aware of how a viewing position defines and limits what you can see, it also makes us aware of how profoundly relational any act of interpretation is. Nakagami's writing makes us aware of the multiple identities that can exist within one writer and of the constant work required to keep both in focus at the same time. He concluded his Frankfurt talk by describing his work as the response to a challenge to invent a new kind of writing that shuttles between these places. *Nakagami, Japan* shows the contexts and debates that made Nakagami's techniques for writing his own "off-kilter" (*okashi*) language into mainstream Japanese literature new and significant.[29] It shows how his experiments in postmodernist literary historiography departed from the mandate that postwar literature about the *buraku* find meaning within self-consciousness. It also shows how his work created new ways of linking Japanese literature to international issues and contexts. Each chapter focuses on one way Nakagami chose to critique, visibly abandon, or rewrite the existing edifice of Japanese literary history through its relation to ethnography.

As I examine how the concept of parallax is structured into Nakagami's writing and its reworking of Japanese national literature, I hope to expand the ways in which we, postwar readers, read and situate Nakagami's fiction as well as the ways English language readers can encounter Japanese literature. Unlike writers and thinkers about Japanese identity and ethnicity in the prewar era who discoursed loudly and often about the multiple ethnic origins of Japanese people, in the postwar era, an idea of Japan as a homogenous middle-class society has prevailed.[30] This has happened largely by means of ideas of *Nihonjin-ron* (theories of Japanese-ness) encouraged in international contexts that stressed that Japan was a monoculture.[31] But as class stratification reemerges in the economic downturn of the 1990s and the birth rate hits its peak and declines as of 2007, thinking about difference is no longer anachronistic or something to contemplate elsewhere. The new working-poor *precariat* (the Japanese word for a class of precarious proletariat and salaried workers who now make up some 30 percent of Japan's employed work force) class and new immigrants present new kinds of identity that challenge the idea of a monoculture. Nakagami, as a *buraku* writer, was exceptional in his attempts to write and talk about difference on his own terms and to transform the terms of the mainstream. In order to understand his position vis-à-vis the orthodox literary world, it is useful to first survey some key ways in which language was meaningful in establishing what writers, historians, bureaucrats, and activists thought it meant to write the *buraku*.

The Chapters

To account for the ethnographic elements of Nakagami's works, we have to look beyond his fictional writings to the historical and rhetorical conventions in the extraliterary sources upon which he drew, and in which he appeared, that make parallax reading possible. These writings connect the operations of ethnography to social worlds in twentieth-century Japan. Each chapter of *Nakagami, Japan* focuses on one feature of language used in the service of bringing the literary and the ethnographic together to show their mutual dependence.

The first chapter deals with the prehistory of Nakagami's work, which I call the archive of *buraku* rhetorical history. This chapter provides a context for my in-depth treatment of Nakagami's works and gives a brief discussion of the theoretical framework of the book. I approach issues of literary history and political representation through close, rhetorical readings of foundational works of *buraku* historiography and essays. I show how many of these texts were written with comparison in mind, across class, race, status, and ethnic groups. I look at an archive of *buraku* rhetorical activism that was constructed through state nomenclatures, a key manifesto, and examples of *buraku* historiography that put the task of becoming historical at the center of the actions envisioned by these works. I call these people who thought, wrote, and debated "rhetorical activists" to emphasize the performative dimension of the highly idealistic work they did. Some were educated formally; some were well-traveled autodidacts; and some trafficked with the most prominent intellectuals of the day. All the rhetorical activists saw history in terms of class and ethnicity (*minzoku*), following on post–World War I movements of ethnic self-determination. They distanced themselves from the Meiji-era idea of race (*jinshu*) because it was used to refer to people of foreign origins and implied that *buraku-min* were not Japanese and had no part in shaping the nation-state or making claims on it. All of them were interested in writing *buraku* history into a national history.

Chapter 1 also provides a brief account of literary criticism of the *buraku,* which encompassed many forms of writing and rhetoric beyond the purely literary. This includes the collective, sometimes anonymous, of collaborative works of historians, manifesto writers, and orators who transmit culture into the field of politics, exercising what I call "linguistic sovereignty." By this I mean the use of language as a model for retooling political representation in tandem with a shift from state sovereignty and collaborationist social welfare groups to self-determination.[32] I conclude with a treatment of a 1963 novel by a *buraku* "insider" Hijikata Tetsu, a newspaper editor and cultural activist who published an avant-garde novel, *Rhizome* (*Chikakei*). *Rhizome* is the only novel explicitly about the *buraku* by a self-identified *buraku* writer to win critical acclaim before Nakagami appeared.

In chapter 2, I contend that a flare-up of discriminatory representations of the *buraku* in the mid-1970s prompted both Nakagami and the liberation movement to develop a critique of *buraku* representation based on rethinking the scope and forms of culture. Both approaches focused on the pathologizing effects of confession in literature, journalism, and the courts. Both also addressed the discursive reader, one who moves through different domains of culture, albeit in different ways.

Following the All Romance Incident of 1951, movement activists tended to focus on the semantic level of words, specific references, and the idiom of

realism.[33] The incident referred to a story called "Specially-Marked *Buraku*,"
(*Tokushu buraku*) published in the pulp magazine *All Romance* and set in
a *zainichi* (resident) Korean neighborhood. The story featured a doctor
whose vocation licensed a lurid naturalistic examination of the living conditions and conflicts of the neighborhood. Tomotsune Tsutomu argues
that the story was more directly about the suspicion of communism in
occupation-era Japan in the early years of the Korean War. But irrespective
of the actual story, in practice, the effect of the incident was that protest by
a Kyoto activist group established a policy "under which anyone using any
term that *buraku* people could regard as containing insulting nuances . . .
would be forced to apologize."[34] In contrast to such direct action against
semantics that uses realism to produce policy results, Nakagami tends to
work more in the realm of narrative, questioning the contexts through
which prose fiction acquires the authority of realism. The works I examine
include examples from fine fiction (*jun bungaku*) and popular literature
and the long and highly publicized proceedings of a lengthy trial called
the Sayama *saiban*, which prosecuted a *buraku* youth for the rape and murder of a schoolgirl. The key point in this chapter is that culture, in the era
of high-speed economic growth that characterized the 1960s through the
1970s, is perceived to have effects seen across a range of high- and low-
culture texts as well as in the legal system and is increasingly important
as an area in which politics transpires. While the time period in which
this change takes place is often called by the names of information society
(*jōhō shakai*) or postmodern society, Nakagami is interested in how the
particular character of the *buraku* in this time of rapid change is unrepre-
sented, an omission that occurs because of particular relations with writing and reprises patterns of ethnography that date back to the Meiji era.

Chapter 3 pursues the theoretical models that Nakagami employed to
understand what he calls "'imperial' syntax" ('tennō' no shintakusu) or the
arrangement of mainstream and *buraku* within linguistic and cultural structures to privilege the former while exiling but remaining dependent on the
latter.[35] I look at how Nakagami places *monogatari*, or narrative storytelling,
with an emphasis on oral culture, at the center of this understanding in a
series of reportage works, narrative documentaries based on fieldwork that
tap into histories of writing on poverty. These works represent Nakagami's
fieldwork in oral culture and what I call "open-source history." This chapter draws on Chris Kelty's work on the cultural significance of free software
as "a set of practices for the distributed collaborative creation of software

source code that is then made openly and freely available."[36] My particular take on "open source code" refers to the materials in folk knowledge and stories conveyed in a form that leaves certain key elements open for substitutability and scaling. In other words, specific referential units that are part of collaboratively created or shared knowledge, such as places' names or people's names, are subject to change within larger descriptions of structures, enabling comparisons that lace across geographic spaces without fixing specific contents. When Nakagami listens to *buraku* residents tell stories or talks to other authors familiar with performing histories, the substitution of diverse elements into similar narratives connects local contexts in different regional or national scales in ways that show the limits of thinking in terms of a national literary tradition (*kokubungaku*). I examine how Nakagami uses comparative ideas of fieldwork and language from anthropology, the tradition of leftist investigative reportage, research in oral history from Alex Haley, and techniques for using figural language common among *buraku* activists. I show how the idea of "imperial syntax," derived from structuralist ideas about language, works as a model for social life at large and connects text and society, past and present, and the peripheral regions of local South and foreign South. From this point in the book, the category of the South works on multiple scales and takes on a greater weight as Nakagami turns to writing and travel in Asia and the South Seas and Pacific Islands.

Chapter 4 is dedicated to showing how Nakagami's dissatisfaction with leftist student movements in 1968 led to cross-cultural comparison and a turn to thinking in terms of racialization, the effects of marking differential identity that work like racial categories. I examine how Nakagami sought to dramatize the experience of discrimination by comparing how differential identity situates fictional characters in similar situations across national and linguistic lines when those relationships are explicitly sociological, diplomatic, and interracial. To this end, I explore Nakagami's first nationally known novella, *On the Japanese Language* (*Nihongo ni tsuite*; 1968). I show how he uses figural language grafted from or shared with some specific African American writers (James Baldwin and Ralph Ellison) to develop imagined anticolonial solidarities along South–South rather than East–West lines.

By examining a range of Nakagami's writings on Korea, chapter 5 continues to look at the idea of the South, Southern in its late-developing status as Nakagami depicts it in essays, in a novel, and in photo-prose collaborations. I show how Nakagami's treatment of time, direct contact, and violence in the Korean version of South underwrites his envy of Korea's ability to preserve Southernness as a vitalism within modernity where Japan failed.

Chapter 6 concludes the book by examining the surprising attention in the new millennium to Nakagami's subculture works, a comic and a genre novel. Nakagami's subculture works had been downplayed in the initial phase of his canonization in the late 1990s when he was framed in terms of high literature, as "Japan's last writer."[37] But they raise questions about Japanese nationalism and its pan-Asian history at the same time that right-wing revisionist histories like Kobayashi Yoshinori's *Manifesto of Arrogance* (*Gōmanizumu sengen*) are flourishing in mainstream subculture, presenting a kind of community that spurns Kobayashi's neonationalism but is ambivalent about the specific form sovereignty takes.[38] This chapter sets Ōtsuka Eiji's and Azuma Hiroki's interest in subculture works against a backdrop of debates about the relations between high literature and subculture. Nakagami's works play only a cameo role in this tectonic shift between mediums and the kinds of markets and literacies that fiction, manga, and anime demand. But the new emphasis on his popular works does bring to the fore issues of differential identity that had been largely ignored by critics who elevated him as a writer of high-literary fiction. In terms of their engagement with Japan's relation to empire, to perpetrator guilt, and to works of literature that imagine parallel worlds—such as the *roji*—I argue that his subculture works ask the reader to imagine identity as a parallax form, one that revisits past historical forms and refers to contemporary social forms. Before we proceed to look briefly at some of the main concepts that organize the book, it is useful to look at some of the coordinates of Nakagami's life.

Punctuating a Life

Born in 1946, the first year after the Second World War ended, Nakagami lived a life that he describes in terms of a parallax of generations. He would grow up to be the first Akutagawa Prize–winning writer born after World War II. But no one else in his family could read. As he remarks in the only article he ever published in a *buraku* movement publication, he was a beneficiary of the leveling experienced by the first generation of children born after the war.[39] School curricula were revised; "human rights" were guaranteed by Article 11 of the Constitution; and literacy was expected of all children.[40] On public occasions, with perhaps a touch of self-mythology, Nakagami would describe how his family spent the money for school supplies "given by the city, or the prefecture, or the country" for their daily needs.[41] He describes being asked at school to draw a picture with a crayon and realizing his mother didn't know that was a part of the school curriculum. He raced home to get money to buy the crayons, and, when it came up short at the stationary store, the elderly shopkeeper let him have the crayons at a discount. He writes that from that day forward, the "cheap crayon" is the stuff his literature consists of, even to the present day.[42] In fact, the only book that was in the family's house while he was growing up was a copy of French naturalist Jean-Henri Fabré's classic picture book, *Scenes from the Life of Insects*, left by his brother who had committed suicide.[43]

By the time he finished high school, Nakagami had befriended a student who was a classic literature-obsessed youth (*bungaku seinen*).[44] On top of the four favorite writers of his high school days, fiction writers Ōe Kenzaburō and Ishihara Shintarō, critic Etō Jun and sci-fi writer Kaikō Takeshi, he had thoroughly read the works of contemporary avant-garde poets Tanikawa Shuntarō and Irisawa Yasuo.[45] In these models I see early signals of Nakagami's ultimate interest: relinking literature and ethnography in the modern novel with reference to realism and to fantastic fiction. Nakagami burned through the works of Sade and Genet and attended a lecture by Ōe Kenzaburō. He began to write poetry when he encountered the works of Arthur Rimbaud.[46]

Nakagami's poetry is often characterized as a phase of youthful dabbling that served as a stepping stone to longer narrative works, followed by a turn to haiku in middle age, an interest largely ignored by metropolitan critics.[47] This reading tends to overvalue the extravagance of Rimbaud's poetry and his voyage to a lurid death in mysterious and unsavory colonial circumstances. We also forget that he is perhaps the most ethnographic of canonical nineteenth-century French poets and one dedicated to using language for self-transformation.[48] Rimbaud is a precedent for Nakagami's interest in themes of racial history in poetics as well as questions of origin and inheritance and the transformative powers of language. Flawed entries in national anthologies of culture will be a staple of Nakagami's later stories and commentaries, as I explore in chapter 2. Rimbaud's poems in *A Season in Hell* gloss the nineteenth-century textbook representation of French history as seen through "nos ancêtres les Gaulois" (our ancestors the Gauls).[49] Rimbaud's narrator is an "I" who negates his Gallic inheritance ("but I don't butter my hair") and flees from "any part of French history!" He yearns to leave the country and acquire the primitivist persona of "une bête, un nègre" (an animal, a black man), outside of rationality and his despised history to make contact with pure exteriority and transformation.[50] The constant flux between discontented majoritarian and seeker of a more vital experience outside Japan will underpin Nakagami's work over the course of his career. This tendency will cast in and out of metropolitan literary life and on to his own far-flung journeys to alchemically loaded foreign spaces, albeit in the United States and Asia not Africa.

Nakagami began to connect his literary persona to the metropole when at the tender age of sixteen he wrote a fan letter to Shibusawa Tatsuhiko. Shibusawa was notorious for his decadent works (*itan bungaku*) and would soon be prosecuted for translating the Marquis de Sade. Nakagami was chagrined to receive in reply a pamphlet for improving his sex life.[51] In high school Nakagami was largely dismissed as unexceptional apart from his bulky size, but on Saturday nights he would frequently visit one teacher who edited a poetry magazine. High school connections sustained him even after he moved to Tokyo at the age of nineteen. A friend from home introduced him to a jazz coffee shop (jazz *kissaten*, or *kissa* for short), which would be one of his haunts for years. Jazz *kissa* were underground spaces where the immersive powers of free jazz recordings, especially recordings by tenor sax players John Coltrane and Albert Ayler, gave him a model for breaking and remaking tradition. He often cited the acoustic convergence of the words "codes" and "chords"—both pronounced *kōdo* in Japanese. Free jazz voicing of chords to produce a new polyrhythmic sound, selectively drawing on a preexisting repertoire, worked as a model for his own understanding of how to rework the syntax of Japanese literature and create a new expressive language and model for composition.

Unsure of where to publish, Nakagami submitted a story to a former high school teacher who promptly sent it back and told him to submit it to a "grownup's" magazine.[52] He saw a copy of *Literary Metropole* (*Bungei shuto*), an important little magazine (*dōjin zasshi*), in a bookstore. He joined as a member for 150 yen a month. This began a long relationship with the magazine, the only literary institution he would maintain a long-term attachment to. For that sum, a member of a magazine like *Literary Metropole* not only got the magazine in the mail but purchased the right to submit a story and have it read by the editorial board. Nakagami's first story, "Me, at Eighteen" (*Ore, jūhassai*), was published in 1963. Going to the meeting staffed with "people as old as my father," he was miffed that no one spoke about his work, and when time came for "a word from the author," he let fly with remarks about the Marquis de Sade. Comembers recall that they were impressed and "surprised that such a big guy like that was stung by the literature bug."[53]

The little magazine world Nakagami grew to inhabit seems a world away from the isolation and anomie of the postwar literary world that Van Gessel describes. Where Gessel writes that the more usual experience is driven by "individual bread-and-butter goals," Nakagami underscores the editorial commitment to "fostering newcomers" by "training newcomers."[54] Soon after his debut in *Literary Metropole*, Nakagami became an editorial member of the journal. The magazine had served as the launching pad for important twentieth-century writers of serious fiction, including Uno Kōji and Hirabayashi Taiko. Other well-known editorial members included the fantastic fiction writer Kiwa Kyō (Kasumi's pen name), who Nakagami would later marry; the doctor turned novelist Nada Inada; and Tsushima Yūko, later celebrated for stories and novels that dramatize the stark and reflective psychologies of solitary women. As he would say much later, in the somber context of a funeral for writer Mori Atsushi, "for better or for worse, the writers of the little magazine world were, I guess it can't be helped, all turning to the commercial literary world."[55]

Before his writing earned enough to support him and his family, Nakagami divided his days between writing and gainful employment. In the early mornings, he wrote stories in coffee shops. During the day, he worked full time driving a forklift or hauling luggage for the Flying Tigers service at Haneda Airport, where he recounts hiding in the employee bathroom stalls during his breaks to write his stories. On the train commuting back home to the suburbs, he read Eric Hoffer, the famed longshoreman philosopher. By 1968, Nakagami had begun to attract attention in more prestigious and more mass-oriented venues. Publication in magazines such as *The Group* (*Gunzō*) led to a string of "new writer" prizes. He made his debut in the *bundan* (the established publishing world outside of the little magazine world of his apprenticeship) with the story "The Very First Happening" (*Ichiban hajime no dekigoto*) in *Literary Arts* (*Bungei*) in 1969.

"The Very First Happening" was a lyrical first-person story of three boys who hatch a secret plan to build an immensely tall tower in the woods during the hard times of the immediate postwar era. The story is told in a rueful and retrospective voice, by a narrator who invents alternate worlds whose residents are far more responsive than his family or school friends but spurns the doting of his older brother who ultimately commits suicide.[56] The story was largely ignored, according to biographer Takayama Fumihiko, and when it wasn't, it was dismissed as a "warmed-over version of Ōe Kenzaburō."[57] The array of prizes, however, had the overall effect of ushering Nakagami into the literary star system where he would subsequently become the most celebrated writer born in postwar Japan. Nakagami secured his place in the limelight in 1975 when *The Cape* won the Akutagawa Prize, and he quit his job to write full time.

In retrospect, critics tend to see "The Very First Happening" in a revisionist way as almost a literal prophecy seeding something left to unfold. Watanabe Naomi writes that the lyrical relation between character and setting differs categorically from the "rapid unfolding of tonalities and intensities" of his celebrated later works.[58] The later works place Nakagami's flagship character, Akiyuki, at the center. For many readers, these works stand in not only for the author himself but for "a certain era of Japanese literature." This era includes the "indelible memory" of "this one character and one author."[59] It is infused with considerable melancholy because most of the first generation of critics to canonize Nakagami's works knew him personally and were staggered by his early death in 1992 at the age of forty-six. These include Eve Zimmerman, who sees the story's ethnically alienated characters, *zainichi* Korean children, as early cognates of, metaphors for, the later story world that begins to develop with *buraku* identity at its center in *The Cape*.[60] Both of these writers are acutely aware of how Nakagami's characters always seemed to stand for something beyond, but, like themselves, for a mythic author, for an era, for all of literature. Building on their insights, I want to suggest ways that we might frame this shapeshifting stand in for the author-protagonist in more broadly social terms. Specifically, I would like to reembed some key characters and tropes in the kinds of rhetoric and writing that have characterized *buraku* residents in twentieth-century public life.

The Linguistic Turn and the Ethnographic Twist

In large part, the interpretation of whether Nakagami wrote the *buraku* or "threw off the quotation marks" of being a "*buraku* writer," as Hirano claims, can be traced back to fundamentally different ideas held by the respective critics about language and its relation to culture and politics. Both *buraku* activists and the critical world in which Nakagami traveled were profoundly invested in a "linguistic turn" to imagining culture and politics. But they came to that focus from very different directions. Critics thought that denying the connection between the signifier and the signified meant rejecting the possibility of representation at a political level as well as a linguistic level. In the twentieth century, *buraku* activist movements often used language as a space to model possible claims or plans for citizenship or transforming toward it. Nakagami, though, claims to be interested in *buraku* issues only insofar as they are "cultural issues."[61] Of course, for someone who understands cultural forms like language to represent how the social world at large works, this claim allows him to sidestep public political debate while still analyzing the political significance of fiction, writing, and other cultural forms.

The linguistic turn of the liberation movement was inaugurated much earlier and was rhetorical but not specifically literary until the 1970s. I explain some main parameters of the archive of *buraku* rhetorical activism at length in the next chapter. But I would like to briefly contextualize this effort on the part of metropolitan literary critics to rethink the canon of literature, though without essentially challenging highly conventional ideas of Japanese-ness that most of them would have been horrified to think they endorsed. For Anglo-American readers the term "linguistic turn" may be associated with analytic philosopher Richard Rorty. It comes steeped in philosophical critiques of the way language brings the world phenomenally to those who experience it. This context was radically different in Japan. Because of the early, popular reception of semiotics in the immediate postwar era and the boom in academic writing outside of specifically academic venues in Japan in the 1970s through 1980s, the linguistic turn was taken up differently in Japanese literary studies. While studies of semiotics had been present in the first postwar efforts to study popular culture, literary criticism was brought into potential contact with many new fields and platforms with special intensity in Japanese print capitalism, perhaps better imagined through

Tessa Morris-Suzuki's term, information capitalism.[62] The efforts to formulate language as a general model for life brought literature and culture into dialogue with semiotics, structuralism, and poststructuralism, not academic philosophy. Not only was its reception interdisciplinary, but the forums and print culture where the linguistic turn was evident were closer to the marketplace than they were for their U.S. counterparts. Scholars and writers in the domain of what was often called New Aka, or new academicism, had the leeway to write experimentally, prolifically, and in stylized vernacular language about popular culture during the boom of the information economy print culture.

The greater cultural-economic context cleared room for interdisciplinary writing that popularized what might initially seem to be esoteric or technical ideas destined to be read by obsessives or specialists. Public policy, such as the plans whose vision aspires to what Morris-Suzuki calls "computopia," had taken a key turn around 1973, stating government intent to liberate people from industrial labor through the information economy. David Harvey sees a key condition of postmodernity to be a shift from a "mono-functional" planned vision of space in the service of a social purpose to the experience of space-time compression based on "strong internal differentiations within cities and societies based on place, function and social interest."[63] That same year, the journal *Contemporary Thought* (*Gendai shisō*) was founded, providing a venue for Japanese postmodern writers who worked to shift politics from within culture. In the words of longtime editor Ikegami Yoshihiko, "From that time on, political issues never appeared as politics itself, but as a cultural issue."[64] Critics who published in these venues took the liberty of wresting *chi* (knowledge) from its instrumental use in diversifying and informationalizing the economy and relocating it in interdisciplinary histories in the field of *shisō* (thought), a category that we might translate as "theory," a vision of popular postmodernism heavily skewed to epistemology.

The most renowned case of popular postmodernism was the hot-selling *Structure and Power: Going beyond Semiotics* (*Kōzō to chikara: kigō-ron o koete*), a thorough and lucid account of several French poststructural thinkers by one of the editors of Nakagami's complete works, Asada Akira. *Structure and Power* flew off the shelves and into the hands of young readers and had sales that, as Marilyn Ivy writes, "surpassed anyone's grandest expectations."[65] The new genre of New Aka featured popularized versions of postmodernism, structuralism, and poststructural writing that all landed at the same time. Asada's musings on the subject were popular enough to land him a feature interview in the Japanese edition of *Playboy*.[66] In a more lofty register, *Paideia* magazine was created in 1984 and opened a new venue for interdisciplinary scholarship by publishing key early translations of French poststructuralist thinkers such as Michel Foucault and Jacques Derrida.[67] The journal *Episutēme,* published by Asahi shuppan, took its name from Foucault's *Words and Things* and published works on how "meta-knowledge" came to be formed, emphasizing the history of science and works of "anti-philosophy."

New Aka writers such as those who published in *Paideia* and *Episutēme,* like Hasumi Shigehiko, Toyosaki Kōichi, and Karatani Kōjin, used semiotics to approach disciplines that were not conventionally regarded as linguistic. At the same time their angles were intensely textual and interpretive. They found models in French or Italian poststructural writers like Gilles Deleuze, Roland Barthes, and Umberto Eco. Each of these writers pursued the mapping of ideologies and narratives in popular culture in a more essayistic style that also departed from the focus on individual writers that literary studies dubbed *sakka-ron,* author studies. The objects treated by the linguistic turn were very *un*literary indeed, while the style of these writers ranged through eccentric and playful modes rather than the more sober scholarly lingua franca. Musicologist Hosokawa Shūhei brought an erudite and polylingual capacity to writing about music as a form of writing in *The Semiotics of Music* (*Ongaku no kigō-ron;* 1981). He described the flaneur-like acoustic spaces of personal electronics in *The Rhetoric of the Walkman* (*Uōkuman no shūji-gaku;* 1981). Hasumi Shigehiko translated and popularized essays by Derrida and Deleuze before starting his now celebrated career as a scholar of French literature and film critic.[68] Karatani Kōjin published a series of essays on Marx and one on the writer Natsume Sōseki and an extremely influential collection, *The Origins of Modern Japanese Literature* (*Nihon kindai bungaku no kigen*), from 1978 to 1980. Because Karatani was one of Nakagami's closest friends and one of the editors of his complete works and because he was also a main formulator of postmodernism in Japan, the connections between their oeuvres are worth treating at greater length.

After early training in Japan as an Americanist, Karatani spent 1975 through 1977 at Yale University teaching Japanese literature and working with Paul de Man, the scholar of romanticism. His stay coincided with the

U.S. academy's active engagement with deconstruction, primarily in English departments, following a 1966 conference at Johns Hopkins University. De Man's version of deconstruction took on romanticism's tendency to privilege tropes that overcome a distance between literary subject and referential object and deny figural language. He aimed to turn attention away from symbol, icon, and metaphor because they achieved a fusion of representation and world via the immediate referential function of language at the expense of the process of making meaning, one that is diffused rhetorically and figurally throughout a text.

De Man's emphasis on the kinds of immediacy and referentiality found in Anglo-Continental writings differed, of course, from those found in the received traditions of auteur studies and bibliographical studies in Japan. The deconstructionist move to deidealize romantic subjectivity provoked Karatani to historicize how key themes of romanticism in Japan combined with the simultaneous reception of realism to place the idea of the inner self at the origin of modern Japanese literature. He took de Man's idea of "blindness and insight" to mean that both the historical origins (for example, low-ranking samurais' susceptibility to Christianity as a guiding metaphysic) as well as rhetorical origins (for example, systems of figural language that played with the graphic properties of Japanese kanji characters) are effaced. Instead, the concepts of interiority, landscape, and confession are blindly assumed to be sources of meaning in modern fiction. In literary studies, these notions combined in Karatani's most lasting legacy, the assault on *genbun-itchi* (the unification of speech and language). This ideology of writing in the late Meiji era objected that "writing was only a transparent instrument for the transmission of ideas . . . an internal subject and external object were simultaneously produced."[69] Karatani transposes deconstructionist ideas about literature to the broader problem of modernity.

Karatani's afterword to this collection ends with the rousing call that "criticism of the modern has to begin with criticism of literature in modern Japan" (193).[70] The intricate textual friendship between critic and creative writer over twenty-plus years shows in the borrowings that Nakagami freely admits from Karatani. It shows in the roundtables they published as well as Karatani's curatorship of Nakagami's works after his death. The fact that a 1979 roundtable was titled *Overcoming Kobayashi Hideo* (*Kobayashi Hideo o koete*) signals that Nakagami saw himself very much as a critic, not just a fiction writer, and was aware of Kobayashi's

key term of "the socialized self" as well as his eventual capitulation to
wartime ideologies of overcoming modernity.[71] At many turns, we see the
guidance of Karatani. He introduced Nakagami to the works of William
Faulknerand Eric Hoffer; his work paralleled the heightened status of confession in Nakagami's most renowned book, *The Sea of Withered Trees*; and
one of Nakagami's most emotionally freighted essays was published as an
open letter to Karatani in which he addresses Karatani with the Korean
word for "older brother."[72]

While Nakagami's gleanings from Karatani are a recognized critical
topic, oddly enough the reverse possibility is never entertained. Karatani
is presented as an interpreter of Nakagami but never someone who learned
from Nakagami. What I find even more interesting in their exchanges is
the way that Nakagami's fiction makes concrete in ethnographic terms the
abstract or generalized themes of difference that appear consistently in
Karatani's work. Karatani's work deconstructs authorial intention, metaphysical ideals, and differential identity (*sai*) in philosophical discourse.
Nakagami, in contrast, used Jacques Derrida's famed theory of the supplement as his conceptual point of entry into fieldwork in *buraku* areas.
He describes the contributions that *buraku* cultural forms have made to
Japanese culture with the term *doku*. *Doku* is a homonym for "poison" in
Japanese, referencing the role of inoculation that poison plays in the logic
of the "pharmakon." The pharmakon is Derrida's term for an element of
a binary system that is necessary but exiled or abjected in order for the
system as a whole to work.[73] Nakagami writes this set of figures in a set of
essays that are about anti*buraku* discrimination coexisting with vernacular cultural forms from the *buraku* that inspired Noh theatre and other
imperial arts. *Doku* is also a homonym for "reading" and "independence."
Both are modes of empowerment strongly advocated by *buraku* partisans
in their twentieth-century rhetoric. In my view, Nakagami's reception of
the same group of texts in these essays, published while Karatani was in
the United States, suggests a very different object of deidealization: the
socially rooted relationship between mainstream and *buraku* cultural
forms, especially those articulated through language, a system he refers to
as "imperial syntax."

The legacy of the linguistic turn in a more proper literary setting has
continued to inform Japanese literary studies in two primary ways that
also underpin Nakagami's work. Nakagami's own approach is perhaps
closest in ideology to some scholars of classical literature who examine

all constituents of premodern fiction, poetic or prosodic, to rework the classical canon, show its investment in imperial myths, and call attention to discontinuities in the imperial line that is idealized to exist from the beginnings of written narrative to the present. These scholars distinguished their work even farther from the realist subject by arguing that premodern texts had their own specific kinds of narration that predated the conventions of realism. Mitani Kuniaki examined narration (*monogatari*) in classical texts to emphasize how the processes of storytelling could not be attributed to a single, overarching narrator but rather a variety of points of enunciation. Fujii Sadakazu changed his object of analysis rather than deconstructing the narrator (*katari-te*). He calls this event "Genji on the barricades." When placed in the tumultuous context of the New Left and student protests in 1968, Fujii was prompted to reconsider the central place that literary studies accorded to this story of the imperial court.[74] Fujii's work, like the efforts of many Japanese members of the *Monogatari kenkyūkai* (a narrative study group active in the 1980s and 1990s), ultimately turned away from *The Tale of Genji* (*Genji monogatari*, Murasaki Shikubu, early eleventh century), which had been exceptionally foregrounded during the occupation years and had promoted an aestheticized image of Japan as a peaceful, demilitarized country.[75] Fujii and others turned their attentions to look at processes of narration in other classical texts, ones that seemed more political than aesthetic, and departed from court-centered views of culture as a way of finding cultural alternatives to the emperor system. Hyōdo Hiromi connected the ideas of lyric and community formation in analyses of oral poetics in the *Tale of the Heike* (*Heike monogatari*) and nomadic storytellers and published more popular works on how the "voice" of twentieth-century popular performing arts was mobilized into imperial ideologies in mass culture.[76] Nakagami, like many canon reformers in the linguistic turn, was acutely concerned with how an encounter between text and reader or audience worked to coproduce meaning in a dynamic process and how the forms of performing arts and literary arts intertwined. As I examine in chapter 3, Nakagami's choice to begin his story of the Japanese *monogatari*'s relation to power and domination with the eighth-century works the *Kojiki* (*Record of Ancient Matters*) and the *Nihon shoki* (*Chronicles of Japan*) is consistent with this approach.

Nakagami's way of doing this, however, did not merely expand the repertoire of *kokubungaku* to include folk and oral culture as a corrective to imperial tradition. Rather, at the same time as modeling written narrative on premodern oral vernacular *katari-mono* narration, Nakagami also trained his poststructural lens on oral narration itself, showing it to possess properties of writing commonly attributed to print culture. Rather than expanding the literary repertoire by pegging the *roji* to a fixed origin that would in turn unfold a narrative that paralleled the development of *kokubungaku*, Nakagami collected "open-source" origin stories and folk stories that had variants in names and places. Though his emphasis is local and grounded in orality, his move is consistent with the energy that New Aka writers showed as they translated poststructural concepts into the 1970s cultural scene.

Unlike its French source texts, the reception of semiotics and poststructuralism, including that popularized by Karatani, was, as I stated earlier, not particularly literary. Nor, with a few exceptions, was it particularly ethnographic in its attention to popular culture. Nakagami was exceptional in his attempt to reckon the antihumanist tradition with a critique of differential identity. Many scholarly and more popular New Aka writers in Tokyo used myth as an analytic like Nakagami did, read Derrida with great avidity like Nakagami did, and mapped space semiotically like Nakagami did. But the practice of fieldwork outside of institutions, which was a crucial operation for French structuralists writing in an era of decolonization, had largely dropped out of the Tokyo literary establishment's critiques of epistemology and knowledge systems. While rejecting an anthropomorphic focus and retaining a concern with narration (*katari*), Nakagami restores a dimension of structuralism, its rooting in ethnography (literally, the writing of ethnicity), that had been lost to an astounding degree in its Japanese reception. His use of premodern and fieldwork-based aspects of writing to talk about contemporary life in institutions outside of literature was exceptional.

With every connection, Nakagami adds an ethnographic twist to the linguistic turn, one that is not necessarily apparent to fine fiction readers but is to a discursive reader of *buraku* rhetoric, history, and ethnography. Beginning in the late 1960s, Nakagami's works begin to experiment with the kinds of consciousness typical of the historically aware and self-reflexive characters that politically engaged fiction places at its center. But ultimately they abandon this strategy. Simply put, by the mid-1970s, this is because historical reflection is consistently alienating and even fatal for his characters. Rather than being empowering, reflection makes Nakagami's characters realize that they have no place in the all-inclusive structures that give them meaning, whether this is school textbooks, the student movement, or tropes taken from the archive of national literature. Nakagami will later label these structures such as jobs, nations, and student movements as "syntax" and will refer to those that submit to state uses of writing as "imperial syntax." These fixed structures are places in daily life and citizenship where there is, as of yet, no clear space of enunciation for a *buraku* protagonist.

In the era when Nakagami lived and wrote, the most prominent thinkers joined philosophy and literature and often experimented with styles that were both highly conceptual and appeared in nonacademic venues. These writers were crucial in framing his work as a project that featured similar tendencies to those they noted in poststructuralism. But most of them did not extend their interest in the linguistic turn to areas beyond textual realms. My book endeavors to reconnect these realms, to show how Nakagami's work cannot be read outside of a linguistic turn in the domain of social movements, namely the *buraku* activist movement, where language often served to model desires and forms for citizenship and modes of belonging. Nakagami's own meditations on language and its powers drew from the parallax resulting from a foot in each of these camps. His writing must be read as ethnography because he draws on these rhetorical traditions to, literally, write ethnicity.

Socializing the "Socialized Self"

In terms of literary history, much of Nakagami's work toward shaping a discourse on ethnography can be viewed as an attempt to reform and widen the boundaries of the *shi-shōsetsu*, I-fiction, to accommodate different engagements with the social world. I emphasize the term of the "socialized self" (*shakai-ka sareta watakushi*) because it is a central term, coined by Kobayashi in a 1935 essay called "On I-fiction" (*Watakushi shōsetsu-ron*), around which Nakagami organizes his revision of the Japanese literary canon.[77] Nakagami's choice of texts is much more idiosyncratic, less systematic, and more fluid in moving between fiction and criticism than a scholarly survey of I-fiction would be, a fact that generates gaps, ellipses, and unexpected links in his work. Although critics dispute the exact origins of I-fiction, its place in literary history was cemented by Kobayashi, generally considered the first literary critic in modern Japanese letters. I-fiction, a dominant mode of storytelling in modern Japanese writing, is a prose narrative often told in first-person voice; but, even if it uses third-person voice, it is understood to have some referential fidelity to the writer's life. Neither autobiography nor fabulation, it nonetheless makes the self the center of literary meaning and may be treated either sincerely or with great irony to show a lack of self-awareness as well as keen reflexive insight. When postwar writers experimented with ways of narrating the literary signifier of the "I," they began, as Van Gessel writes, to acknowledge authorities outside of the central character's individual will, what he calls the "deified self."[78] But when Nakagami establishes his critical program, he leaps back in time and bypasses fellow fiction writers like Shimao Toshio, Kojima Nobuo, Ōe Kenzaburo, and Dazai Osamu to anchor his idea in this touchstone of modern literary criticism rather than in the novel. This is because Kobayashi Hideo offers a broader (if more doleful) view of the social than the tight-knit human circumstances of these writers and has a broader critical agenda. These writers typically socialize, or establish the process of social construction of, their characters in the intimate terrains of family or the escapist worlds of the characters' own creating.

"On I-fiction" diagnosed what Kobayashi saw as a fatal malaise of Japanese literature. To Kobayashi, I-fiction was insufficiently social because of its "dangerous proximity to actual life."[79] People often mistook its protagonist for the author himself, collapsing signifier with signified. Kobayashi thought that Marxism provided a possible resistance to I-fiction because its emphasis on historicism offered ways to connect even first-person characters to dynamics larger than themselves. To him, Japanese fiction had failed because of the fact that "I" appears everywhere, yet it is aware of no world outside itself—"I" is not fully socialized. Marxism, too, failed by raising the mundane to such an elevated historical level that it privileged ideas over physical life, too aware of the world outside itself. Kobayashi's melancholy conclusion is that literature had walked headlong into the "special pit" (*tokushu-na ana*) of I-fiction, being trivial, private, and hermetic, full of subjects unaware of themselves as objects mediated by cultural codes and forms. Japanese fiction had retained "the limpid visage of a single persona" disappointing because it did not see itself as both subject and object and thus lacked the connection to social life that fiction alone could provide.[80]

Kobayashi *did* find this socialized self, for example, in André Gide's 1926 novel *The Counterfeiters* (*Les faux-monnayeurs*). *The Counterfeiters* showed "not the figure of the self, but the problems it posed."[81] And this laboratory work led to yet another discovery: "a certain mechanism that calibrated the intake of the individual and the social in literature." *The Counterfeiters* is the story of a band of schoolboys who are employed by a band of criminals to circulate fake coins. One of the main characters, Édouard, keeps a diary, also called *The Counterfeiters:* "My notebook contains, as it were, a running criticism of my novel—or rather of the novel in general."[82] While he never actually writes the novel, Édouard's rumination on the process of composition generates a kind of parallax view of himself as subject and object, writer and written about.

The regulator or certain mechanism between individual and social that Kobayashi mentions above is concretely imaged later in his essay. Kobayashi imagines the writer as someone who confronts the material of reality not with a pen but with a pair of scissors: "A novelist tries to express reality as it is, without any trace of scissor cuts. Or at least he tries to wield the scissors so as to simulate a multiplicity of cuts that would seem to represent reality as it is. And so events, ideas and characters must not be defined and molded to possess a single, static shape. The author should create as though he were reflecting the lives of others, when in fact each fictional character is holding up a mirror at different angles to the light."[83]

The metaphors of writer-cutter and cut as mirror suggest that the job of the writer is not to respect the integrity of an object—a mind, a character. It is through cutting, to create a raw line that traverses objects, characters, and other textual materials, that makes for a distributed narrative between characters, one that is not focalized through one single narrator but that reflects this three-dimensional space at different angles. Kobayashi suggests that a novelist tells a story through the relations of the story's parts, a three-dimensional space of the oeuvre, not just the volumetric space of character psychology. This form is close to Nakagami's ideas about another key term, exchange (*kōtsū*). Simply put, Nakagami's sagas and interlocking stories are constantly cut and their internal relations changing as he adds elements to the saga. The problem with Kobayashi's reading in my view (and the place where Nakagami is more deliberate about where "social" registers) is that the self is often not the originator of the social fields it inhabits. Kobayashi's focus on self-reflection is not interested in seeing these cuts, mirrors (what I have called parallax) in terms of the culture beyond the novel.

Nakagami's engagement with I-fiction across different media forms is closer to the realm that literary historian Hibi Yoshitaka calls "writing the self."[84] Hibi's model examines how the self crystallizes as writers and their texts start to be laced across a number of venues in the late Meiji-era mass media marketplace. He argues that I-fiction emerged just after the Russo-Japanese War ended in 1905. At that point, magazines started to bring together information on writers and to deliver information on the people who were models for particular works. In Hibi's argument, writers before the 1920s did not necessarily see the self as the initial referent for writing about "I." They saw the self as a combination of autobiography and represented simulacra brought together from different media forms in print journalism and gossip rags. This understanding of the self as a representation compiled from multiple venues, rather than fixed as an identity in a work, alters considerably our understanding of the term.

The distributed "I" is consistent with Nakagami's presentation of his own nonfiction signifier of "I" as well as the stand-in characters that are often read as his counterparts. Nakagami connects with I-fiction in two primary ways that are profoundly social, if not always in the confessional way the I-fiction reader looks for. First, he presented himself as the first writer from a *hisabetsu buraku*, although he never uses the word *buraku* in his fiction.[85] And second, he articulates his "I" across a wide array of venues, from lectures and literary journals to celebrity gossip rags. His social life encompassed rarified literary prize juries as well as popular and glamorous *enka* showcases with the *zainichi* Korean singer Miyako Harumi.

Nakagami, Japan follows Hibi's approach by reorienting the study of postwar I-fiction to expand the places in which we might look for the character "I," understood as both subject and object. This expanded field includes the kinds of parallax in terms of media form and differential identity we find in celebrated examples of fiction, in roundtable discussions, in essays and book reviews, and in repertoires of activist language that Nakagami draws on, all examples of parallax that have histories and powers that exceed his own life and making. My claim is that the discursive reader who has the capacity to read across media forms to compile the distributed "I" actually needs the same skills as a *buraku* activist reader. The contextual knowledge, however, has to be supplied from elsewhere in order to read *roji* as *buraku*, for instance. The discursive reader is aware of these conventions, tropes, and collective figures across genres and media forms.

By emphasizing the range of meanings that "social" has in Nakagami's writing, I aim to delink his work critically from the frame of postwar I-fiction. I want to think about the representation of the self as a field traversed by multiple texts and intertexts, both literary and extraliter-ary. This expansion is necessary because Nakagami is so closely tied to I-fiction in its narrow meaning by the Tokyo literary establishment. From his Akutagawa Prize through his 1992 obituaries, and even in post-humous homages, it is astounding that critics and journalists still found it possible to align Nakagami's personal appearance so closely with the substance and even the literal bulk of his writings. In their praise of his singularity, they often rubbed out many of the social fields that I would argue make his writing so deeply invested in prose fiction's relation to social and historical worlds.

As Eve Zimmerman has astutely shown, the influential critic Etō Jun was instrumental to the presentation of Nakagami as a physical, unintel-lectual writer, "barely in control of his material": "Nakagami's is not a borrowed Naturalism; he creates characters through the pulse of his own heart which drinks in earth and blood . . . he is able to sing about the pain people feel in this world."[86] Kawamura Jirō, too, links Nakagami and I-fiction through the tropes of blood and soil, writing in an authoritative literary reference work that in order to compose *The Cape* Nakagami turned to "the landscape of short stories set in the folklorically-loaded region of Kumano, his place of origin," and took "as his raw materials the compli-cated relations of his own family [and] sought the secrets of his own trou-bled blood."[87] The *Nikkei shinbun* obituary remarks on the "highly physical style of his writings," obliquely referring to Nakagami's notoriously large size, echoed again by Etō, in an *Asahi shinbun* piece he titled "My friend, the gentle giant."[88] And writer Tatematsu Wahei in his elegy called Naka-gami "an excessively carnal writer."[89]

Taken together, many assessments of Nakagami's writing frame his works as natural extensions of his body rather than highly crafted rep-resentations and even less as representations that exist in a social field beyond its author's making. To my mind, an important context—the changes in social and educational infrastructures during the postwar occupation era—is neglected when Nakagami is made most critically meaningful by connection to early century naturalism. Etō in particular was instrumental in establishing Nakagami's critical reputation. Doing so, he severed the work from a postwar context dominated by the U.S. occupation and praised Nakagami for transcending its "fetters."[90] How-ever, as Nakagami himself wrote, he was not resentful about the occupa-tion. Had there not been postwar reforms that made *buraku* education possible in "our house way out in the countryside" due to "perhaps the public assistance system . . . or an extra-earnest public health officer," he would never have had access to basic education, much less access to transforming the very terms of Japanese prose fiction.[91]

Evaluations that praise Nakagami for leaping over postwar history both omit his anger at the Japanese state's neglect and oppression of internal others and give the unfortunate impression of Nakagami as a primitive expressionist. They frame him as a natural representative of all *buraku* writing, a claim he sometimes endorsed, but one that was often challenged. In 1979, Nakagami wrote, "for me, born in the postwar era, the war I experienced was not World War II or the Pacific War" but the Great Treason Incident of 1910–11 and the Great Nankai Earthquake of 1946 that killed over thirteen hundred people, caused fires that burnt 70 percent of residential housing, and sent waves as far as Hawaii and California.[92] Nakagami aligned his works on a periodization of history that tracked how Kumano's low material and human value was superimposed on its symbolically exalted status over time. To him, this throughline dated from the beginnings of written narrative in the eighth century. He called this history "invisible" (*fukashi*).[93]

This parallax between what a metropolitan literary audience expects and what a national *buraku* audience wants provides a fruitful place for experimenting with textual construction for multiple audiences. *Nakagami, Japan* is an exploration of how this sometimes privileged and sometimes contradicted parallax view structures of Nakagami's understanding of himself; critical understandings of his work; and, more immediately to us, his production of a textual world that can be read doubly either as fine fiction or in terms of a history of *buraku* rhetorical activism. Chapter 1 maps out significant issues, strategies, and rhetorical conventions of this twentieth-century archive that intersect profoundly with Nakagami's work.

An Archive of Activism

Becoming Historical

The most important task carried out by early twentieth-century *buraku* activist thinkers was crafting a history of their own that would establish a place for the *buraku* within a national historiography. While the Meiji government made efforts to create a body of citizens that was less stratified than it had been under the Tokugawa status system, ethnologists and writers began to consolidate and narrate history. Three years after the Meiji Restoration, in 1871, the Meiji government issued a decree that eliminated the two outcast groups that sat outside of the Tokugawa status system and composed the "abject classes" (*senmin*): *eta* and *hinin*.[1] A year earlier, it had changed the categories of the nobility and consolidated the three classes of farmers, craftsmen, and merchants into the category heimin, or commoners.[2] From that point forward, writers who took on the cause of *buraku* identity were sure of two things. First, they were sure that they had been done a grave injustice despite shaking off elements of the Tokugawa past. This was because, as the new infrastructures of sovereignty emerged in the Meiji period, changes in labor, property ownership, and citizenship status underwent sea changes that were detrimental to *buraku-min* at the same time that old forms of discrimination persisted under new names. And second, they were sure that their collective identity was best articulated in the words of Yanase's 1901 book as a *Society Outside of Society: Eta Hinin* (*Shakai-gai no shakai: eta hinin*), a group still marked with the nomenclature of premodern discrimination, even thirty years after the Meiji restoration.[3]

This chapter surveys a set of responses that use language to dispute and transform both these situations at key points in the twentieth century. Each of these shifts, in turn, accords an important place to language and the claims that it makes on the state. And each of them demonstrates an attempt to write Japan into a transnational set of ways of thinking about differential identity, whether in terms of race, class, ethnicity, or nationalism.

The umbrella name I use to describe the ideology that underwrites the repertoire of *buraku* rhetorical activism is "linguistic sovereignty." This concept refers to how theories of language and narrative were important to *buraku* activists as they challenged their treatment by the state, by state-influenced civic groups, and in popular representation and advocated for a popular sovereignty of the *buraku* through practices of self-determination. Sovereignty in my argument refers to a form of political power whereby an entity has the right or force of rule over a given domain. The term of linguistic sovereignty means to exert power on a form of political representation by shaping the means of signification or representation as rhetoric, definition, illustration, persuasion, or force.

Within the *buraku* liberation movement that began in the 1920s in the wake of the Paris Peace Conference, rhetorical activism began as a critique of state power. The critique also created a historiography. It addressed specific examples of how language, in the form of classifications, proclamations, and other state-issued utterances, failed to adequately exercise sovereignty when state law first created a modern *buraku* identity. This repertoire of *buraku* rhetorical activism focused on critiques as well as on new strategies, such as manifestos and formalized modes of extralegal justice. From the movement's beginnings, writing and orating were integral parts of the liberation movement. Writing and speeches drew people to assemblies, kept them absorbed in debate, and compiled lists of demands that movement leaders desired to put into action. Movement leaders thought that having control over the group's means of signification—on top of the means of production—was a key part of controlling its political representation. With regularity from the 1920s to the 1970s, the key symbolic elements of liberationist rhetoric worked in the service of providing a historical account of discrimination and sketching an outline for a movement toward liberation.

One aim of undertaking rhetorical activism was to counter the Japanese state's particular constricting use of language. Government policies from the Home Ministry as well as civic groups funded or advised by the Home Ministry launched programs of reform (*kaizen*). In 1913 ethnologist and folklorist Yanagita Kunio remarked that the Home Ministry attempted many times to change the name of *buraku-min*, from *eta* to *shin-heimin* (new commoners) to *tokushu buraku-min* (specially marked *buraku-min*) to *saimin buraku* (poor *buraku*), but "even a hundred names" would be insufficient as long as *buraku* were still marked with a "special" (*tokushu*) status.[4] Nakagami responds to the question of naming by making his chief literary topos, the *roji*, a concept that refers to a nonexistent neighborhood. Defining the neighborhood through its articulation defies the belief that this neighborhood—and, by analogy, any *buraku* neighborhood—exists "out there" as a fixed object. His emphasis on processes of becoming the *roji* as opposed to a fixed representation of being the *roji* delinks his topos from a static state and calls attention to how it is narrated. Early activists, too, focused on mechanisms and conventions through which *buraku* and their residents were narrated.

Four main nodes of linguistic sovereignty establish long-term reference points in *buraku* activist movements: the 1871 Emancipation Edict (*kaihō-rei*) that abolished the names of premodern *eta* and *hinin* outcast groups; the criticism of the 1906 novel *The Broken Commandment* (*Hakai*), which features an *eta* protagonist thirty-five years after the edict; the Suiheisha Manifesto, proclaimed at the inaugural meeting of the first nationwide *buraku* organization in 1922; and the strategy of denunciation struggles (*kyūdan tōsō*) pioneered by the Suiheisha, a formalized pursuit of extra-legal justice designed to confront and mandate change in discriminatory actions. Together these attempts to shape and exert linguistic sovereignty compose a set of strategies for rhetorical activism. This is also the frame in which I see *buraku* historiography, a narrative form that emerged in the 1910s to bridge theory and practice and is seen most significantly in the works of scholar and colonial bureaucrat Kita Sadakichi (1871–1939) and political organizer Takahashi Sadaki (1905–35). The task of historiographers is to locate *buraku* history within a specifically Japanese set of political and ethnographic chronologies, explaining a set of grievances and a set of social relations whose consciousness can relieve suffering, lead to self-determination, and transform the mainstream terms of power. In Takahashi's words, "history is the route to liberation."[5]

The archive of twentieth-century *buraku* writing includes literature and fiction but goes beyond it. Starting with Kimura Ki's book chapter "The Suihei Buraku Liberation Movement and Literary Arts" (*Suihei buraku kaihō undō to bungei*) in 1926, literary criticism of the *buraku* dwelled on particular kinds of writing, both literary and extraliterary, that stressed the capacity of language to exert and shape power.[6] Even as they weighed historical events and periods differently, the central thinkers I turn to were all acutely aware of their desire to represent—to stand in for a collective larger than themselves by taking a very deliberate and visible stance vis-à-vis their "voice."[7] They were aware of being part of a "recursive public." This is a term that writers in media studies use to talk about publics that are acutely aware of the modifiability of their own terms of existence.[8] In some cases the relevant terms of "modifiability" may be technological. But, more broadly, a recursive public is shaped by the way that reflexive thinking about information processes—about epistemology, essentially, while incorporating the existential effects of knowing—shapes ideas and stances on the medium's own terms of existence. In my reading, the medium for twentieth-century literary critics and historiographers is narrative, and the recursive public is keenly aware of the rhetorical strategies, narratives, and figural language through which its story is told.

Linguistic Sovereignty

Rhetorical activists responded to state and civic directives, funding, nomenclatures, and management but defined their goals and intended courses of action independently. They used rhetoric to construct histories in pamphlets, leaflets, speeches, and plays and to suggest and inspire a mandate for future action. Most histories of the *buraku* see the modern *buraku* emerge when a document colloquially called the Emancipation Edict was issued in 1871 by the central government organ of the time, the Dajōkan (Great Ministry of State).[9] The document abolished the *eta* and *hinin* outcast groups that had existed under the Tokugawa-era status system from the early 1600s. These groups included people such as butchers, entertainers, and criminals, who were classified outside of and subordinate to the four-class system that consisted of samurai, farmers, craftsmen, and merchants.[10] Although many scholars refer to the ruling as the "emancipation edict" (*kaihō-rei*), in a suggestive comparison to the Emancipation Proclamation, this colloquial name was applied later; the edict has nothing to do with chattel slavery, and reads simply that "the abjected names of *eta* and *hinin* should be abolished, and both *mibun* (status) and occupations should be the same as *heimin*," or commoners.[11] An understanding of *eta* and *hinin* categories as defined by hierarchies of status and occupation was replaced by an understanding of commoners as citizens. In other words, rather than being under or outside of the other status groups, the former outcasts were meant to be placed on the same level plane as commoners. For several reasons, it is hard to call this change in semantics liberatory.

The main complaint *buraku* activists have made about the edict is the way it instituted new kinds of economic inequality despite its face value of liberation. In theory, when the edict was issued, people who had been classified as *eta* and *hinin* should not have been consigned to a lower place than they occupied in the Tokugawa era. Three critiques emerged to argue that the new situation was no better. The first group felt that discrimination experienced under the Tokugawa regime did not disappear after the edict. A second group argued that although *senmin* had been both excluded and singled out for unfair treatment under Tokugawa, after the edict their situation grew even more dire. Under Tokugawa, *senmin* also had access to a kind of social welfare system because *eta* and *hinin* had been given monopoly rights to certain sectors of the labor market, including the right to collect and trade with animal carcasses left on state lands. This right was rescinded the month before the edict, and the animal carcasses were put on the open market before the citizenship status of *eta* and *hinin* was transposed into that of "new commoners."[12]

A third group protested the registration of former outcasts. The day after the edict was issued, each local administration was directed to move *eta* and *hinin* entries into *heimin* family register books. *Koseki* (戸籍), or family registers, are the primary data by which the Japanese legal structure makes a citizen socially and financially intelligible and accountable. The family register is the key official document in forming the modern episteme of *buraku* identity—the way *buraku* citizens are known—in the context of national infrastructures. In the modern era, *koseki* were employed to insure that people paid taxes and reported for military conscription. Even today, when a person is born or changes his or her legal status, his or her name and place of residence are recorded in a family list, in relation to other family members. He or she also has a *honseki* (registered family domicile) where family members are inscribed and are most likely buried. These two markers affirm residence and ancestral origin as primary attributes of a person's legal identity. As the process of incorporating people into family registers was carried out, some new entries that logged former *eta* or *hinin* into the books were tagged with the marker of *shin-heimin*, or *new* commoners. In effect, a society outside of society was literally discriminated from commoners by means of the inscriptions of official record keeping. The family registers are a key example to many *burakumin* of how the powers bound up in writing can be used in the service of domination and discrimination. The family registers were publicly accessible until the 1970s, and information about residence and origin could have effects in the public world by connecting people to *buraku* neighborhoods.[13] Compounding this difficulty in making a livelihood, land redistribution policies were enacted to take land that had been formerly regarded as commons and allocate it to specific property owners. When people suddenly lost their positions as tenant farmers and had to pay the taxes on new lands, they were hurt economically.

In practice, this new Meiji-era citizen position still had to be supported by legal and social infrastructures. Because of continued discrimination, a new insecure relation to the labor market, and the family register system, the edict neither lived up to its promise to create a level society of citizens nor abolished the practical effects of the hierarchies of the status system. This very failure in the realm of policy, however, inaugurates nearly all movement-based activism.

The question of an individual citizen's struggle to locate himself or herself within Japanese national history and its system of symbols provides the backdrop for the second moment of linguistic sovereignty. The relation among language, power, and character transpires in a passionate confession in the pages of Shimazaki Tōson's *The Broken Commandment*. Although in mainstream postwar literary criticism it would be eclipsed by Tayama Katai's 1907 *The Quilt* (*Futon*), Shimazaki's 1906 work *The Broken Commandment* is the cornerstone of the literary canon initiated by Kimura in 1926 and built upon by *buraku* activists in the 1970s. It is the work that Nakagami repudiated most strongly and whose major trope, confession, is featured in his most celebrated novel, *The Sea of Withered Trees* (*Karekinada*). Moreover, it is foundational in the mainstream canon of *kokubungaku* (national literature) that was assembled by postwar critics. *The Quilt* presents private, intimate life as the most significant site in which confession might take place. It dramatizes the story of a frustrated writer who takes on a young female literary apprentice and falls in love with her. When she becomes spiritually and carnally attached to a young theology student, the writer sends her back to the provinces and only confesses the melancholy depths of his attraction by sobbing into her bedspread in her empty room after she is gone. *The Broken Commandment*, in contrast, places confession in the public sphere of the Meiji-era schoolroom. With its imperial portraits, patriotic songs, and national holidays, *The Broken Commandment* is deeply concerned with how the sovereignty of the imperial state is exercised in small-scale routines of the daily lives of its characters. Sovereignty is strongly linked to a confession the main character, Ushimatsu, makes.

Ushimatsu Segawa is a schoolteacher in the rural Nagano town of Iiyama who is poised to marry his fiancée. Unknown to his colleagues, Ushimatsu comes from an *eta* family who lives in the hills "on the outskirts of the village" (*machi no hazure*).[14] His father, a shepherd, has compelled him to promise never to reveal his *eta* origins. He warns his son that making this knowledge public would jeopardize the success he has so far achieved and would force his dismissal from the civil service school system. Ushimatsu's background becomes vulnerable to exposure following a train of rumors spread by a nefarious political candidate who opposes Ushimatsu's mentor, the sole person in the area who has publicly presented himself as an *eta*. Shortly before the murder of the daring *eta* candidate, the opposition candidate tells Ushimatsu he knows his secret and hints that someone in the school is also "an *eta*."[15]

As Ushimatsu becomes suspect, his fellow teachers initially dismiss the rumors since he exhibits none of the conventional external signs of *eta* identity. He is too disciplined. He has no "special smell," and the principal observes, "When it comes to his skin, his build, I don't think there's anything that especially seems *senmin*-like."[16] His rival Bunpei calls attention to uncertain motivation for Ushimatsu's lodgings, his reading habits, and even his last name: "Appearances are deceptive, Principal, what about his character?"[17] Bunpei encourages the others to believe that Ushimatsu has a secret, an impression conjured by his moodiness and amplified by a mysterious melancholy his friend Ginnosuke tries to explain away by attributing to a lost love.

Ushimatsu undergoes a crisis of conscience, throws himself to the floor, and confesses to his students, "I am such an outcast," one whose people make the shoes and drums the students use but follow strict guidelines about belonging in both public and private space.[18] This act makes his continued existence in imperial Japan untenable; though they all sing "the same Kimi ga yo" national anthem, he is "an *eta*, a *chori*, an impure human."[19] He takes flight to frontier-era Texas, an exile that might be explained by looking at the larger chain of intertexts that advocate *buraku* emigration. Early *buraku* organizers called themselves the *Tsubasa-kai* (Flying Group) because of their desire to get away from discrimination. The earliest fiction that activists place in the domain of liberation literature, *Story of a Shin-heimin Dream of the South Seas* (*Hankai yume monogatari ichimei shin-heimin kaiten-dan*; 1886), was a transcribed oral story about a fantastic emigration scheme to the South Seas, a trope that explored desires of political escapism and flourished in the 1880s and 1890s (as I explore in chapter 6).[20] At the policy level, Japanese bureaucrats advocated emigration to Hokkaidō and the colonies. Even given this background of emigration as problem-solving fantasy, because Ushimatsu's imagined liberation is prefigured on his removal from national boundaries, it forms a problematic prototype of what I call the "tragic enlightenment" narrative. In order to register and be known as a social being *in* Japan, he has to *leave* Japan. Japan allows no one to be both an *eta* and a full citizen; that kind of parallax is simply untenable in the literary imagination.

The desire to be both determined and a full citizen in Japan spurred the *buraku* liberation movement in the Taishō era (1912–26). Debates on ethnic self-determination surfaced in many national contexts following the settlements of World War I and gave a cosmopolitan character to both the ideas (Marxism and anarchism) and the ideals (brotherhood) that underwrote the movement. On March 3, 1922, three thousand people gathered in Kyoto under the banner of the Suiheisha. The document that came out of this meeting, the Suiheisha Manifesto, marks the third moment of linguistic sovereignty. Nearly all contemporary *buraku* movements trace their ancestry to this meeting and this text written by the painter, poet, and playwright Saikō Mankichi (1895–1970). Saikō produced screenplays for silent film, such as *Love and Revolution* (*Ai to sen*), as well as theatre works, such as *Tenchūgumi*. *Tenchūgumi* is based on a world renewal (*yo-naoshi*) movement that burst into a magistrate's office just before an imperial visit in 1863 and proclaimed itself to be a new government, only to be slain by government troops. The elements of passion, sacrifice, and sublimation to a higher ideal, seen in Saikō's dramatic works, transfer to the Suiheisha Manifesto.

The Suiheisha Manifesto is important because it is the mandate of the first national *buraku* organization and, furthermore, because it provides the first major statement on *buraku* status, which has a transformative relation to language; at the same time it makes language an integral part of its program of political self-representation. Twentieth-century public speaking was, as Massimiliano Tomasi reminds us, not only "a social phenomenon that was supported by favorable political circumstances," such as the Taishō-era formation of political parties, but also "provided for the introduction of knowledge and the growth of a new awareness of the power and scope of the spoken word."[21]

Using a syncretic mix of Marxist language, Christian emblems of suffering, and descriptions of daily life, the manifesto set out the Suiheisha's demands and a process for achieving them. It was signed and dated with a reign year, Suihei 1, conspicuously different than either the imperial reign year of Taishō 12 or 1922. Suihei 1 marked the beginning of a new era that displaced the name of the emperor yet kept the discursive structure of renewal that would be popularly expected of a reign. The manifesto begins with a ringing phrase that cites but does not quote the last line of the *Communist Manifesto* of 1848 (and thus provides a prototype of the hidden transcript that will appear in later Nakagami works). Rather than the international subject of the proletariat, however, the subject in formation is *buraku-min*. Marx's international proletariat concluded by urging workers of the world to unite and lose their chains. This work begins by asking "long-suffering brothers" to unite and liberate themselves:

Buraku-min throughout the country unite!

Long-suffering brothers:

In the past half-century, reform undertakings on our behalf by many people in various ways have not yielded any appreciable results. This should be taken as divine punishment for permitting others as well as ourselves to debase our human dignity. Previous movements, though seemingly motivated by compassion, actually degraded many of our brothers. Therefore, it is necessary for us to organize a new collective movement through which we shall liberate ourselves by our own effort and self-respect.

Brothers, our ancestors pursued liberty and equality, and practiced these principles. But they became the victims of a contemptible system developed by a despicable ruling class. They became the manly martyrs of industry. In recompense for their work in skinning animals, [our ancestors] were skinned alive. For tearing out the animals' hearts, their own warm hearts were ripped out. They were spat at with ridicule. Yet all through these cursed nights of evil dreams, their human blood has kept flowing. We, who have been born of this blood, are trying to become divine. The time has come when the oppressed shall throw off the brand of martyrdom. The martyr's crown of thorns shall receive blessing.

We, who know how cruel and cold it is to be discriminated against, must not use disrespectful words and crookedly behavior to retaliate against ordinary human beings. To do so would be to discredit our ancestors who died for freedom and to desecrate humanity. Therefore, we should work passionately for human rights and seek the light of true humanity.

Let there be warmth in the hearts of people, and let there be light upon all mankind. From this, the Levelers' association is born.

Signed in Suihei, year 1.[22]

Most of all, the manifesto is the story of a crisis based on conditions of suffering imposed by labor and false-friend philanthropists, followed by an awakening and transformation in political consciousness in which the former relations of oppression are turned upside down. As a form of theoretical writing, like Marxist philosophy, it demands that we not only see the world but also act to change it, propelling the world toward the revolution that has yet to materialize. In turn, it emplots steps that must be taken to carry out the program.[23]

The formalized strategy of "denunciation," the fourth moment of linguistic sovereignty, was a concrete step undertaken by *buraku* activists to combat perceived discrimination on a grassroots level. Since Suiheisha activists had little faith that due process of law would enforce their claims to equal treatment, they established a highly organized formal and extralegal system of justice that Frank Upham describes as "convincing one or more majority Japanese to adopt the BLL [*Buraku* Liberation League] interpretation of a particular event, language or policy that the BLL considers discriminatory."[24] Still in use today by the postwar successor to the Suiheisha movement, the BLL, this formalized strategy dates to prewar Suiheisha and forms what Ian Neary calls "the distinguishing feature of Suiheisha group activities."[25] A denunciation is carried out when a person is understood to commit an act of discrimination. A representative group of BLL members meets with him or her and negotiates with him or her until she or he agrees to apologize and makes amends for the damage. In the context of Nakagami's writing, the strategy of denunciations will be an important precedent because he thinks that the precision and specificity of its confrontations make it a "one-time-only solution, and don't do anything to systematically solve discrimination."[26]

The incident that was hotly debated at the time Nakagami weighed in, the Yata incident, took place in an Osaka school in 1969.[27] 1969 was a tense year in overall *buraku* activism because a split occurred between the Japan Communist Party (JCP) and the BLL and surfaced in this dispute. A three-person roundtable with Noma Hiroshi, Hijikata Tetsu, and Kokubun Ichitarō placed it in the context of education and "school jumping," long-distance commutes by non*buraku* children to avoid *buraku* schools in favor of mainstream ones.[28] Hijikata Tetsu, a writer and newspaper editor, researched that forty-five thousand children from *buraku* neighborhoods changed their place of residence in their *koseki*. Hijikata states that the BLL attempted to regulate school jumping because school jumpers tended to be more affluent and left poorer *buraku* children in sub-standard schools with substandard teachers. This issue collided with an election pamphlet a teacher distributed in his campaign in which he gave *dōwa*, the word for assimilation taken from the language of government administration, as a reason that teachers were overworked and even forced to quit. The teacher's statement ended with a rousing call of solidarity for the Okinawan fight against reversion to Japan from U.S. possession, sig-naling that he was critical of the Japanese government and sympathetic with ideas of local rule, qualities that seemed to clash with his position on *buraku* neighborhoods.[29]

The violent clash between the two groups began when the BLL local chapter confronted both the candidate and those who supported him with a written protest, asking for the candidate's apology in writing. The need to get it in writing illustrates the role that such written documents had in legitimating and disciplining the rules of the institution, a power that Nakagami will scrutinize closely. The candidate turned in his apology but made an about-face. Legal accounts of the incident emphasize intimi-dation tactics that BLL members used, drawing in the upper ranks of the organization's central committee. The BLL account describes in militant terms the "attack" by the JCP, pointing to an antagonism of larger pro-portions. The National Diet had just passed a series of funding measures called the Special Measures Law for Assimilation Projects (SML) to fund *buraku* neighborhood revitalization. The JCP was incensed that the BLL was given exclusive control of a vast amount of funds when their party actually represented the interests of all worker classes in a broader way, not just those mired in a half-feudal system.

This decision had the effect of stressing that ethnicity was the defin-ing criterion for *buraku* identity, not class. The BLL countered that unless *buraku-min* were liberated no one was and, furthermore, that many struc-tures of discrimination were modern. In this instance, words and force came to a head when BLL members faked stepping on the supporter's foot and, when he took it away, accused him of prejudice. The end result after negotiations with the JCP union was that the teachers who supported the candidate were all transferred to *buraku* schools and subsequently sent for tours of "sabbatical" at the BLL's research center. When the JCP took the case to the courts, the BLL was acquitted at both the district and high court levels, leading to a general acceptance of denunciation as a tactic, within unspecific "reasonable limits."[30]

Choosing Your People

By the mid-1970s, when Nakagami began to weigh in on *buraku* issues, the three topics of occupation, religious belief, and the Tokugawa political system were no longer the only explanations offered for *buraku* origins.[31] As I discussed in the previous section, activists also stressed the new inequities that accumulated in the modern Meiji era. However, emphasis on the historical origins *for* discrimination and a history *of* discrimination still form a part of movement self-consciousness, one developed in the early twentieth century to explain the structurally fixed nature of *buraku* experience and grievances over time. Kita Sadakichi and Takahashi Sadaki placed *hisabetsu-sha* (people who have been discriminated against) squarely in a Japanese history by narrating the specific character of discrimination proper to each period and noting the sociological origins and experiences of each respective group. When Japanese ethnologists and activists reprise the story of the beginning of the "historical" *buraku* in ethnography, they mean that the *buraku* (or, more precisely, its premodern antecedent usually as seen through the nomenclature of the *eta* status category) was "historicized" within the Japanese domestic context in a 1919 issue of the journal that scholar-bureaucrat Kita Sadakichi edited, *Folk and History* (*Minzoku to rekishi*).

Kita made two major contributions to *buraku* historiography. One was debunking the foreigner theory (*ijin-setsu*) that claimed foreign origins for *buraku-min*, along with the thesis on differing ethnic origins (*i-minzoku kigen-setsu*) that claimed that *buraku-min* were not Japanese but rather Korean; Chinese; or Ezo, indigenous people who dwelled in northern Japan.[32] The evidence for this myth was gleaned through the historical philology of the term *eta* itself and interpreting that the status group (*e-tori*) responsible for providing dead horsemeat to birds kept by the classical court was partially composed of émigrés from Korea or China. These myths had functioned to not only keep *buraku-min* outside of Japanese history but to see them as ahistorical, outside of development.

Kita's second contribution was to classify the historical quality of the "marked" *buraku* (*tokushu buraku*) in terms of a culturalist definition. He saw its emergence as a "problem of circumstances or environment" (*kyōgu no mondai*), one that can be managed. Praise of Kita appears with little variation in a range of publications that spans from authoritative dictionaries like the *Kōjien* to Kimura's first effort at *buraku* literary criticism in 1926.

Harada Tomohiko's *History of the Hisabetsu Buraku* (*Hisabetsu buraku no rekishi*) praises Kita as the only prewar ethnologist who has contributed at the highest level to *buraku* historical research.[33] As a scholar and a government bureaucrat, Kita argued that domestic political conditions in the era of warring states (mid-fifteenth to early seventeenth century) created dropouts (*rakugo-sha*) of the public sphere. Though later activists would stress the intensification of the Tokugawa status system over the origins of discrimination as the crucial time for *buraku* identity formation, Kita provided a framework for seeing different historical precipitations of marginality as effects of economic, legal, and social structures.

The narrative pattern for Kita's historiography is announced in his introduction to the 1919 issue of *Folk and History*. He establishes the origins of discrimination in the premodern status system but sees discrimination through the categories that define the modern citizen. This modern framework corresponds to the distinction between commoners and new commoners. The difference between the two works is the organizing principle that allows him to see a bifurcated but continuous history over roughly one thousand years—the parallax relation of the "society outside of society." Despite the kinds of social exile that Kita finds as early as the sixth century, Kita's history is surprisingly indebted to modern notions of citizenship. The key division in his scheme is between participation and exile. Regardless of difference in historical time, Kita sees this split at work in a series of dropouts who lag behind or fail to progress. These laggards of history are excluded from the body of Tokugawa citizens (*kōmin*) and from the "common rights" (*kōken*) that Kita posits were allowed to each citizen after the 646 Taika reforms that established the first basic system of legal codes in Japan.

Kita calls for abolishing discrimination in the domestic context, but placing his work in the context of arguments that legitimize Japanese empire brings out the limits of his interpretation of self-determination. Kita's investment in *buraku* liberation is complicated by his role as a bureaucrat invested in assimilating other ethnic groups in the Japanese empire, especially Koreans. The essay that historicizes *buraku-min* as Japanese subjects places them in a specifically imperial order: *buraku-min* are "all children under the reign of the same emperor" though they are made to suffer "alienation from mainstream society." On one hand, Kita's call echoes efforts made by Japanese representatives to the League of Nations that same year to be seen as equal in the world gaze. He calls on these leaders, "our brethren who are lately calling upon the world to abolish racial discrimination" to live up to the rhetoric of the ethnic self-determination clause that they themselves put forth.[34]

The consequences of Kita's advocacy for *buraku-min* and simultaneous justification of imperial rule are apparent in two lectures he published in 1926 and 1928. The lectures treat the problem of assimilating benighted minorities who had suffered discrimination for historical reasons. *The Promotion of Assimilation* (*Yūwa sokushin*) and *On the Historical Consideration of Issues of Assimilation* (*Yūwa mondai ni kansuru rekishi-teki kōsatsu*) clarify that, to Kita, history means attaining a place within the Japanese protonation, meaning at first the Heian court and later the Tokugawa *bakufu* military government.[35] In short, attaining a place in national history also involves finding a place in imperial history. Kita's histories of ethnic assimilation regarding the *buraku* map effectively to colonial policies that eradicate the historical differences between the mainland of Japan (*naichi*) and its colonies (*gaichi*) through the same claim of originary cultural sameness, pan-Asianism.[36] Kita's concern seems less motivated by human rights or social justice concerns of "leveling" and more by a desire to integrate all residents of the empire in a general scheme of comparative nationalisms within the empire. The second figure responsible for putting *buraku* historiography on the map, however, used the narrative of history to counter arguments for imperial rule.

A Thousand Years of Servitude

Takahashi Sadaki was a political organizer, a Bolshevik and head of the publicity bureau of the Suiheisha from 1922 to 1926. While he, too, railed at the rejection of the racial equality clause, he used it to provoke Japanese readers to realize their alliance with other oppressed peoples and make the domestic government live up to the demands Japan had made in the international sphere. After reading works by Kita and by socialist Sano Manabu, he published the first diachronic history from within the *buraku* movement, *A Thousand-Year History of the Hisabetsu Buraku* (*Hisabetsu buraku issennen-shi*) in 1924. It was banned shortly after publication but, after being reissued four times, sold eight thousand copies in edited versions its first year. Takahashi served as an interpreter for Comintern in Moscow from 1926 to 1928. He was arrested in 1929 and died in jail of tuberculosis. Takahashi contributed to the first wave of publishing Marx's works, the fifty-volume *Marxism* series (1924–29); introduced Rosa Luxemburg to a Japanese reading public; and drew on his knowledge of Russian, English, and German to lecture at one of the most active think tanks of the 1920s, the Avant-gardist Society (*Zen'ei-sha*) run by Yamakawa Hitoshi who founded the Worker-Farmer Party, one of prewar Japan's two major schools of Marxism.[37] Yamakawa committed *tenkō* (ideological volte-face) in prison by signing a statement that renounced his socialist affiliation. According to Okiura Kazuteru, because of this renunciation, interest in his works only revived after the mid-1950s critique of Stalinism.[38]

Takahashi drew on Kita's work as well as Yanase Keisuke's 1901 *Society Outside of Society: Eta Hinin* (*Shakai-gai no shakai: eta hinin*) and the arguments about self-determination put forth in Sano Manabu's 1922 *On Liberation of Tokushu Buraku* (*Tokushu buraku kaihō-ron*). The difference was that Takahashi extended their historical schemes into a program for international anticolonial alliance. The first half of *A Thousand-Year History* is a history of the shifting meanings of *senmin* since the beginning of the Taika reforms. Takahashi argues, according to a Marxist view of materialist history (*yuibutsu shi-kan*), that the origins of the *buraku* can be found in the ancient slavery put into place between the Nara and the Heian periods.[39] Each historical stage has its proper mode of exploitation but the Tokugawa era fixed and intensified both the categories and the degree of exploitation.[40] He traces a series of underclasses that emerge through different relations in production. The different groups of *senmin* are consolidated into variants of a single object turned subject of history. When he reaches the Meiji period, characterized by the bourgeois and the proletariat, Takahashi credits the liberation movement with sparking the transformation in consciousness that did not appear in either medieval or early modern periods, despite dissatisfaction seen in class clashes like peasant revolts. The agent of change is not clear, but Takahashi writes that in his own historical moment *buraku-min* seek "the right to manage relations of production," to engage creatively with capitalism, and join the economic development of the proletariat at an international level.[41]

In keeping with Marxist theories of poesis, Takahashi felt that the job of writing was not only to provide a narrative form for history but to change current existence. He appealed to international law and anticolonial movements for ethnic self-determination to change the machinery of authority that extended through and structured sovereignty in the Taishō and early Shōwa eras. His statement of the book's mandate clearly lays out the terms of historical materialism in terms of dominator and dominated and charts a clear course from a dark past (*antan taru kako*) to a shining future (*kōki aru mirai*) that culminates in the "historical inevitability" of the Suiheisha movement:[42]

> Now the Suiheisha movement is beginning to spread like wildfire throughout the country. The material that flows at the bottom of this vast movement is the tears of rage against the disdainful, traditional point of view. There is no one who has endured an everyday life as cruel or been as cruelly oppressed as *tokushu buraku-min* of the past. This book narrates the integrated thousand-year history of *tokushu buraku-min,* and is an effort to show the way in which the Suihei movement followed out of historical inevitability.
>
> It is not overstating the facts to say that until now, there have been no powerful books that treat the *tokushu buraku-min.* Our country's history books have in the past been political history or military history, and have lacked a history of the dominated classes. This book is the history of a slave who has been exploited until the last drop of his blood, writing against the history of the dominators.[43]

The rhetoric of historical materialism that sees history unfolding as a class struggle from exploitation to liberation mingles with an affectively freighted discourse of sympathy. Takahashi states that although "the bourgeois of the world met in Versailles" to sign the Treaty of Versailles in 1919, many are still suffering "in domination and enslavement."[44] Liberation (*kaihō*) ideology is also explicitly tied to programs of national-ethnic self-determination. He writes that before the 1914 war six hundred million people were living in the conditions of colonial lands; and "half-colonial" populations including Persia, Turkey, and China amounted to 1.2 billion.[45] Legitimating the *buraku* cause through its alliance with national decolonization movements outside Japan, he writes that those "whose hearts are pained" at colonial situations abroad should apply the same principle domestically, to remember "the thirty million brethren hit by the whip of our country's slave customs reminiscent of ancient times."[46] Takahashi charges the "dominant class of Japan" who submitted the failed request for the abolition of racial discrimination to the League of Nations with ignoring the internal state of their own country.[47] They proposed such a "deceptive and fictional proposal for racial equality" (*jinshu byōdō*) while "thirty million *buraku-min* groan[ed] under such irrational discrimination and oppression."[48] Takahashi's contribution to historiography was to emphasize the international dimensions of the Suiheisha mandate and to locate *senmin* in a worldwide struggle. He places the Suiheisha Manifesto's rhetorical subject of "our brothers" in an explicitly international frame that galvanizes the imagery of suffering and ethnic struggle.

In addition to the commitment to a dialectical materialism that works toward absolute knowledge, freedom, and civil society, the Suiheisha rhetorical tradition of which Takahashi was a part also played freely with writing systems and what I call heterophonics as a way to demonstrate their active ability to shape symbolic and therefore narrative and material meaning. Heterophonics is a strategy that substitutes kanji characters for different ones that indicate the same phoneme in order to alter the meaning of the whole. This is a paradigm that Nakagami and later writers will engage.

One celebrated paradigm appears as the title of the journal edited by Matsumoto Ji'ichirō, the first *buraku* member of the National Diet. The journal was titled *Senmin* (Choosing people), a title that sounds slightly anachronistic because *sen* had been the adjective that referred to the abject status of a heterogeneous collection of outcast groups, *senmin*, under the Tokugawa-era status system. But Matsumoto wrote the title as a neologism using the characters 選民. This title sounded the same, but it looked *rather* different and meant something *entirely* different. His polemical choice of characters substituted one homonym, *sen*, for another, markedly changing the meaning of the *kanji* compound in the title. The name of the title actually takes on the sense of agency that it proclaims, a performative dimension of poetics like the manifesto. The name had contrasted *senmin* to *ryōmin*, 良民, members of the four official status groups of the Tokugawa era: samurai, merchants, farmers, and artisans. The alternate homonym of 選 inverts this abjection by switching the character for *sen*.

Matsumoto's journal tropes on the meaning of *senmin* as "chosen people" and unites otherwise potentially disparate people into a collective identity in two significant ways. The effect of this switch is to powerfully embed the *buraku*, which Matsumoto aims to represent politically, in two representational histories. First, the new compound of *senmin* draws on the popular sentiment of *buraku* residents as a tribe in exile, referring to other chosen peoples, such as lost tribes of Israel, who offer the historical precedent of being redeemed after enduring long spells of suffering. Second, the inversion of *sen* was also given an emphatically modern cast, as *sen* is the modern character designating the kinds of selection and processes involved in modern electoral politics, like *sentaku* (選択, selection) or *senkyo* (選挙, election). By singling out these characters, Matsumoto not only reclassifies his constituents as modern subjects but actually performs the acts of election that the characters refer to. Matsumoto's choice implies that *buraku* residents have the agency of self-determination necessary to choose and chart out a future.

Buraku Writing and Literary Arts

Two orientations were key to the role that literature and literary criticism played in the liberation movement. First, literature was viewed as part of a larger task, which was to establish *buraku-min* as an integral, if unrecognized, subject of Japanese history. Second, to this end, the kinds of writing produced by movement activists and writers of *buraku* fiction included a range of extraliterary genres, over and above bellelettristic literature. Of these, literary criticism played a role in establishing how the projects of political representation and literary representation could be allied.

Takahashi Sadaki had remarked in 1924 that there were no "powerful books" that treated the *hisabetsu buraku*. Although not a *buraku-min* himself, in 1926 Kimura Ki began formal literary criticism of *buraku* literary arts by including a chapter on the Suiheisha in his collection *Literary Arts from Four Corners of the Earth* (*Bungei tōzai nanboku*). Kimura's framework was less militant than the Suiheisha and was directed at sparking awareness in sympathizers of the movement rather than in movement members themselves. Kimura's style was expository and unengaged with the emotionally freighted archive of socialist and Christological symbols of sacrifice, and privileged feeling over politics. He addressed his essays to an audience that would be receptive to his claim that sympathy from mainstream readers was more important than a direct movement (*chokusetsu undō*).[49] (The term "direct" was strongly associated with the anarchist political philosopher Kōtoku Shūsui who was executed in 1911 as part of an alleged plot to assassinate the emperor. Negating the term reinforces the clampdown on public protest, socialism, and anti-imperial critiques that descended after the Great Treason Incident.) Kimura drew on a cosmopolitan range of examples to argue that literature was an important diplomatic tool and interwove his assessment of literary categories with an argument that the people (*minshū*) constitute a source of support apart from the government based on a history of failed promises. Like activists, he cites many failings of the Japanese government, from the deceit of the *shin-heimin* name to the ineffectiveness of the improvement (*kaizen*) movement. Unlike activists, he sees the people and the government as separate institutions and refrains from making claims on the government's promise of modernity, much less historical analyses of structural exploitation.

In Kimura's argument, although the Japanese government had failed to successfully execute liberal social welfare programs, successful examples of literature from abroad showed that literary fiction could reach the people in ways the state cannot. He praises examples of potential revolutions that were made nonthreatening to the mainstream citizenry through an appeal to the sentiments of the people. Literary works like Harriet Beecher Stowe's *Uncle Tom's Cabin* and Ivan Turgenev's *Sketches of a Hunter*, for instance, contributed to movements like "black slave liberation" by tapping into the "sentiments of everyday people."[50] Kimura writes that since the Russo-Japanese War readers have been accustomed to thinking of Russians as barbarians. (Kimura's focus on the 1904–5 war eclipses the Bolshevik revolution altogether.) But Russian literature "makes people able to think of Russian people as people, not as enemies."[51]

In his canon, Kimura rules out popular works such as *Recollections of a Husband's Love* (*Sōfuren*; 1904) and *Biwa Song* because they sustain a "beautiful illusion" that the actual *buraku* cannot live up to.[52] *Recollection of a Husband's Love*, named after a genre of court music (*sōfuren*), is a pure love story featuring the heroine Masako.[53] Although her name suggests that the truth will ultimately come out, she hides her identity after she is adopted by a military couple. After she marries, her real father threatens to expose her, and her negotiations with him are mistaken for romantic intrigue. She runs away to the seasonally poignant mountains where she pines for her husband. By and by, her foster father and husband come to realize her true value, and under a full moon the sounds of her husband's serenading koto waft through. She announces her true provenance and is once again embraced by her husband. Kimura thinks the writer lacks the thought and morals of a Victor Hugo and "panders to sentimental tears."[54]

Biwa Song is a prototypical popular novel, a work of domestic fiction, set in the Meiji era. Satono and her brother live alone until he is called into the army. When she goes to see him off, she gets lost in a strange part of town. A young man falls in love with her at first glance. She refuses, due to their difference in status, but love wins out. They marry and live in bliss until her mother-in-law decides she cannot live with such a daughter-in-law and forces the son to choose between them. Satono is sent home, and she quickly falls to pieces. She is brought back to life, however, by a next-door neighbor who has fallen from a noble position and is her alter ego. Kimura is not precise about what sort of reality he finds the works lack, but both stories posit an essential feminine virtue that shines through, one that is recognized as essentially noble by another person of higher status who allies with the protagonist and redeems her suffering.

Other categories in Kimura's inventory are reference lists of dramatic works about *buraku-min;* works by Suiheisha members; works by writers who have done fieldwork in *buraku,* including foreigners; and Suiheisha scholars. Despite differences in genre, his examples converge in finding that the most powerful works are those that dramatize suffering in a real-istic way, so as to cause change in a mainstream reader whose broadened horizons and sympathy are premised on not having contact with actual *buraku-min* or their movement. At the same time, he values most highly the *buraku* experience that is felt so intensely that it challenges the lim-its of representation. He even manages to make socialist Sano Manabu sound like a melodrama at wit's end. To illustrate the magnitude of suf-fering of *buraku-min* who have lived the transition from the Tokugawa to the Meiji era, he cites Sano's plaint of "how cruel are the two characters that spell *eta.* If you searched the extensive pools of Chinese vocabulary you couldn't find a pair of characters so contemptuous."[55] This hyperbolic suffering that challenges the imagination is, conversely, enlightening to the reader. Despite the fact that he does not suggest what actions might follow upon moving hearts and minds to lead to a future course of action, the works he chooses suggest a selection of texts that persists almost unaltered until Sumii Sue's seven-volume *River without a Bridge* (*Hashi no nai kawa*) appears beginning in 1961, and a work amenable to the liberation move-ment finally appears.

Liberation literature stands in conceptual opposition to Kimura's ini-tial program because it is premised on making action a natural result of thinking or feeling. Noma Hiroshi first formulated the program of libera-tion literature (*kaihō bungaku*) in the immediate wake of World War II. Noma was a socially engaged writer with a history in social services. He

had begun his career by joining the Osaka city government just after gradu-
ating college with a seemingly irrelevant degree in French. He was asked to
translate studies on Parisian municipal pawnshops because his boss thought
that French social welfare systems might provide a good policy model for
Osaka.[56] He continued to work for the city in its departments of surveys
and direct services to *buraku* areas, called by the administrative government
name of *dōwa chiku*. His most renowned work, *Ring of Youth* (*Seinen no
wa*; 1977–81), featured a protagonist who also worked for Osaka city, during the war, on behalf of *buraku* residents. Its style pursued the structure of
ideas that Noma terms the total novel (*zentai shōsetsu*).[57] The narrative of
the total novel essentially follows the agenda of the 1946 essay. It dramatizes
characters who become aware of their actual relation to the world and use
that new consciousness to change it. Because it is Japan specific and deals
with discrimination as a premodern legacy and because its characters confront problems publicly, it becomes the exemplary work of *buraku* fiction for
Kitahara Taisaku. Kitahara was a member of the central committee of the
BLL when he published a 1959 survey of buraku issues in literature.[57]

The realism of Noma Hiroshi and Hijikata Tetsu emphasized the positivist texture of daily life but it also had faith in a postwar narrative of liberation from premodern elements of culture that Noma felt lingered even
after 1945. Noma's historical outline for liberation literature also mapped
in significant ways onto the *buraku* liberation narrative, as signaled in the
very categories of liberation literature and the *buraku* social movement's
guiding historical concept of *buraku* liberation. In novellas like *Dark Pictures* (*Kurai e*; 1946) and essays written throughout the postwar era, Noma
plots history as a series of stages that progress from primitive, medieval
chaos to modern, universal enlightenment.[59]

Noma's outline of liberation literature follows the narrative of a manifesto, though it contains close analysis of literary texts. He narrates in a
collective voice of "we" (*watashi-tachi*). His narrative establishes a set of
grievances, assesses failed attempts to attain liberation, and elaborates the
conditions for a true liberation. Liberation starts from a particular concept, the repressive powers of the feudal regime that still linger and hinder
the ability to progress personally or socially or to integrate the two and
achieve the highest order of liberation. The paradigm of the Renaissance
structures the narrative by providing a pan-national model for appealing
to the laws of the physical world to combat metaphysical illusion, such as
that diffused during wartime. Noma illustrates this state with the example

of a lurid incident in which a shopkeeper took in a boarder, a kabuki actor, Nizaemon. The boarder first ate him out of house and home and then killed his whole family. Noma repeats the lesson from the incident that Kono Mitsuru, head of the Japan Socialist Party, offers: the "kabuki actor lives his everyday life in a feudal world." He agrees that many "relics of the feudal world" live within "our hearts." In this example, kabuki is a metaphysical concept rather than a craft or art and is presumably waiting to kill those it lodges within.[60] Noma proceeds chronologically through literary history in an essentially tragic mode to explain how each historical stage was marked with a flaw that blocked the necessary consciousness for liberation. For instance, in the Genroku era (1688–1704) literature flourished despite writing that was modern before its time, in writers like haiku writer Matsuo Bashō, dramatist Chikamatsu Monzaemon, and the priest-poet Saigyō. While thinkers like Ando Shōeki presented challenges to the feudal system, no systematic movement emerged.

In the Meiji era, he continues, two visionaries emerged and devoted themselves to an iconoclastic takedown of old structures. Yet they, too, were unable to transcend their focus on personal matters to sublate their interests to higher, social causes. Kitamura Tōkoku (1868–94) committed suicide after despairing that "in Japan there is no revolution, only shifts."[61] Finally, although Tōson's protagonist attacked the feudal system by promoting the elements of self that are the only means to liberation (by exiling Ushimatsu to Texas), Tōson, too, failed to merge that consciousness with "people as a whole" (*jinmin zentai*) to develop a social self-consciousness. Noma's essay sends a powerful message that the nature of protagonists is to be exemplary and to change the world through channeling self-consciousness into an understanding of interconnectedness with the physical world in the largest possible way, through what he calls a "cosmic" (*uchū-teki*) understanding. Noma's agenda will provide a set of expectations about the progressive nature of history and the exemplary nature of protagonists that Nakagami's works depart from. At the same time, other writers affiliated with the liberation movement began to use and alter the rules, showing that liberation literature could make use of nonlinear avant-garde temporality and modernist style and still be deeply engaged in a social self-consciousness.

Hijikata Tetsu and Rhizomatic Writing

Although usually cast as a realist mode, liberation literature in fact provided an infrastructure of ideas, institutions, and narratives with which a writer could operate with some degree of autonomy from movement imperatives. The most accomplished *buraku* writer recognized by the movement, Hijikata Tetsu (1927–2005), came from within this conversation but developed an avant-garde style that differed from the kind of historicist narrative that Noma promoted. Though he only had a primary school education himself, Hijikata's writing, advocacy and editorial work underwrote the cultural turn of *buraku* activism, one that established literary prizes, debated the value of language and culture in *buraku* activism, and encouraged a literacy movement. After publishing his novel *Rhizome* (*Chikakei*), Hijikata wrote several books and quit his former job as a shoe repairman to edit the *Liberation News* (*Kaihō shinbun*), the weekly newspaper of the BLL, a post he held from 1974 to 1990. He wrote scripts for five documentary films about the Sayama trial, a widely contested case in which a *buraku* youth was sentenced to death for the rape and murder of a schoolgirl. (I address this trial in chapter 2.) He led the movement against republishing *The Broken Commandment* after the war and promoted a special category on criticism in the awards that the BLL began to sponsor in the mid 1970s. Hijikata published several more books containing essays and roundtable discussions on the role of culture in the *buraku* movement, which had taken a back seat to organized politics until the 1970s.

Rhizome won the third annual *New Japan Literature* (*Shin nihon bungaku*) Prize in 1963, the first time the competition had a category for full-length fiction. The magazine, edited by Noma Hiroshi, had broken away from the main structure of the JCP after the critique of Stalin. The editors were disenchanted with the JCP's failure to be truly populist and incorporated texts that they had formerly spurned as the products of war criminals into their own program of liberation literature. *Rhizome* was, in Noma's words, the "first novel from inside the *buraku*."[62] Hijikata would later describe this approach as a kind of fieldwork-based ethnography based on having seen the "real thing" (*jittai chōsa*).[63] Given the strict criteria of self-consciousness, historical engagement, and exemplary behavior that liberation literature advocated, the dense and experimental style of *Rhizome* comes as a surprise.

Rhizome uses avant-garde, stream-of-consciousness style to narrate the kind of scenes of close-knit family life and aggrieved illness that have served as staple themes of *buraku* literature in modes of realism or melodrama since the late Tokugawa era. In his afterward to *Rhizome*, Hijikata writes that he remembers feeling strongly that the way Ushimatsu's sense of life (*ikitsukai*) and his very "temperature" (*taion*) were depicted did not correspond to someone from the *buraku*.[64] *Rhizome* is written, Hijikata writes, in particular response to the idea put forth in *The Broken Commandment* that you cannot be openly from a *buraku* and lead the life of a normal citizen in Japan. It contains set-piece scenes of confession, confrontation, and labor that respond to and reinterpret famous scenes from Tōson's novel.

Rhizome reworks the reader's perceptions of realism by using a multiple point-of-view structure. The reader has to recognize that parallax in triptych and work to put together the relationships of three characters' stories, a representation of their world that corresponded to neither historicist linear time nor the completely personal time of I-fiction. *Rhizome* contributed an avant-garde challenge to a realist mandate while still maintaining the imperative to make *buraku* life manifest by using specifically ethnographic rhetorics. A further model for *Rhizome* is Kafka's *Metamorphosis*. The first chapter of *Rhizome* opens from a place midstream in someone's consciousness. But where the youth Gregor Samsa wakes up to an unfamiliar insect body one day and narrates from the point of view of a cockroach throughout the work, the first narrator of *Rhizome* wakes up morbidly ill in a hospital sickbed. His view of the story is only partial and is relativized not just by the narrator but also by two other characters, his mother and his sister, who will socialize his narration. The aleatory skips of the narrator's description of humiliation fade into delirium and emerge in a hospital room. The novella opens with a hallucination that is later framed as the effect of illness and medication:

> Suddenly, an upturned hand with its fingers sticking up came into my field of vision. The palm of that hand is outspread, but only the thumb is folded down to touch the palm. The white of that palm is something I didn't want to get into my field of vision, but even though I shut them because I'm allowed to since I'm sick, it slid in under my eyelids and flickered. These are all works in a haiku magazine Yamagata held out. "How can he do such a thing as kill a milk cow when it's still nursing, it's insufferable." "My body's smell verges on being taken over by a beastly smell." These are the works of Kyōtani Akio, shot through with the complex feelings

of contempt an abattoir worker feels. That shocked me, in a state where I couldn't even speak, it felt like Yamagata was sticking out its own outstretched, upturned palm to me. With its nimble thumb all folded down. And Yamagata seemed pretty happy with himself. "This guy, he's one of *those.*" When that palm and those short words were aimed at me, it felt like my body even underneath my skin was all exposed ... That moment, that contempt. That time I got all flustered. My blood rushed to my face, I averted my eyes as soon as possible from that palm, and in a raspy voice I said "yes" and nodded. That was a double dose of contempt ... In front of Yamagata I pulled off being I-the-imposter. That four-fingered palm flickers in front of my eyes. The four fingers flicker. It's as if it's trying to pull my guts out, gouge itself into my insides and stab me.[65]

Stream-of-consciousness narration is a modernist device that emphasizes an interpretative, rather than objective, relation to the world by showing how a personal experience of time can diverge from what the clock shows. This passage shows how, even within the strictures of liberation literature, modernism and realism can be compatible. The character Hiroshi's reverie conveys tropes that would be common knowledge to a discursive reader familiar with the codes of *buraku* literature or experience: the dehumanizing imagery, the communiqué in secret that leaves no trace despite its aggression, and the sense of being uncovered by someone with extremely local knowledge and left in a vulnerable state. Intricate figural language that switches between visual and acoustic registers reinforces the pathological effect of the palm (*hira*) and the lingering effect of a cinematic afterimage when the palm flickers (*hirahira*) in the patient's mind's eye even as his eyelids are closed. The reverie uses tropes of the Suiheisha Manifesto not only to connect the pain of discrimination to somatic pain but to include print culture, the haiku journal, as an agent of toxicity. Each mention of a sensation is connected to a social field, and both human action and print culture seem to have equal effect.

Hijikata writes that the difference between Gregor Samsa and the character Hiroshi is that defamiliarization for the *buraku-min* happens every day, and the experience of a nonhuman life does not require transport into a fantastic realm. As if to underscore this experience of disjunction and perform it on the reader, the modernist form adopted by each subsequent chapter of *Rhizome* structures the experience of alienation into the reader's understanding while depicting the particular social sources of the characters' alienation. Chapters alternate among three points of view belonging to three family members. Each is written in a slightly different Kyoto dialect, and each represents a different orientation to *buraku* life. Hiroshi, who introduces the novel, has left the *buraku* as fast as he could. He gets a job outside until he is brought down by tuberculosis and has two ribs removed. Hijikata transposes the terms of personal health into social terms. Hiroshi's operation, in Hijikata's explanation, is closely tied to Hijikata's own method. He writes that Japanese society is "ill." The solution to somatic illness is a classically naturalist solution: to open the body and expose its "insides" (*naizō*) to the light of critique.[66]

Hiroshi's flashbacks are organized around an idea of constant exile. After leaving the *buraku*, he allies with leftist politics but is disenchanted because their disdain for *buraku-min* makes him a second-class participant in the revolution. He has nothing but contempt for his mother throughout most of the novel until a hospital scene that is familiar from the genre of melodrama but told in avant-garde style. His mother, Maki, is introduced in the throes of a sex scene when a telegram arrives to tell her that Hiroshi is on death's door. Hiroshi has scorned her because she is lustful and has had children by different fathers, all of whom have left the scene. The narrative sections focusing on Hiroshi and Maki are embedded in the past. But the narrative energy of the novel is clearly placed on the youngest character, fifteen-year-old Kinuko, poised between adolescent curiosity and the looming pressures of adulthood. Cheeky and self-reliant, she "throws back" discrimination by taking her shoes off and wiggling her toes at Ken-chan, a boy who has taunted her. While she shares her brother's exasperation with her mother and desires escape from her immediate life like her brother does, she is "different than him" in that this escape does not lead to hiding her *buraku* identity but rather proudly claiming it and moving forward.[67]

As in *The Broken Commandment,* the locus classicus of the *buraku* in modern prose fiction that Hijikata returns to in the afterward to his own novella is a school, the most symbolically loaded venue in the book. We first meet Kinuko in class as the teacher gives a lecture on poetics. The scene works to establish a difference between formal written knowledge and informal social knowledge. The narrative works as Kinuko begins to recognize the differences between the two spheres and moves between them through a series of trials where she learns how to live in the parallax of the two worlds and even thrive on code-switching.

In an early example of how formal and informal knowledge are incompatible, the teacher puts two kanji characters on the blackboard. He asks if anyone can read them. No one can; they make no literal sense in reference to the everyday world. He explains that though their literal characters do not spell phonetically, they mean *tsuyu*, the early summer period of intense rain. He explains the reasoning behind the abstraction by giving the etymology of the word (plum maturity, plus rain). He connects the phrase to the everyday world by reminding the class of practical details. In rainy season, food molds faster. Even his shirts mold faster because of the starch.[68] His pedagogy is derailed, however, when Kinuko causes the class to burst out laughing by suggesting that he is not up with street knowledge—a different kind of abstract social practice—if he is not buying fashionable nylon shirts that don't need ironing. Moreover, she challenges him: if he has no girlfriend to keep track of his clothes and school him on style, he is missing out and clearly lacks the form of practical poetry that would have gotten the job done. The teacher takes her piped-up outburst in stride and becomes the mediator between Kinuko's vernacular oral version of *buraku* life and abstract reason. He introduces her to practical knowledge as well as lessons in how to connect self-respect and recognition to issues of discrimination he knows she will encounter.

The teacher becomes the emissary of compassionate, movement-based liberation pedagogy through a Socratic method, but he never uses writing to quash Kinuko's relation to vernacular oral culture. He teaches Kinuko her constitutional rights and how to conduct her own small-scale lesson based on the Suiheisha Manifesto of humanizing those treated inhumanely. Some pedagogical scenes between the teacher and Kinuko enter into extremely intimate territory and fall into the category of examples often used to illustrate the primitive, barbarous, or antisocial elements of *buraku* life. Strikingly, Nakagami's signature term, *roji*, is used interchangeably with *buraku* in this work; realism and representation are fused in a way that Nakagami never brings close. On one occasion, the teacher yells at Kinuko for defecating in the schoolyard. When she explains her reasoning, however, that the privies in the *roji* are dark, scary, and cold, the teacher softens. Their discussion leads to an understanding about self-discipline and understanding spatial contexts for behavior as a precondition for public life as a grown-up. The conversation represents a synthesis in which authority and potential come to an understanding within a structure. Later in the book, Kinuko yells at another student for the same offense, taking on the role of teacher herself, making exemplary conscious choices and commitments in her life. She practices her resolve by staking out and confronting her father, a shopkeeper in the respectable part of town. Though he spurns her, she takes it in stride. The book ends with a final confrontation. Kinuko confronts the principal of her school, who has called her a slur, and stomps on his foot. He is stunned until she explains to him that it hurts when he stomps on her, too. *Rhizome* inverts *The Broken Commandment*'s message that you must hide or emigrate if you are a *buraku-min*.

A broad framework of stances, conflicts, and positions has articulated *buraku* rhetorical activism as critique, as historiography, and as mandate since 1871. Rhetorical activism is propelled by the belief that language can stake a claim on the state or the social world and the way it distributes its sovereign powers. Rhetorical activism is also a practice that has the capacity to create new imaginaries. If we examine Nakagami's fiction in light of this archive, we can see that he draws extensively on a refashioning of its tropes and figures. We see this in the dehumanized worker and the manifesto-like language of *On the Japanese Language*, in the idea of a society outside of society that the protagonist Akiyuki imagines in the Kishū trilogy, and in the countermyth of the heroic resister of national consolidation that a character invents in *The Sea of Withered Trees* and *The Ends of the Earth, Supreme Time.*

For the bulk of the twentieth century, activists' work has been directed at state allocation of money, power, and representation as well as discrimination against *buraku* residents. Like these activists, Nakagami's investments in language extend beyond the artifacts of books and journals or the themes and styles of prose fiction precisely because language traverses the realms of fiction, nonfiction, and the extraliterary. The next chapter focuses on a trope, confession, that bridged literature and the legal sphere. A notorious confession by a *buraku* youth during a cause célèbre trial prompted Nakagami to begin his own countercanon of literary history, to begin to comment on *buraku*-related events in print, and to mark his writings more deeply with concrete experiences of discrimination. As we have seen, each theory of the *buraku* as a historically constituted identity and experience stakes a claim to political or economic injustice and redress and aims toward an open-ended future of liberation. Nakagami's agenda diverged at nearly every level from that of liberation literature activists. But his focus on emigration and exile, the long duration of *buraku* sufferings, consciousness of differential identity in a transnational frame, and efforts to convert a past of grievances into a future of more powerful representation stayed true to the main currents of *buraku* rhetorical activism and the drive for linguistic sovereignty as mapped by these earlier thinkers and writers.

CHAPTER 2

Confession and the Crisis of
Buraku Writing in the 1970s

Confession and *Kokubungaku*

This chapter shows how the theme of confession preoccupied writers in the 1970s who sought to place *buraku* settings and characters at the center of their work. Since *The Broken Commandment,* confession had been an instrumental part of literary characterization—and a heavily freighted one—for representing *buraku* characters and adjudicating how they fit in terms of national belonging. The confessional narrative pioneered in *The Broken Commandment* is a set-piece in which the *buraku* character reveals a long-held secret of his identity, one that is pent up but has guided his life as a young adult. The confession provokes immediate consequences and judgments in social life, clarifies past mysteries, and connects this newly identified character's behavior and psychic life to the setting of the *buraku.*

Nakagami's claim that modern literature began with *The Broken Commandment* is echoed by *buraku* activists who took offense at the work but from a different angle. They responded to the kinds of realist description that Watanabe Naomi calls the "outwardly legible signs" (*shirushi*) that marked residents of the *buraku.*[1] These signs are a pool of attributes that have different semantic contents, ranging from the beautiful woman to outrageous amounts of money to illness, but function in a structurally interchangeable way. The *Buraku* Liberation League (BLL) attempted to regulate these signs at the level of discrete units of speech as they challenged several different editions of *The Broken Commandment.* In 1939, phrases that had attributed a pathological identity to residents of the *buraku,* such as *eta* and *shin-heimin,* were replaced by the more objective-sounding *buraku no mono* or "*buraku* resident," as were other words that suggested class conflict.[2] Drawing on that edition, in 1959, Kitahara Taisaku finds *The Broken Commandment* flawed in ways that echo criticisms of proletariat literature: it sees confession exclusively in terms of personal choice and has no place for a collective movement. It also endorses class discrimination among those who should be allied, because Ushimatsu's father anchors the family's identity in a misty samurai past, unlike others of foreign origin.[3] In more contemporary criticism, Umezawa, Hirano, and Yamagishi's comprehensive survey of "images of the *buraku*" in literature also begins its history with *The Broken Commandment*. These critics find fault with the typologizing description of slaughterhouse workers on different grounds. They object that while the mandate of naturalism was to provide interior expression (*naimen byōsha*) to characters, the *buraku* characters were only described in contemptuous terms from the outside as having "the glazed half-wit expression common to the lowest of their kind."[4] They also object that Ushimatsu himself uses the language of discrimination to refer to fellow *eta* when he has not yet confessed his identity.

In the 1970s, the language of discrimination dependent upon confession traversed fictional works of different genres and audiences and included examples that I discuss below: avant-garde poetry (a long poem "E-tta," published in *Modern Poetry Notebook* [*Gendai shi techō*]) as well as left-ist journals (a novella published in *Prospects* [*Tenbō*]).[5] Each work in this cluster featured a confession by a *buraku* character, an act that indicted the neighborhood as a deviant or pathological place and reaffirmed the under-standing of *buraku* culture as a society outside of society and one of dubious morality at that. In addition, these stories introduced an extra dimension that I earlier called "tragic enlightenment," the narrative tendency to cast the confessing character out of the public sphere. In this tendency, enlighten-ment—the knowledge or nomenclature that clarifies and fixes his supposed identity—occurs by resolving in a transcendental signifier that produces tragedy, an impossible coexistence. Each of these texts captured popular attention and provoked activist wrath because they featured youthful *buraku* protagonists who were unaware that their confessions gave long descrip-tions of apparently crime-bound surroundings while recounting the cir-cumstances that were judged to motivate their perverse acts. These fictional representations affirmed the heightened sense that a culture of pathology was linked to *buraku* identity and drew on the sensationalism that a contro-versial trial, the Sayama trial, generated at local and national levels.

The Sayama Trial and Confession

The press and the Diet lavished attention on the case when it first broke in 1963. Heightening its news value was the kidnapping of a young girl that had taken place the previous month in the Taitō-ku ward in Tokyo. The perpetrator had gotten away, and the body had not yet been found when the Sayama case broke. The Taitō-ku case was bungled so seriously that mistakes made by the police were brought into question at the Diet; the ruling Liberal Democratic Party's safety committee reprimanded the police; and the director general of the Tokyo Metropolitan Police Department resigned. The ripple effect of panic in Sayama caused the local police force to be joined by hundreds of firefighters and self-defense forces troops. The pressure was so great that the Sayama police chief said that "*we* feel like the suspects."[6]

Lawyers for the defendant Ishikawa Kazuo, who was twenty-four at the time of his arrest in 1963, appealed the original death sentence. In the Sayama trial, Ishikawa confessed to the following chain of events. On May 1, 1963, Nakada Yoshie, a sixteen-year-old schoolgirl, disappeared on her way home from school in the city of Sayama in rural Saitama, an area then famous for its tea fields. A ransom note was delivered to her family demanding two hundred thousand yen. When her sister brought the money at the appointed time, she sparred verbally with the perpetrator. He ran away although surrounded by forty policemen.[7] Three days later, the girl's body was discovered in a nearby forest; she had apparently been raped before she was killed.

The document that was instrumental in producing the judge's final narrative is called the *jihaku chōsho*, or self-professed confession. This document is composed by investigators who question the suspect, take notes, compile the notes into a narrative, and have the suspect sign it. Ishikawa was arraigned at Urawa district court on July 9 on charges of rape, murder, disposing of a body, and extortion. He pled guilty (*kisō jijitsu o mitomeru*) on the basis of the confessional narrative presented to him. His signed statement consisted of a scrawled, barely legible note using almost exclusively phonetic hiragana characters. Other objections to this "confession" occurred because Ishikawa could not read what had been written; because he allegedly signed the statement thinking it would cut his jail time to ten years; because he was held for a long time in a "temporary" cell at a police station, not an official jail; and because, in the words of Tokyo University professor Hirano Ryūichi, even if the "arrest for a separate incident and long incarceration were not formally illegal, they violated the spirit of the Constitution and criminal procedural law."[8]

The judge in the first trial issued the death penalty in the surprisingly short time of six months after questioning only four people. The case was appealed to the Tokyo High Court, and the sentence was reduced to life imprisonment in October, 1974, despite the fact that Ishikawa had switched his plea to not guilty and had raised the issue of discrimination as a governing factor in his prosecution—that, in essence, discrimination on the part of investigators had accounted for the narrative attributed to already flimsy evidence. A petition for permission to appeal was submitted to the court in January, 1976, and denied on August 9, 1977. (In terms of Nakagami's works, this was just after *Sea of Withered Trees* was published.) Eventually in 1986, seven detectives who had been present at the original search of Ishikawa's house stepped forward to admit that a key piece of evidence, the schoolgirl's fountain pen they claimed to have found, had not actually been present in the house. Ishikawa was finally paroled in 1991 after thirty-one years in prison, but in 2005 the Supreme Court dismissed a request for a retrial, and as of 2010, the conviction still stands.

Beyond its immediate role in sealing Ichikawa's guilt in the Sayama trial and its effect of affirming what many felt were chronic features of anti*buraku* discrimination, confession was a heavily freighted act because of the rhetorical tradition it evoked and the place of *buraku* confession at the beginning of the canon of Japanese literature. Nakagami connects the principle of confession from the Sayama trial to the confession that concludes *The Broken Commandment*. Overall, as Higashi Eizō writes, the confession scene of *The Broken Commandment* received the most critical attention.[9] Nakagami's attack, too, focuses on the effect of this scene, but its critique is different. He indicts *The Broken Commandment* in a 1979 roundtable with Karatani Kōjin where he links literary and legal confession through narrative (*monogatari*) and its work in the service of law and system (*hō to seido*). This connection will traverse his work for the next decade:

> The hundred-odd years from the Meiji restoration to the present have covered the ground of the loss of the war and the occupation. Moreover, humanism and the privileging of belletristic "literature" have run rampant. For instance, Katai, for instance, Tōson. Why did *The Broken Commandment* have to end with the confession of

being an *eta*? I'm different from the run of literary scholars and critics, when I think that Segawa Ushimatsu's confession is an emaciation of the author Shimazaki Tōson, and that *eta* is the effect of social law and system at the same time that it is the *monogatari* borne by Segawa Ushimatsu. In effect, what I think Tōson did is to ignore law and system, and plunge *monogatari* into humanism and the belle-lettrism of "literature."[10]

From the 1930s to the 1960s, as Michael Bourdaghs notes, every young critic who wanted to "make a name for himself" would begin with a book on the author of *The Broken Commandment*.[11] The "run of literary scholars and critics" against which Nakagami thunders includes Noma Hiroshi. Although other writers emerged in the 1970s to overtake Tōson as the standard bearer of modern literature, Noma had praised *The Broken Commandment* because he felt that the protagonist's confession showed a desire to externalize his identity and take responsibility for it in public, rather than harboring it in secret. Where Noma sees the enlightenment that follows on publicly claiming the identity of *eta* as a positive sign, Nakagami disagrees. He argues that this interpretation gives a false impression that the confessor is the proprietor of his own voice. In other words, interpretations like Noma's imply that because Ushimatsu takes on agency in the schoolroom scene, he is empowered in other spheres of life as well, when in fact that very agency and enlightenment is used in the service of abasing himself.

Nakagami reads Ushimatsu's embrace of his identity as a deluded self-negation. The confession obscures the fact that the socialized self encouraged by the imperial law and system is in fact profoundly antagonistic to Ushimatsu's social life: it will not allow him to remain in Japan once he has self-identified as an *eta*. When Nakagami calls *eta* the effect of law and system, he is emphasizing how language has the capacity to shape and fix identity and to connect signifier and signified, not only to name what is preexisting. And when he calls *eta* a *monogatari*, or narrative, he implies that *eta* is not a noun but a cause and effect relation—the name of *eta* has a consequence, which is expulsion from Japan. Because this self-propelled agency actually functions very much like a law, the term "law and system" thus applies equally to literature and classifies a narrative that functions like a law, though it may emerge from a different context. Nakagami's concern is how the same narrative operations, which he describes with the term *monogatari,* also function in other dimensions of the public sphere, such as the interpretive structures of the legal-judicial system as revealed in the Sayama trial. In the trial, Ishikawa's confession had served to substantiate all the signs that had been read as evidence of his character.

Nakagami's focus on language as a model for the world that actually *worked* in the world set him apart from the poststructuralist literary critics of the 1970s who were reformulating literature's relation to ideas, concepts, and power using the very same idea of confession. Chief among these was his friend and interlocutor in the 1979 roundtable, Karatani Kōjin. Nakagami's emphasis on the confession as a narrative of law or system adds a concrete historical character to the account of modern Japanese literary subjectivity as it has been established in Karatani's work, especially in the essay "Confession as a System" (*Kokuhaku to iu seido*), found in Karatani's 1980 essay collection, published in English as *The Origins of Modern Japanese Literature* (*Nihon kindai bungaku no kigen*).[12] Written during Karatani's study of Japanese literature in the United States, this collection was an extremely influential work for the post-1968 generation of critics who saw literature as a component of contemporary thought (*gendai shisō*) that was not restricted to the academic arena. The work has probably been even more influential in English-language criticism of Japanese literature, given Karatani's strong ties to the U.S. academy and the fact that during the first ten years of its life it was the only book of Japanese theory translated into English.

In this essay, Karatani tries to explain how modern subjectivity was established by the new language created to represent confession, rather than by expressing an a priori identity. His reading of the blindness of Meiji fiction to this insight retains *The Quilt*'s emphasis on sexuality as the object of confession, concluding that "in the process, the body and sexuality are discovered."[13] He connects the idea of discovery to the Foucauldian notion of self-discipline to conclude that self-scrutiny and transcription of its results actually produces what writers of I-fiction understand to be preexisting interiority. "To maintain this kind of conscience requires one to exercise constant surveillance over one's inner thoughts. One must keep watch over one's 'interiority' at all times. One must scrutinize the passions that well up 'within.' It is this surveillance, in fact, that produces interiority."[14]

Nakagami's analysis of *The Broken Commandment* asserts that the same dynamic is true of confession—that it produces the impression of interiority by creating a language for it. But he diverges from Karatani's conviction that the narrative triumph of *The Quilt*, and in turn sexuality, offers the paradigmatic object for confession. In Nakagami's work, the big unnameable that founds modern literature is ethnic—namely but not exclusively *buraku*—identity. Why this issue should be prominent in his mind becomes clear when we examine the striking prominence of the theme of confession and *buraku* identity in 1970s fiction.

"A Young Writer I Know"

As the Sayama trial unfolded, editors in broader print culture used their periodicals as venues to examine the relation between discrimination and the criminal justice system. In March, 1977, Nakagami began to weigh in on *buraku* issues in a public forum. Senbon Kenichirō, an editor of the left-ist weekly *Asahi Journal* (*Asahi jānaru*), recruited two older writers, Noma Hiroshi and Yasuoka Shōtarō, as hosts for a series of conversations. These three-person conversations took place over the course of a year and focused on current issues of ethnic discrimination. The series used *buraku* discrimination as its point of departure because a key verdict had just been issued in the Sayama trial. A judge affirmed the defendant's conviction despite a widely contested investigation that cast doubt on the confession because it had been coerced from the illiterate defendant and therefore was seen to violate Article 38 of the Constitution, which prohibits self-incrimination.

The featured writers who participated in all twelve episodes of the 1977 roundtable series, Noma and Yasuoka, were both noted for their long-standing interest in social issues. They were especially noted for connecting literary representation to political representation at the level of character self-consciousness. Yasuoka was less clearly identified with socially engaged subjectivity because his most recognized fiction resided in extremely personal registers of I-fiction. His writing career, however, had taken him to reside in the United States in the late 1960s, an experience that gave rise to an essay collection about his impressions of being neither black nor white in the segregated American South, and he subsequently translated and wrote an introduction to the highly successful Japanese edition of Alex Haley's *Roots*, a work that would inspire Nakagami's reportage in *buraku* neighborhoods.

Nakagami was the fourth guest in the series and by far the young-est. He followed three fiction writers, Mizugami Tsutomu, Sugiura Min-pei, and Ōoka Shōhei. Succeeding him were *zainichi* Korean writer Kim Shi-jon, folklorists Miyamoto Tsuneichi and Takatori Masao, and lawyer Aoki Eigorō. At the time of the *Asahi Journal* roundtable responding to the Sayama verdict, no mainstream author, Nakagami included, had self-identified as a *buraku* writer. In my reading, the Sayama trial marks an important turning point in Nakagami's writing. Immediately after this roundtable, he was commissioned to conduct a six-month field trip to visit *buraku* neighborhoods and describe his findings in a series of reportage essays in the *Asahi Journal*.

The reportage writings compose what Noguchi Michihiko terms "the first work where Nakagami as a writer encounters *buraku mondai* (issues), and his clear-cut 'coming out' as a *buraku-min* himself."[15] Later critics, in contrast, note that Nakagami's public self-identification did not take place until 1981 in an interview in the Wakayama edition of the *Asahi shinbun* when Nakagami said point blank, "I was born in a *hisabetsu buraku* in Shingū."[16] Read in the context of later writings where Nakagami asserts a more direct connection with *buraku* folk history and identity, statements from the conversation with Noma and Yasuoka have often been inter-preted as crypto-confessions of Nakagami's own identity.[17] I would like to refrain from this leap, however. A later 1991 roundtable with Karatani clarifies how Nakagami's own role in the editing process of the roundtable with Noma and Yasuoka cut out important parts of Nakagami's contribu-tion and shifted the point of view from a confession to an observation. He explains using terms that I read as a clear articulation that his strategy of parallax writing had begun and very much depends on a distributed "I" across media:

At this date, I suppose [the 1977 roundtable], I would add archival information; I did speak about [his *buraku* identity] directly, but I asked that they "please edit it out." "Please write it as someone else's story." It's not a big deal that I come from a *hisabetsu buraku* background. This is unimpeachably true, but I told them to explain it in terms of the things that I had heard happened to someone else. So it's not really true; it was my own story. When that conversation happened, in one sense I was aware that it had finally started. By which I mean . . . that if you look at the bottom of my literature, or the thorough way I see things, *hisabetsu buraku* issues absolutely come through.[18]

The irony of the *Asahi Journal* roundtable is that despite the public and consciousness-raising nature of conducting a twelve-part series on discrimination, Nakagami narrated his own identity only cryptically. The interface of print, though, functioned to restrict and channel the voice through the editorial process so that a reader could read into what we could call the *buraku* under erasure without naming it. In other words, it is possible to read a suggestion of *buraku* identity through form, syntax, or allusion, without affirmation in semantic or positivist content.

The term "under erasure," or more properly under erasure, comes from Jacques Derrida's interpretation of philosopher Martin Heidegger. Heidegger critiqued the term "being," the staple of modern philosophical inquiry, because he felt that philosophy's project repeated the theological claim that being itself, pure existence, could be apprehended if the proper language were found and applied. Derrida takes the argument one step further. To him, erasure permits the parallax reading of something that is effaced while still remaining legible. In Derrida's words,

> To question the origin of that domination does not amount to hypostatizing a transcendental signified, but to a questioning of what constitutes our history and what produces transcendentality itself. Heidegger brings it up also when in *Zur Seinsfrage*, for the same reason, he lets the word *being* be read only if it is crossed out (*kreuzweise Durchstreichung*). That cross is not, however, a merely "negative symbol." This erasure is the final writing of an epoch. Under its strokes the presence of a transcendental signified is effaced while still remaining legible, is destroyed while making visible the very idea of the sign.[19]

The open secret of Nakagami's identity is one of these instances of effaced legibility. The *roji*, as an open but marked signifier for the *buraku*, is another, as it is interested in exploring what has constituted the historicity of *buraku* experience and discrimination but without making it a transcendental. Because of the open nature of Nakagami's confession, the roundtable and its ripple effect in his later writings suggested that the Sayama trial was an event to which he needed to respond. In particular, this was because of the role that confession played, as it traversed from the literary to the legal sphere to the public sphere of protest, where one BLL activist says he took Nakagami regularly to attend meetings in protest of the Sayama trial.[20]

In keeping with his refusal to represent, rather than speaking of himself as either a participant or an observer of the Sayama trial in this roundtable, Nakagami invents a character, "a young aspiring writer I know."[21] This persona illustrates the difficulties that face an up-and-coming writer as he attempts to connect politics and personal life. Nakagami initially distances this character from himself by describing him in the third person. For the "young aspiring writer," the only way to enter politics is by tossing a bomb: "For now, he's writing novels, so it's not an issue. But if he were to enter politics, honestly, the only answer would be to toss a bomb . . . Thinking about discrimination, a bomb is the only answer."[22] While the public response to discrimination is envisioned as nothing but violent, in reality, he continues, the "young writer I know" makes his identity known only in private. "He's still anonymous, but the country hometown of this aspiring writer is really interesting. At his house in the city, there is nothing like BLL magazines lying around. But when he goes home, it seems that he reads them all. That kind of structure I find interesting. His wife knows about it, he took the right steps and told her before they got married; if he would have hidden it would have come out anyway."[23]

He continues in a third-person voice. But when he begins to narrate emotions, the narrating voice loses the objective distance that is initially anchored by the pronoun *kare* because the subject is implied rather than indicated. "But for his part, he says, there's still some kind of hesitation, things [he] doesn't want to look at. So in that sense, half of him is passing (from the *buraku*). But even though there are things [he] doesn't want to look at, there is still a very cherished part of it, you know."[24] "You know" is expressed using the final particle *yo,* which, combined with the dropping of the third-person pronoun, makes the source of the emotional insider voice ambiguous; grammatically, it could be first person or third person, but in either case the emotive quality is stressed. In other words, it is grammatically possible to conclude that Nakagami is the "aspiring young writer" even though he refrains from saying so directly. This ambiguity of parallax, or doubled possibility, corresponds to the collapse of author, narrator, and character that is conventional in I-fiction. The use of ambiguous grammar to enable multiple readings most likely accounts for critics' tendencies to read this statement as a veiled confession.

As Nakagami concludes his reply, the *kare* subject identifier that locates the story in the third person is kept out of the sentence, as are the end-of-sentence particles. Where "he" might be imagined in the remainder of the speech, "I" is equally plausible when he describes how the "young aspiring writer" stopped short of attending a Sayama protest rally. To illustrate this plausibility, I insert both hypothetical terms in parentheses: "Recently, too, when [he/I] saw how Ishikawa was fighting it out in jail, [he/I] [told me/said that] it brought him to tears." In the next sentence, information that typically comes from an inner voice is expressed using "I thought" (*to omotta*), a state that the following sentence continues: "[He/I] had thought of it as something very distant from himself, and thought [he/I] would go have a look at the rally in Meiji *kōen* (park). It's not just that Ishikawa should have been declared innocent, but [he/I] think[s] these guys must have been pretty depressed too, seeing everybody give their all. Then when [he/I] was about to get on the JR [railways train] and head in, [he/I] stood in the station and couldn't help crying, and [he/I] decided not to go."[25] As a whole, the passage or conversational reply shifts away from a detached, clear third-person voice to one where a first-person voice is equally plausible. The interchange between "he" and "I" is especially noticeable when emotion begins to leak in. This style, in which a passage shifts from external scene to heightened emotional state framed by the verb *omou*, resembles the literary conventions of Nakagami's fiction. The works that made him famous, like *The Sea of Withered Trees*, feature an extremely consistent use of the verb thought/felt (*omou*) to channel feelings and affect from an omniscient perspective located outside the character.

As for interpretation of this passage, the missed connection between Nakagami and the train to the rally in Meiji Park is an apt metaphor for the larger body of connections that Nakagami hesitated to make with *buraku* activism as a mass movement and will account for chronic activist dissatisfaction with Nakagami's work. Although the "young writer I know" is never empirically connected to Nakagami, the stop short of making the reference clear is characteristic of his work. And the plausible substitution of "I" for "he" coupled with the synch to Nakagami's fictional style likely accounts for critics' tendencies to read this roundtable as a confession of Nakagami's own identity. As this roundtable went to press, the same verdict provoked a number of reactions on the activist front. Many of these reactions emphasized how language and its ability to exert force were instrumental in anti*buraku* discrimination—in writing, in testimony, in legal narrative, and in techniques of information gathering and storage. The rally where Nakagami likely never arrived in 1974 was attended by one hundred thousand people who assembled to protest the second verdict of the Sayama trial. By activist count, two thousand more people went on a hunger strike.

Confession, as Miyako Inoue reminds us, is "also a speech act that entails power relations, in that it is made to institutional authorities such as priests and judges."[26] Ishikawa's confession is interpreted as a structure by the *Asahi Journal* roundtable participants Noma, Yasuoka, and Nakagami. They see it in these terms because it has little chance of transforming the power relations that it enters into. At the level of writing, Ishikawa's confession affirms the structure as it is transposed from the oral realm to the written realm through the intervention of such authorities representing the structure, namely the police who added their own characterization to the events and causalities that it traced. Although the first verdict of the Sayama trial, written in the form of accusation/sentence/reason, never mentions the word *buraku,* the impression of Ishikawa's life and "environment" (*kankyō*) as determining factors in his alleged crime surface clearly. Since the 1920s, the idea of environment was a vital part of assimilationist social welfare discourse that tried to specify why the purported society outside of society existed and how it could be ameliorated.

The first piece of information given in the verdict is Ishikawa's *honseki,* or originary ancestral home, that is inscribed in his family register. This is followed by the charges; the sentence; and the most substantial part of the document, the reason (*riyū*). The predisposition to see a person as a likely candidate for crime based on his place of residence is a kind of geographic profiling. Just as American police may size up a suspect based on race, resulting in racial profiling, Japanese police and investigators use place of residence to assess probability of criminal activity. At this place and time in Japan, the kind of differential identity that triggered profiling depended on place of residence as the key determinant of ethnicity and likelihood of committing a crime. *Koseki* checks, stopping people to ascertain their place of residence, functioned as a kind of geographical profiling because they authorized suspicion based on someone's address. They attempted to find or provoke infractions of the law based on the existential quality of what one could call living while *buraku.*[27] The *koseki* check practice not only tied identity to geography but also served as an open door to conflict based on geographic profiling.

As Noma points out, it was a common practice for police to conduct an inordinately frequent number of *koseki* checks, or police visits to individual houses in *buraku* neighborhoods near crime scenes, to ascertain whether the people listed as residents in the family register were indeed living there.[28] The preliminary investigation in the Sayama trial targeted a *buraku* near the crime scene, the Sugehara 4-chōme area, one of two *buraku* neighborhoods in Sayama city. Police argued that because the body was found near the *buraku* and because Yoshie's bicycle route to school took her through the *buraku* neighborhood, then a *buraku* resident must have been the perpetrator. Each of these claims was based on the perceived disposition to criminality of the inhabitants of Sugehara. The suspicion gave the pretext for searching Ishikawa's home, although he lived in his place of work. Defining Ishikawa in terms of his *honseki* furthered the impression of the news reports that the motivation for Ishikawa's crime could be found in his domestic circumstances (*kankyō*) and in his disposition (*seikaku*).

The investigation was narrowed by extending this geographical profiling to hypothesize a series of questions about the kind of person who would commit such an act and who would correspond to the transcendental signifier of *buraku*. The reporting in the local *Sayama shinbun* newspaper clearly reveals the pathology associated with the space of the *buraku* environment that creates a disposition legible as *buraku* identity. In an article that typologized Ishikawa, titled "Ishikawa Kazuo Is This Kind of Man," a reporter from the *Sayama shinbun* vividly roots the portrait of Ishikawa's "spirit" and "disposition" in his family environment: "Kazuo was born on January 12, Shōwa 14 (1939), as the fourth son of his father (64) a carpenter (or literally, 'a scaffolding man' who did *tobi shoku*), and a mother (57), and was raised in squalid quarters near the Seibu-line Iruma station, with an older brother, younger brother, and two younger sisters ... Gradually in this environment, poor and almost slum-like, from the time he was small, a brooding rebellious spirit and resentment distorted the disposition of the strong-minded Kazuo."[29] Articles such as these that presented background to the case from the point of view of police, prosecutors, judges, and members of the press were highly indebted to prejudicial modes of reading the character of the defendant. Their authors assumed that the defendant was predisposed to criminality based on his geographical origin and permanent address in the *buraku*. Classifying Ishikawa's personality as "distorted" drew on the rhetoric of modernization theory that sees poor areas as deviations from the path of progress. In this journalistic context, however, it conveys the same meaning of an entity that deviates from a normal and expected progression or movement, something whose growth is socially stunted and perhaps perverse.

The trial instigated a series of commentaries that all drew attention to the role that language and writing had played in Ishikawa's frame-up and particularly to the ways that journalism and the legal process had focused on his alleged deviance from expected norms. Prior to the verdict, police evidence, too, had drawn on writing as evidence to show Ishikawa's guilt and to paint a psychological portrait of his deviations. The emphasis on writing is no doubt one reason that Nakagami connected the Sayama trial back to the confession of *The Broken Commandment*. Police had argued that Ishikawa had composed the ransom note by copying printed hiragana phonetic readings alongside the *kanji* in a manga of his sister's that he found called *Ribon*, whose readers were more typically imagined to be middle-class adolescent girls. However, the kanji that were written in the ransom note were idiosyncratic in two ways. One of the compound words was made of several kanji strung together to read as homonyms for "the girl" (*shō-jo* 少女). When read aloud, the combination made sense, as *sho-ji-yō*, although the articulation would sound forced and strange. But as writing, the characters (小時様) added up to semantic nonsense and did not even make any sense as a neologism or as a play on words. The hypothesis of the cut-and-paste ransom note from the magazine emphasized Ishikawa's low level of literacy at the same time as it represented his resourcefulness in the area of deception. Moreover, it suggested that either he was so perverse as to be familiar with girls' comics due to habits of cross-reading, in violation of the strictly sex-segregated market orientation of manga, or he was oblivious enough to norms that his lack of literacy would be underscored. In both cases, writing was used to characterize Ishikawa as a criminal.

The status of confession is so loaded in the Sayama case because it illuminates connections between the legal sphere, illiteracy, and a set of assumptions about the nature of writing in general. When Ishikawa confessed to the crime after nearly a month of solitary confinement without a lawyer, his confession was taken as a testimony of agency, a place from which he could speak as a sovereign subject by taking responsibility for his violations of law and system. But unlike Noma's formulation of engaged empowerment in liberation literature, confession actually worked to hide the narrative operations of law and system within which Ishikawa's confession became meaningful.

Though both the BLL and Nakagami clearly disagreed with the Sayama process, in the course of the roundtable with Noma and Yasuoka, Nakagami distanced himself from the policy strategies of both the BLL and the Japan Communist Party (JCP). He tells Noma and Yasuoka that "the only thing that literature of denunciation (*kyūdan bungaku*) or the 'outcry' (*sakebi*) novel can accomplish is a one-time-only effect. It would be nice if it would all die down with one round of denunciation or shouting, but issues of discrimination in Japan go deeper and wider than that."[30] After claiming that the BLL's tried-and-true strategy of denunciation battles works in isolation, not systematically, he continues to criticize both the BLL and the JCP strategies for being too logical (*gōri-teki*). Nakagami suggests that rather than engaging in power politics to influence the jurisdiction over the allocation of public funds for improving infrastructure, the problem of discrimination should be approached as an illogical structure. Although he uses this key logic from historical materialist thinking, one that was key to postwar Marxist scholarship as well as early *buraku* histories, his way of pursuing the illogical flew in the face of BLL activists.[31] Urged on by Noma, movement activists were beginning to turn their attention to regulating elements of culture that they felt injurious to the *buraku* cause. The next section describes a series of other instances where writing was used to single out, identify, and discriminate against *buraku* residents following their confessions, leading ultimately to two separate strategies: the activist cultural turn and Nakagami's turn to *monogatari* (stories, tales) as a way to understand the expanded field of narrative as it traverses not only prose fiction but also other venues where stories are told through the same conventions, like the legal system, mass journalism, and even leftist periodicals.

Buraku Liberation and the Cultural Turn

The turn to understand how confession stigmatized *buraku* characters and settings informed two of the three major struggles that the BLL pursued in 1977. While one aimed to extend the policies of 1969 legislation that provided ten years of funding to improve living conditions, the remaining two made 1977 a landmark year for activists conscious of how language, power, and *buraku* identity were related in postwar life. Even before the Sayama trial verdict, an incident broke in May 1977, in the midst of an ongoing movement to make family registers unavailable to the general public. Since narrative will be understood as a kind of law and system by both Nakagami and poststructuralist critics, it is important to note that the family register (*koseki*) contains information that is made meaningful by contexts such as narrative but is not itself a narrative. The family register systematizes the link between geography and identity and places this information under public surveillance.

One of Nakagami's first celebrated stories, in fact, uses *koseki* consciousness as the source of its angry young protagonist's rage and estrangement. The family register itself does not make an appearance in the story. However, Nakagami stated in the 1991 roundtable with Karatani Kōjin that throughout the entire nine years before he won the Akutagawa Prize in 1975 he "consistently wrote about the *hisabetsu buraku*. Or you could also say I didn't."[32] I take this "I did, but I didn't" to indicate that the way he referred to the *buraku* was not through direct positivist representation but rather through an allegory that traces the protagonist's experience in terms that recall typical experiences of exile from structures as a result of specific ways of attaching geography to identity.

The 1973 title story of Nakagami's first collection, "Map of a Nineteen Year Old" (*Jūkyūsai no chizu*), is set in the back streets of mom-and-pop Tokyo where many urban provincials settled as they flocked to the city to exploit opportunities generated by the 1964 Tokyo Olympics.[33] These alleyways link the life of the young country immigrant to the possibilities of mobility the metropole offered in the abstract. But Nakagami's experiences shut him out at the same time, in a reprisal of the society outside of society narrative—this time, with a tragic twist. At nineteen, the narrator Boku (I) is separated from his family, unsettled in his educational and occupational track, and a year shy of legal adulthood. When the story opens, Boku is a cram-school student who is doing record keeping for his part-time job in his room in a cheap boarding house littered with the sections of bygone newspapers he has never read. Boku is cold to the bone, even though the windows and doors are shut. He is lying face down, marking an X on a very detailed map of his newspaper territory in a physics notebook. He marks an X for each offense committed by a customer: refusal to pay a bill on time, a growling attack dog, or flat-out nastiness.

When the X's reach three in number, he strikes back with a prank call or some other threat.

The connection of "Map of a Nineteen-Year-Old" to a legacy of dispossession, a society outside of society, is conveyed primarily through Boku's desire to territorialize the bourgeois "residential strip just off of the busy shopping street" where he does his paper route.[34] This district is defined purely by its relation to newspaper culture. Not only is it mapped out and elaborated through the paperboy's bicycle journeys, but the industrial production of paper even saturates the acoustic register of his day's work. "Just when you thought you might run across a cocktail lounge or a bar, there was a printing factory with machines whose motors make a clapping sound, on and on, echoing from early morning." As he crams for his school in his cramped apartment, Boku is unable to find himself represented in the newspapers he delivers to support himself or in the school history textbooks he crams:

> A child's crying voice entered into the range of hearing. The
> couple's quarrel that had been going on seemed to have completely
> subsided. The television that must have been on in the room
> downstairs, or in Saitō's next door, seemed to emit a hushed con-
> spiratorial dialogue. I felt that I was at some place of rock-bottom
> desperation. What the hell had I seen? And why in the world was
> I cooped up like a maggot in this filthy garbage-y room? I stood
> up silently, sat down on a chair, pulled down a Japanese history
> book from the shelf on my desk, and opened it up to the Middle
> Ages. What a bunch of crap. Was I supposed to care about who
> held control of power, and what they were aiming to produce? I
> have not the faintest idea why I have to understand this stuff, have
> to remember it even. I assume that my ancestors lived someplace
> pretty remote from the narration of this textbook. Even now, I live
> in a place that the narration of this book doesn't even approach . . .
> I chucked the history book up on the shelf like I was throwing it
> away, and instead I took out my atlas and opened it up.[35]

In this logbook, Boku appropriates the means of rendering the *buraku* legible by mapping out and classifying the houses in his delivery territory with information, in a structure that makes an allegory of the *koseki* register. He then turns the cruelty of his own process of becoming socially

marked onto his customers. His prank calls escalate; he injures neighborhood pets and commits other petty crimes. The story ends as Boku wails
hysterically in a phone booth after threatening to bomb a Japan Railways
train. The narrative ends in the same paradox of tragic enlightenment as
do other Nakagami short stories that appear in the 1970s: becoming intelligible as a *buraku* resident, in this case through *koseki* consciousness,
requires expulsion from the community. Usually, as in this case, the community the character is expelled from is a national community.

Koseki consciousness was highlighted to *buraku* residents when news
broke in 1977 that 103 Tokyo companies had purchased *buraku* lists from
a private investigator. The companies included Nissan, Mitsubishi, Yasuda
Insurance, banks, and other industrial concerns that used the inventories of *buraku* neighborhoods nationwide to cross-check the actual living
situations of potential hires with information that they submitted on job
applications.[36] When confronted with objections that these lists could
provide information for discriminating against *buraku* applicants, companies argued that they used them for descriptive reasons, study purposes,
or reference.[37] In 1977, Japanese corporations and policy-makers were still
reacting to the 1973 oil shock that had prompted Japanese leaders to accel-
erate plans for a postindustrial economy. The country was in the middle of
its biggest postwar recession and undergoing downsizing and restructur-
ing, and activists felt that assessing identity purely by address amounted
to geographic profiling and made *buraku-min* feel the economic pressure
disproportionately.[38]

Responding to these events, activists directed their attention in three
directions that targeted the power of language to categorize and subordinate and would later connect to the Sayama trial activism. First, they
started a movement to keep *koseki* registers behind closed doors. Second,
they worked to extend the prewar legacy of denunciation struggles by regulating specific kinds of words that they felt demeaned *buraku* residents
or characters. And, lastly, moving from critique to creativity, they developed an alternate set of literary and cultural prizes and publications. Their
activities in the mid-1970s started to move away from confrontations over
specific terms and words—away from semantics to structure.

The language of hate speech (*sabetsu-go*) was first foregrounded by an
April 1975 article in the JCP newspaper *Red Flag* (*Akahata*). The op-ed
argued that the mainstream press was reined in by a self-censorship of
taboos regarding the *buraku*. The editorial further charged that the BLL's

confusion of hate speech with substantive critique effectively prevented *Red Flag* from any critique of the BLL. In 1975, a coalition of groups, including the BLL and the Japan Actors' Coalition (an ensemble of unions of theater and entertainment workers, broadcasters, and other culture industry workers), issued a series of policy statements and a spate of handbooks. The BLL statement stands out because it programmatically states its goal to take hate speech "out of the field of politics" and address it within the field of culture, which it defines as language.[39] By linking its current cause to the postwar guarantee of freedom of expression, the BLL distanced itself from some of the organization's prewar concessions to war mobilization and also from the denunciation struggles.[40]

The BLL established the Liberation Literature Prize (*Kaihō bungaku shō*), the "pillar of our cultural movement," in 1974 "at a time of national crisis."[41] In 1973, oil supplies from the Middle East had been cut slightly at a time when both demand for oil and inflation increased, right after the yen had been made into a floating and potentially volatile currency. This gave rise to the oil shock, a general spike in wholesale prices resulting in consumer panic. The editorial introducing the prize invoked the Suiheisha movement to incite the production of literature that took a stand and offered a program for progress. It stated that at a moment when both the nation of Japan and literature itself were in crisis the latent power of artistry in the *buraku* should become visible to transcend the contradictions of the present day.

In 1977, a second award, the Matsumoto Ji'ichirō Prize, was established. This award commemorated the first *buraku* member of the Diet and a leading figure in the Suiheisha movement and aimed to reward the "affirmation of human rights and *buraku* liberation" by an artist or scholar. [42] The first prize was given to Noma Hiroshi at the annual BLL meeting in 1977. The prize recognized the international dimensions of Noma's work and his efforts to draw general attention to the Sayama trial by publishing readings of the investigation and trial in major periodicals.

After Ishikawa's first conviction, Noma made the legal proceedings the focus of a sustained critique of discriminatory practices. His essays pursued factual errors in the police investigation, mistakes whose consistency pointed to a structure that pathologized *buraku* neighborhoods and characterized residents in turn. Between 1975 and 1991 he serialized 191 articles about the trial in the popular current affairs monthly journal *World* (*Sekai*).[43] *Sayama saiban* was produced with the help of a committee, some of whom Noma had worked with in his capacity as a civil servant in the Osaka City Hall Employment Division. The essays are framed by broader journalistic and legal discussion that demonstrates how embedded Noma was in the issues and rhetorics of postwar social services. The range of people interested in the trial extended from movement activist and fiction writer Hijikata Tetsu and historian and author Umezawa Toshihiko to editors from the prestigious Iwanami publishing house and nonfiction crime writer Saki Ryūzō and fiction writers Ōda Makoto, Yasuoka, and Mizugami. The range from high to low culture across a number of fields testifies to the broad impact of the Sayama trial on the perception of whether a postwar democracy did indeed exist, as gauged by the workings of the judicial system.

Noma reinterpreted key pieces of evidence the investigators had constructed their narrative on, such as the footprints found near the body that matched Ishikawa's and a shovel found nearby that police claimed was stolen some days earlier from the stockyard where Ishikawa worked. Noma's critiques paid close attention to minute bits of evidence, a strategy that literary critics would know as "close reading." He foregrounded the police procedure and the pressures that had coerced Ishikawa's confession, the subtexts of prejudice that had informed the preliminary investigation, and the faults of narrative logic that could only be explained by appealing to anti*buraku* prejudice. Noma's work of close reading provided a precedent for Nakagami's engagement in the Sayama trial, though his interest in positivist evidence is certainly different than Nakagami's own literary style.

Noma's reporting led directly to the leftist press revival of interest in the trial because it "brought to the general public a critique of the way Japanese trials were conducted," according to Hidaka Rokurō.[44] Hidaka's critique of confession hinged on Article 38 of the Japanese Constitution, which resembles Article 5 of the U.S. Constitution and maintains that "(1) No person shall be compelled to testify against himself. (2) Confession made under compulsion, torture or threat, or after prolonged arrest or detention shall not be admitted in evidence. (3) No person shall be convicted or punished in cases where the only proof against him is his own confession."[45]

Noma's method of carefully connecting empirical evidence facts to the ultimate narrative judgment of the Sayama process and verdicts challenges the claim that Nakagami often made that he himself was unprecedented in connecting the power of writing to discrimination. Nakagami's later formulation of literature about the *buraku* as *monogatari* (narrative) was preceded by Noma's work in connecting the literary and legal spheres to show how narratives of discrimination and prejudice shaped the apparently detached facts, documents, and processes of the legal system. The idea of a language of discrimination was worked out by activists and writers who were more rooted than Nakagami in two postwar investments: the style of postwar realism and a postwar legal framework instituted under the 1946 Constitution. Noma's presentation of liberation is partially invested in the libratory possibilities of democracy as introduced against Japanese feudalism under the U.S. occupation but calls for a greater sovereignty and liberation from one's own interiority (*naibu*) than that introduced by the outside. He credits literature with the ability to resolve issues of political and class relations through the embodied subjectivity of individual self-consciousness, leading to a renaissance of humanism.[46] Unlike many Japanese leftists who railed at the hegemony of occupation, Noma was more concerned with the longer and more intimate hegemony of Japanese imperial rule within the country, particularly in its subordination of *buraku* and outcast populations.

In the framework Noma follows, Japan did not yet qualify as a developed country. It was still considered backward in the Marxist outline of stages that provided the structure for his thinking because it did not yet fulfill the mandate of the new human rights–based Constitution to guarantee a very different set of rights than the Meiji Constitution, which had led to the demise of so many prewar leftists. The mass roundup and torture of writers such as Kobayashi Takiji, Nakano Shigeharu, Sata Ineko, and Miyamoto Yuriko happened repeatedly and was only halted upon the writer's *tenkō*, or written narrative, describing how she or he repudiated communism. It is difficult to assess how much the idea of forced wartime conversion weighed on Noma's mind, but it is clear that in the 1970s, confession drew attention to a configuration of law and system particular to postwar Japan, one that was significant because it traversed literary and extraliterary spheres.

Confession and Innocence: Traversing High and Low

The Sayama trial and Nakagami's literary historiography highlighted issues of characterization, confession, and pathology that focused on *buraku* neighborhoods and residents. Two other representations of the *buraku* appeared in literary journals at roughly the same time, the late 1970s, and showed similar tendencies. A free verse poem, "E-tta," was published in the avant-garde poetry journal *Contemporary Poetry Notebook* (*Gendai shi techō*). "E-tta," whose title approximates the stuttered pronunciation of the word *eta* by the child narrator, conveys a scene of sexual violence in a *buraku* household from the point of view of the child when his safety is endangered. The poem provoked the BLL to make a more extensive policy statement on its treatment of cultural artifacts and the representation of discrimination. The novella *A Complete Account of the Incident* (*Jiko no tenmatsu*) was published by popular leftist editor Usui Yoshimi in his own journal *Prospects*. It caused a bigger stir in the mainstream press because of the scandalous nature of its subject: Nobel Prize–winner Kawabata Yasunari's presumed "secret" identity as a *buraku-min*. The novella intimated that the key to Kawabata's 1972 suicide lay in his *buraku* identity, an alienation compounded by his unrequited love for a young woman he recruits to be his personal secretary and driver as he assumes a role on the world literary stage.

Like the Sayama trial characterization and following Karatani's critique, each of these works was controversial because it suggested that a *buraku* identity is lodged inside personal psychology in an a priori way rather than socialized in a complex and layered set of social codes that were only readable after being formulated in language that could be likened to law and system. The most disturbing feature of the two literary examples is their exploitation of a restricted first-person point of view located in a protagonist who is not yet adult. The narration through a not-yet-aware introverted protagonist makes it easier to see *buraku* identity as personal and psychological rather than social. "E-tta" and *A Complete Account of the Accident* both maintain a romantic conceit that the youthful narrator is innocent and unaware of adult corruption, desire, and violence. The protagonist in each work serves as a witness to an irresponsible and corrupting *buraku* adult and delivers an unfiltered and spontaneous description of dangerous or unhealthy environments without realizing the danger he or she is in.

"E-tta" is a forty-line poem that uses a young boy's stream-of-consciousness narration to depict the domestic violence and sexual exploitation that takes place in his house. The poem is told in the first-person voice using the vernacular dialect of a particularly impoverished mining district in Kyūshū. The poem is composed of seemingly uncensored, to-the-moment expostulations composed in lines of thirty characters each. The poem uses the formal symmetry of line length to imply a steadiness to the child's consciousness in contrast to the mayhem that surrounds him. It is inter-cut with scenes from the child's memory as he hides in his "sweat-smelly futon" and has flashbacks to moments in which he has been made to feel marked as an "e-tta."[47]

The scene opens at a high pitch as the narrator calls out to his mother. The child's way of speaking verges on baby talk, is intimate and clumsy, and dra-matizes the gap between his cognitive grasp of the situation and his increas-ing anxiety and vulnerability. The child's mother has brought home a new father who, unlike them, is not from the *buraku*. Discontinuous reactions of shock are registered in the child's stuttering and broken syntax. His fearful responses make it clear that the new father is drunk and that his mother is exposing him to danger because the man is volatile and because he so eas-ily asserts a role of paternal authority. The fragmentation and broken syntax highlight the violence done to the interior, intimate spaces of home, family, and maternity. The man drunkenly chases the mother around and demands that she perform oral sex on him. In highly vulgar language he orders her to "suck my dick" (*ore no chinbo wa namero!*) seventeen times in the course of forty lines until the infantilized mother gets on her knees and "slurps it down like a baby" (*akanbō no yō ni suitsukusu*).[48] The child responds in panic, screaming, "Mother, don't do it! Mother, you absolutely must not!" (*Kā-chan, nameru na! Zettai nametara deken zo!*).[49] As the child watches the scene taking place between the two adults, he flashes back to another scene of abjection when he had been insulted by a classmate. The classmate accuses him of committing incest with his own mother and repeats the slur of "Beast, beast!" and "Beast, beast, everybody knows you got the blood of dogs and cattle running in your blood!"[50] In these flashbacks, the child reproduces a rhetoric common in descriptions of the *buraku* since 1900s naturalism, in which humans are linked to hereditary degeneration, cruelty, and association with bestiality.

The title of the poem itself, "E-tta," is an oral rendition of the premod-ern word *eta* that referred to an outcast social status that had been offi-cially abolished in 1871. Its use in the 1970s suggests that the boy and his environment are traits carried over from a primitive, premodern world. Throughout the poem, the child reveals that he is too young to specify or articulate the taboos and transgressions to which he is subjected. Although he understands the effects of the disruption and scorn that enter his house and life, he has not yet experienced the fall into knowledge that would allow him to interpret the situation. This gap occurs, for example, when an internal monologue uncritically reproduces his mother's comparison of her lover and herself to the gulf between "clouds and mud" as she asks the child to be nice to his "new father" and to say hello.[51] By situating this dialogue as a confidential moment of intimate discipline between parent and child, the poem associates the mother's love for her child with the precondition of his abjection.

The child comments on this primal scene of subjugation repeatedly in a stuttered repetition of shock but lacks the consciousness to censor or reword the language. He internalizes the social pathology without any resistance. The poem ends abruptly when the child grabs a knife, which we presume he uses to stab the man in parallel with the man's climax. "Knife. Then. I. Of blood. Opened the screen door" (*Hoshi. Soshite. Ore wa. Chi no. Fusuma wo aketa*).[52] The poem ends as violently as it began. However, the positions of aggressor and aggressed are reversed as the child spills the blood of a non*buraku* antagonist. Because in his flashbacks his class-mate used the metaphorics of blood to attribute pathology to the boy and license his oppression, the invocation of blood in the boy's act of aggression against his mother's lover appears as a kind of retribution, completing a circle of metaphor.

The poem ends suspended in stereotype, literally waiting for the forces of law and system, the police, to arrive. As the poem crescendos to violence, narrative irony builds on the gulf between the child's innocence and the reader's experience. The gulf between the reader's appreciation of the signifying power of the word *eta* and the narrator's inability to locate where its power comes from reinforces the quality of pathos that infuses this irony. The problem with this poem is that in order for the magnitude of the child's innocence to be apparent, the precondition is a spectacle of violence. The pleasure of the text—the knowledge that arrives through the innocent yet narratively manipulative eyes of the child—can only be achieved by affirming tired stereotypes about the *buraku* as a breeding ground for excessive violence. Again, enlightenment, or the informed action on the part of the police and a greater knowledge about what *buraku* life is like, is only available in a package deal with tragedy.

The second work, *A Complete Account of the Incident*, is a roman à clef work that proposes the resolution of a historical riddle. In 1972, Nobel Prize–winning writer Kawabata Yasunari committed suicide for reasons

that remain unclear. The story is told through the diary of a young inge-
nue, Ayako, who has been employed as a secretary by Kawabata upon her
graduation from high school. She goes to live in his house where his duties
as head of the Japan PEN Club increase, and he makes increasingly eccentric demands on her. After his death, she buries herself in his works and
uses depth psychology to confirm in her mind not only the backstory of
their alliance but their common identity as *buraku-min*.

The immediate reaction to the novella was explosive, beginning with a
feature on the top society (*shakai*) page of the *Yomiuri shinbun* newspaper.
The first print run of sixty thousand copies sold out, and it was turned
into a hardcover book that sold three hundred thousand copies.[53] Kawabata's wife and son gave numerous statements to the press denying any
connection to the *buraku* and decrying the mix of fact and fiction in the
narrative. The persona of the young girl who acts as a detective solving the
riddle of Kawabata is fictional. However, the novella uses a long excerpt
from a roundtable in the 1977 *Asahi Journal* series between Noma Hiroshi
and Yasuoka Shōtarō to lend credence to notion that the secret of Kawabata's suicide may be found in his concealed *buraku* identity.[54] The Kawabata family tried to stop the novel's hardcover publication and when that
failed, brought charges against the writer Usui in Tokyo District Court on
the grounds of the novella's untruth and discriminatory characterizations,
including perverse sexuality, stinginess, and other socially scorned characteristics, damaging both Kawabata's reputation and the family's privacy.[55]
They asked that the book be taken out of print and demanded fifty million
yen in damages.[56] After protracted negotiations and following the objections against discrimination that came separately from the BLL, the Kawabata family and the publisher of *Prospects,* Chikuma shobō, signed a note
of agreement. Usui apologized for giving the impression that the entire
story was truth, though the protagonist Ayako was a fictional device. In
return, Chikuma shobō agreed not to reprint the hardcover version.[57]

In the story, Ayako and Kawabata become acquainted when he comes
to her family's horticulture shop. His character is portrayed as consistently secretive and mysterious, an ensemble of cryptic traits that make
him a *nazo,* or interpretive puzzle, and confirms his belonging in Watanabe Naomi's playbook of pathologizing signifiers. On a whim, he buys an
extravagant array of bonsai sculptures whose cost amounts to 530,000 yen.
He is taken with Ayako, and offers her a job in his house. Ayako's father
describes him as mysterious and wonders if he is even Japanese, and the

narrator characterizes him as very short, strange, with unkempt white hair and a dark (*kurozunda*) face.[58] Even the shape of his ears is odd (*iyō*). He is eccentric and demanding in his tastes and almost grotesquely rich. The first time Ayako sees him, he is staring into the plants so intently he "might have opened a hole" in them.[59] When she first meets him, she is not a "lover of literature" and has only read two of his stories.[60]

From their first meeting, Kawabata becomes irrationally attached to Ayako. He orders many plants from the family's shop and has them transported all the way from the northern rice fields of Tōhoku to his property in Kamakura, near Tokyo. Though he keeps ordering plants without paying, the apparent prerogative of Nobel Prize winners, he insists that Ayako come work for him for six months while he prepares to host a meeting of the International PEN Club. She assents and becomes his secretary, chef, and driver. His wife repeatedly entreats her to stay, "put up with it for a while, for the sake of *sensei* writing good novels."[61] But when Kawabata pleads, she declines to extend her employment, even when Kawabata offers her his Mercedes. Shortly after, she finds him dead of an overdose of pills, gas, and liquor. The novella's first half ends as Kawabata's wife whispers in her ear as she sleeps that she is responsible for his suicide.

Following Kawabata's death, in Part II, Ayako begins sleuthing the history of her relation with Kawabata to solve the "riddle upon riddle" nature of his existence as well as his connection to her.[62] A kindly teacher introduces her to depth psychology by giving her a book by a medical psychoanalyst, Ishida Rokurō. Ishida's work on the Romantic poet Ishikawa Takuboku provides a method for identifying and interpreting clues provided by Kawabata's behavior alongside his works. Ishida's work is a kind of case study for investigating how "the power of distinctive poets frequently is based on sexual (in the broad sense) trauma they underwent as youths."[63] Read as parallel and coreferential planes, life and work make a composite portrait of Kawabata's psyche linking author to text. In a similar vein, Usui himself had edited a number of anthologies that maintained a special focus on the relation between biographical models and their literary representations (*moderu mondai*), particularly in the Meiji era. He strengthened his belief that life and work could mutually illuminate each other by deliberately looking outside literary criticism for other expertise in narrative analysis. He found, for example, that Ishida's work argued for depth psychology, the unconscious and lifelong governance of one's conscious life by an inaccessible and persistent formative trauma that took place early in life, as the key to reading literary works. Usui explains, "Everything is due to the working of the unconscious under the layers of depth psychology."[64] (This point is nicely illustrated by Ishida's diagram of a flower that depicts the complex and its transformation into consciousness, making an aesthetic object out of neurosis.)

Ishida's model, Ishikawa Takuboku (1886–1912), had often been cast as a quintessential Romantic poet of modern love but was also viewed by literary critics as a socialist poet. Ishida's analysis, however, draws on the personality studies of wartime anthropologist Ruth Benedict to assert that politics became a kind of compensatory mechanism for Takuboku, meaningful only in personal terms. The separation from his devoted mother motivated his desire to create a new socialist world, and the death of his first love at the age of eight was sublimated and expressed as "depositions" (*kyōkutsu-sho*) in his poetry.[65] In Usui's interpretation, the epiphenomenal nature of politics never quite made up for the early losses in Takuboku's sentimental life that persisted in defining his interiority. Nor did repetitions of "personality and behavior" apparent in his love life to try to recapture his early idealism.

Ayako applies the method of depth psychology acquired from Ishida's analysis to the books that Kawabata gave her as well as the magazine reportage that is in turmoil over his death. Her aim is to become an "expert in the plots of his works, and all kinds of gossip."[66] She puzzles over his texts and performs elaborate comparisons of his chronology, family history, and places of residence to find the originary traumas that he has sublimated. She concludes that there "is no choice but to acknowledge that *sensei* had a link to the *buraku*."[67] She finds that he is only able to articulate this fact cryptically in his texts and interprets this as the key to the "bottomless alienation" that plagued him and ultimately drove him to suicide.[68] Ayako also excavates clues from her own past that make it apparent that she, too, was born into a *buraku* family and later adopted by the owner of the bonsai nursery where Kawabata first became (fatefully!) smitten with her. Her ability to read text and life against each other at last reveals that she and Kawabata had something in common—their status as orphans. Through their common origin as foundlings, the revelation of Kawabata's early abandonment emerges as the motivating fact of his puzzle-like quality of being a "cluster of riddles."[69] Ayako feels a kinship with Kawabata; she, too, is an orphan: his story is "just like me!"[70] And in reading the short story "A Letter to Mother" (*Haha e no tegami*), she exclaims, "The kind of orphan described there—that is exactly just like me."[7]

Kawabata is doubly pathological in this novella, as his *buraku* identity compounds with his romantic obsession. His general eccentricity, mysterious and insistent attraction to her, along with their growing number of family resemblances, adds up to imply a potentially incestuous motive on his part, a creepiness that is heightened by the portrayal of Ayako's innocence. The disconnect between her lack of knowledge and the reader's insight also amplifies Kawabata's potentially sinister but ultimately tragic power over her. This feeling of looming danger is reinforced and aestheticized by Ayako's hyper-awareness of her own beauty. She reports confiding in a friend, "I'm not that kind of a woman. Whatever eyes you look at me with, I'd say my looks rate at about seventy-eight out of a hundred. When my friends heard me say that, they said, 'Aya, you've overrated yourself by about eight points!'"[72] Ayako's friend's assessment stresses that her connection with Kawabata was based on something more soulful than pure looks. The strength of her personality is underscored as she refers to herself as "brazen" (*namaiki*) and intuitive, "an average country girl" rather than reflective.[73] Kawabata's "words" (*gendō*) were often above her head, and she frequently says that "at that time, it did not occur to me," or "I had no such kind of self-reflection."[74] The only outright disagreement Ayako has with Kawabata occurs when the imperial prince visits. She balks at meeting him, presumably due to anti-imperial feelings that, Usui writes, derive from her origins in Shinshū, a notorious breeding ground of democracy movements in the 1890s and the birthplace of Freedom and People's Rights (*Jiyū minken undō*) leaders such as Matsuzawa Kyūsaku.[75] Ayako feels like a "human sacrifice," despite not being as "progressive" as some of her friends, but Kawabata insists. Furthermore, he insists on calling her his "niece," a family relation close enough to be intimate but distant enough to be sexualized.[76]

The narrative device of the innocent girl reading Kawabata's fiction in terms of depth psychology serves three functions. First, it reaffirms the investment in referential fidelity at the core of I-fiction's confessional tradition in general. It hooks I-fiction's conventions of referentiality to stereotypic signs of *buraku* identity. Second, it reinforces the idea that *buraku* identity is both hidden and secret but present as an unchanging fact. The story hides the operations of law and system as it is present in conventional language and tropes (grotesqueness, excessive wealth spent impulsively, etc.) by presenting Kawabata's story as something already out there in the folds of his psychology that must be excavated rather than something that is narratively invented. And, finally, given Kawabata's suicide, the novella reprises the tragic narrative of the dispossessed *buraku* character unable to seize the means of signification to affect a different mode of political organization.

Alternatives to Tragic Enlightenment

We have seen how twentieth-century fiction that places *buraku* characters at the center of their stories finds formal solutions for expelling them from the local or national community. Typically, from 1906's *The Broken Commandment* through the poetry, novellas, legal uses of writing, and even Nakagami's own work in the 1970s, a crucial piece of information divulged in confession reveals the link of the character's identity to geography, triggering a causal chain. I called this narrative operation "tragic enlightenment" because of the role that knowledge plays in enabling exile. The resulting works present fictional versions of the narrative histories of the "society outside of society" that seem hardly different from those produced by *buraku* partisans and historians decades later, as discussed in chapter 1.

Because he valued confession as a staple of modern Japanese fiction differently than Noma and other writers, Nakagami was both critically hostile to it and fictionally drawn to it. In the roundtable with Noma and Yasuoka, Nakagami had said that the BLL denunciation struggle against particular words and phrases was too rational. But neither did he seem satisfied with seeing confession exclusively as a formal structure that, for better or worse, provides a referent for engaged identity politics. The "irrational" narrative to which his characters turn, especially in his major trilogy, has two strands: first, a turn to patriarchy as the source of judgment, finding in literal fathers and precursor men a personal, if folklorically or nationally inflected, family rather than a public authority; and, second, a desire to use confession to bind, rather than sunder, character and community.

A set-piece scene in *The Sea of Withered Trees* features a confession that resonates in key ways with *The Broken Commandment*. Halfway through the book, the protagonist, Akiyuki, seeks out his absent and charismatic father who has often haunted him in person and in spirit. He brings his half sister as a silent companion; his agenda is to confess what transpired in the last scene of the previous work when Akiyuki and Satoko had slept together. That scene reprised the figural language of the creation of the Japanese archipelago in the *Kojiki*. But, moreover, since Akiyuki was a customer purchasing Satoko's services as a prostitute in a bar called the Yayoi (the period designating the start of settled agriculture in Japanese history), the finale suggested that culture is a place that was bought and sold and that contained a fundamental violence at its foundation.

In this scene, Akiyuki, like Ushimatsu, contemplates prostrating himself abjectly with his head on the tatami floor in deference to authority. And like Ushimatsu's flight to Texas, the solution presented by the judge, Akiyuki's father, is provided by a land grab. Hamamura owns a large parcel of land in the nearby town of Arima, a frontier where he might resettle out of reach of the law. As Akiyuki addresses his father, his father's wife and his own sister/consort gracefully vanish from the scene, leaving the two alone:

"This is Satoko," said Akiyuki.

Satoko stood behind Akiyuki, as if to hide herself from the man's sightline. Satoko slouched.

The man said, "Well, have a seat," and waved toward the floor. He told his wife to go and bring some sake, and a good fresh piece of fish. A laugh sat on his face, and that purr of a voice had not changed one bit. As if she had Akiyuki and Satoko all figured out, in a low voice she said, "All right," and bowed silently to Akiyuki. The man's wife shut the door without making a sound.

"Well, you've come all this way, make yourselves comfortable" the man said. He pushed forward a list of the restaurant's offerings that his wife had left on the table, and said, "Order whatever you want." That purr of a voice did not sit well with Akiyuki. He looked straight at the man, who was still drawing out his laugh. It was that purr of a voice that had smooth-talked all the girls. Did he think he could smooth over everything with Akiyuki and Satoko merely by pulling out this purr of a voice?

"Do you know Satoko?" Akiyuki asked. As if to brush off that conversation, the man said, "Well, in any case, I'm just happy you've come to see me today."

"I'm not here because you told me to come." As he was saying that, Akiyuki heard some kind of sound tearing through his body from some emotional surge. He had the feeling that something like tears were welling up in his eyes. "I brought Satoko along with me. You know, Satoko. You know Satoko don't you, you know Kinoe," said Akiyuki in a quavery voice.

... The man looked at Akiyuki.

"I know about it," the man said. "It is what it is," the man said in a voice slightly steeped in anger.

Tears started to flow. Akiyuki wiped away his tears.

Akiyuki had no idea why tears had started at that moment. He wanted to tell all, every little bit of it.

Akiyuki pulled himself together and said, "Satoko and I slept together." Just as he said that, he thought that he wanted to beg for forgiveness, that there was still a whirl of things inside of him he wanted to talk about. He might even put his head down on the tatami mat. No, somewhere inside him Akiyuki knew he had the wherewithal to speak out to the man. I screwed you with the dick that you made me with. For the rest of our lives I'm going to be a thorn in your side. As if in a trance, Akiyuki said, "I did it with Satoko." Akiyuki waited for the man to show signs of bursting out in pain. He waited for the man to bash his head against the wall till blood ran, to rip off the penis that had fathered Akiyuki and Satoko in separate women. The man would crush both his eyes, and mutilate his ears. That was his image of a father. As such a father, it would have been just to beat Akiyuki without mercy, and knock Satoko to the floor.

"Well, that's how it is now. This kind of thing happens anywhere," said the man. His voice bubbled up from the deep, and he laughed. "Don't worry about such a thing. If you and Satoko have a child, even an idiot child, that's just how it is. I guess it would be hard all around if you did have a idiot."

"Yeah, we're giving birth to a vegetable," said Satoko.

"Go ahead, go ahead. Even an idiot child is no skin off my back. I have all that land in Arima, so we could have vegetable grandchildren for all I care."

The man regained his composure. "Bent out of shape by an idiot . . ." the man mumbled as if to persuade himself. "Do I worry about anything? If you wreck a car, hurt somebody, reparations usually do the trick," the man said. "Right, son?" he said, looking for acknowledgement. "Do we have to play stupid games, like Mie's husband?"[77]

Critics such as Nina Cornyetz, Yomota Inuhiko, and Eve Zimmerman are quite right to draw our attention to the magnetic capacity of family psychodrama to fuel the "irrational" course of Nakagami's narratives.[78] Though the characters' minds do not teem with complex interior reflections, narration in *The Sea of Withered Trees* jumps back and forth in time according to displacements and substitutions of feelings and people evoked by particular scenes. In this scene, for instance, Akiyuki abruptly detaches from the failed dialectic of confession to immerse himself in a chain of memories whose taboos and transgressions all converge as precedents for the payback of his incestuous attempted revenge against his father, Hamamura Ryūzō.

But I would like to draw attention to a different dynamic, the radical break in confessional narrative that this scene proposes. Simply put, knowledge produces no resolution of tragic enlightenment. The revelation is greeted with irritation but dealt with pragmatically. In its wake, Akiyuki is deprived of the high melodrama of recognition he so ardently seeks: signifier and signified do not correspond. Instead of being recognized, Akiyuki finds that land and capital have the power to clear the ground for self-invention by literally purchasing a geographic frontier that acts as a temporal and ethical frontier. In the remainder of the Kishū trilogy, set in the context of Prime Minister Tanaka Kakuei's massive program of infrastructure building in the provinces, Hamamura develops an elaborate myth by which to explicate his territory. This myth works as a counterhistory to the history of writing in Japanese fiction that has created a "society outside of society" beginning with the *Kojiki*. In the next chapter, I turn to look further at ideas of fieldwork and what Nakagami calls "exchange." Prompted in part by the Sayama trial and the structures of an intransigent "syntax" it made manifest, Nakagami undertakes a six-month road trip around southwestern Japan to excavate this imperial syntax by listening to stories, or what he calls *monogatari*.

CHAPTER 3

Constituents of National Literature

Kumano and the South

In 1955, five years after winning the Nobel Prize, William Faulkner visited Japan as a guest of the U.S. State Department's Exchange of Persons Division. He later described himself and his Japanese hosts as "two people running at top speed on the opposite sides of a plate-glass window."[1] Despite or because of this disconnect, his works became perhaps the most attentively interpreted pieces of American literature in the postwar Japanese academy. Japanese scholar of American literature Owada Eiko notes, "Roughly speaking, there is at least one—or more in many cases—professor who can teach Faulkner in a graduate program at any Japanese university or college. Truly, the 'Faulkner industry' is most prosperous in Japan."[2]

This chapter shows how Nakagami used Faulkner as a model for asserting the presence and literary absence of a Japanese "South" and worked to rewrite this Japanese South back into *kokubungaku*. Faulkner was known in postwar Japan as an emissary of the "lost cause," a defeated feudal South trying to come to terms with its memories. His visit to Japan at the height of the Cold War underscored the conceptual links between these two places that "lost to the Yankees" by seeing postwar Japan as a national South.[3] (The Japanese term for the Civil War is the North-South War, *nanboku sensō*.) Nakagami relocates the idea of national-cum-universal Japanese South to a domestic context and implicitly critiques postwar Japanese stances on history that downplay empire. He explicitly focuses on the state violence that was directed at *buraku* residents in Japan's South in the twentieth century and asserts that this violence underwrote Japanese literature from the very beginnings of written narrative.

This chapter focuses on a series of reportage essays, *Kishū: Stories of the Country of Trees, Country of Roots* (*Kishū: ki no kuni, ne no kuni monogatari*) published in the *Asahi Journal* in 1977–78.[4] These essays use the term "imperial syntax" ('*tennō' no shintakusu*) to connect *kokubungaku* to questions of power and subjugation vis-à-vis a Japanese South.[5] They predate by ten years the interest in imperial symbolics that appears in anthropologists' and cultural historians' analyses of city planning and media studies in the 1980s.[6] Nakagami's reception of structuralism and poststructuralism through ideas such as syntax provokes us to rethink why the ethnographic contexts he writes into his fiction and criticism were left out of Japanese postmodernism, even when discussions of national identity came to the fore.

I argue that abstract models of language actually allowed Nakagami to steer questions about writing and representation back into reckonings with political, economic and social power. First, I show how Nakagami developed the discourse of imperial syntax, a kind of literary criticism that connects written narrative to extraliterary kinds of power and domination, with the South of Japan, the regions of Kumano or Kishū, at its center. Then I survey some key models for his road-trip reportage in hugely popular ethnographic histories that provide a countermodel to this imperial syntax: Alex Haley's *Roots* and Meiji-era reportage writing. I outline why the key term of fieldwork helped Nakagami to establish why and how language was an overall model for conceptualizing how *buraku* cultural forms appear in Japanese literature. I show how Nakagami employs further structuralist and poststructuralist concepts such as code and the Derridean idea of the supplement to show how cultural forms of Japan's South have both underwritten and been excluded from the seemingly organic category of *kokubungaku*. Then, I turn to show how Nakagami's reception of Faulkner's works as a method for fieldwork, excavating "roots," differed from the more established interpretation based on Faulkner's 1955 comparison of Japan to the post–Civil War U.S. South. I show how Nakagami's concept of narrative (*monogatari*) was the key term on which he based his understanding of literature that would work as an alternative to imperial syntax. And finally, I turn to propose a reading of Nakagami's major cluster of works, the Kishū saga, based on Nakagami's key term, exchange (*kōtsū*).

Imperial Syntax

After the Sayama verdict in 1977, Nakagami began a systematic critique of the way that the narrative operations of both literary and extraliterary representations of the *buraku* worked in the service of law and system. Why did *buraku* characters always seem doomed to exile from systems of writing authorized by the Japanese state—even in Nakagami's own writings? This critique started with a road trip through a series of small towns and *buraku* neighborhoods in the Kii peninsula between February and December 1977.[7] The essays are on the one hand a travelogue that enables Nakagami to better inform himself about the specific character of *buraku* other than where he grew up. As Noguchi Michihiko points out, until this tour, Nakagami did not have concrete, first-hand information about *buraku* in places other than his hometown of Shingū.[8] His model for understanding center-periphery relations also draws on poststructuralist concepts as well as concrete field-work. He transposes these concepts from the world of New Aka criticism, restores their ethnographic dimension, and links Jacques Derrida's concept of the supplement of reading to the Marxian idea of "exchange" (*kōtsū*) to construct his own literary criticism.[9] The concept of *kōtsū* shows the specifi-cally local nature of specific points of center and periphery. These essays then read the landscape as a highly textualized place via an analytic of reading (*doku* 読) as poison (*doku* 毒), one that is an alternative to the aesthetics of liberation (*doku* 独) promoted by *buraku* activists. Nakagami mapped out the systematic and half-underground relations between the tree, the sym-bolic domain of imperial culture, and its underground component, the root, of *buraku* culture. He aims to deorganicize this structure by showing how Japanese literature is dependent on that which is supposedly its outside and has multiple origins, as seen in the phoneme of *doku*. He explores the rela-tion among orality, writing, space, and power to show the vital position of *buraku* cultural forms in the exchange of cultural forms between center and periphery, or Northern metropole and Southern periphery.

Kishū's point of entry is multiple, as the region Nakagami tours is known by several names, each of which presumes a different way of mapping the space. All coexist in tension with the imperial capitol and the language tied to it. In the beginning of the eighth century, the Kii peninsula was known as "ki no kuni," country of trees. When an imperial edict in 713 CE man-dated that all provincial place names consist of two characters, the name was changed to "kii no kuni."[10] Around the same time, the same geography was also referred to as Kumano and became known as the locus of a major folk belief system, which mingled elements of Shintō, Buddhism, and local myth. Kumano was known in mandalas, poetry, songs, and material culture like shrines and temples as a site of mythic origins, a place of healing proper-ties, and a palimpsest of varying and simultaneous belief systems.[11]

This semiotically loaded space is intimately linked to the capitol of Kyoto in a structure that Nakagami calls "imperial syntax." This is his name for a fixed cultural arrangement that placed the emperor's words at the foundation of written narrative in Japanese. His notion of imperial includes the modern idea of direct imperial rule but reaches further back in time than the 1890s consolidation of national literature, or the modern literary canon assembled under direct imperial rule. It stretches to the beginnings of written narrative in Japan to include texts such as the *Kojiki* (712 CE) and local gazetteers (*fudoki*) containing information on geography and culture that were commissioned from provincial governments in the early Nara period to legitimate Yamato rule. Like earlier *buraku* historiographers, Nakagami understands the relation of *buraku*-and-mainstream, Kishū-and-Japan as being structurally fixed over time as a social order outside the main social order. But "imperial syntax" implicates the written word as the representative of culture more strongly than earlier writings had done (see chapter 2 for a summary of Takahashi Sadaki's anti-imperial *buraku* historiography).

Nakagami's critical writings are placed in the most prominent venues of their time. For leftist news, he publishes in the *Asahi Journal,* and for commentary on the received tradition of Japanese literature, he publishes in the premiere scholarly journal, *Kokubungaku* (National literature). His writings in these periodicals emphasize the critical terms of fieldwork, *monogatari* (narrative) and exchange (*kōtsū*). Fieldwork involves listening and writing, the same process as the mythic emperor Jimmu and the mysterious Hieda no Are, scribe of the *Kojiki,* performed. According to myth, the *Kojiki* was narrated aloud to Hieda who took dictation and fit the phonemes s/he (it is not really clear if Hieda was a man or a woman) heard into kanji characters. Speech is thus associated with imperial mandates. *Monogatari* are the stories of discrimination he hears and associates with a historical narrative of proto-*buraku* residents. "Telling the stories of how people came to be beaten is *monogatari*" in examples like the vanquished of the Gempei wars, and the twelve members of the Shingū group executed for allegedly plotting against the emperor in the Great Treason Incident of 1910.[12] Exchange refers to the movements and relations that exist between "ki no kuni" and the imperial capitol. Each term poses a challenge to the national literary canon by being an analytic tool for perceiving, excavating, and propagating cultural forms obscured by national writing systems, from literature to the courts. These terms were instrumental in understanding, and perhaps undoing, the larger constellation of what Nakagami called more broadly "imperial syntax."

Why is the term "imperial" important, even when the emperor's status was downgraded to "symbolic" in 1945? For Nakagami, imperial does not simply mean "of or pertaining to the emperor." Although it will shift in later works, in the late 1970s it does not focus attention on Japan's imperial ambitions to lead Asia. It means something more general: the domination of one state over another people or state.[13] But he applies this formulation to the domestic, not the international, context. The imperial relation that Nakagami asserts is best captured in the essays' initial reference to Kishū: "I have the feeling that now the Kii peninsula, Kishū, is another country" (*hitotsu no kuni*).[14] (As I pursue in the next chapter, the resonance with James Baldwin's novel of the same name, *Another Country*, attributes a racialized understanding of Kishū and its relation with the metropole.)

To a linguist, syntax refers to the rules that determine the arrangements between parts of a sentence or utterance. Imperial syntax, then, is the rules that establish relations and values between the different constituents of the imperial realm—in the case of Kumano, between an economic and cultural North and South. This model followed a structuralist understanding of language in suggesting that the rules governing the narrative operations of language corresponded to the abstract rules that governed culture as a whole. At the same time, the model followed a *post*structuralist understanding of language in locating the "imperial" nature of syntax as derived from the fixed relation between words and things, or signifier and signified. Nakagami's frame of imperial syntax is a brilliantly localized reading of the idea of phonocentrism as it appears in the writings of Jacques Derrida.[15] This model sees the phonetic sign as closer to the ideal source of meaning, where the written sign mirrors speech but is only a near-miss version of it. Derrida maintains that language is comprised through an interplay of speech and writing. Nakagami outlines what amounts to a macrohistorical formation in which cultural forms issued from the Nara or Kyoto capitol correspond to "speech," and Kishū/Kii/Kumano to "writing." Japanese culture should more properly be seen as a mingling of both elements.

His map of capitol/speech/center and Kishū/Kii/Kumano/writing/ periphery replaces these two fixed points with a relationship of exchange and dependence. He takes the debate one step further by exploiting the full range of signifying possibilities along the vertical axis that linguistics call the paradigmatic dimension of language to undo the fixity between written word and referent. A key example of the localized inversion of phonocentrism I called heterophonics in chapter 1 occurs via the phoneme "ki," the one that titles his essay collection. The title Nakagami gives the book refers to a place called "ki no kuni" (country of trees). He writes this phoneme as 木, based on what he hears people say. 木 is a character that predates the more official name of 紀伊 that displaced it in 713 CE. He approaches his interviews and readings by "stripping off the kanji" (minareta kanji o toriharau).[16] Removing the writing will *not* get more directly at the unvarnished substance of the phoneme. Rather, Nakagami imagines a variety of possible origins springing out, like roots, once the cover of the kanji is lifted off. In other words, each semantic unit is substitutable by any of a number of others.

This dynamic is known in poststructural terms as *différance*. Taken again from Derrida's lexicon, *différance* means two things. First, that one character of *ki* is always meaningful because of what it is *not*. It is wood, not stone, nor fire, or anything else. Then, it is defined by being deferred. Ki as 木 can always be replaced or its meaning revised by other characters that cause its associations to change. (I include the Japanese writing after each translation because the difference in meaning diffused by the phoneme "ki" is more apparent.)

> What is the structure of discrimination? I don't have space to answer this in depth, but here in Japan, if discrimination is something that Japanese "nature" gives rise to, the structure of Japanese fiction, the structure of culture are at the same time that of discrimination. This includes, for instance, the seemingly featureless words that refer to these toponyms—Kishū, Kii. For instance, if we try to link up the circuit of discrimination and discriminated, ki 紀 is, 記 is, split into the spectrum of 木、気、鬼. Kishū 紀州 is Kishū 鬼州, is a space where demon-spirits run amok... How about this reading? On/陰/dark→鬼 oni/ki/demon→ki キ→ ki 木. Of course, I'm half-joking, but it is only in Kishū, Kii that these references do not seem un-natural. Takagi Kenmyō of the Jōsenji temple in Shingū appears in the Great Treason Incident. This makes me think of how at his temple, the modernist thinkers who followed Kōtoku Shūsui gave speeches about Kropotkin and Bakunin to his *hisabetsu buraku-min* parishioners.[17]

The homonym of "ki" works using the conceit of "roots," but gives its semantic contents in a proliferating and associative way with a whole array of substitutable "ki" bursting out of the phoneme. "Ki" is a phoneme that demands, like Matsumoto Jiichirō's heterophonics, to be read under erasure. *Kana* writing in these essays is more approximate to the oral because the *kana* writing system can suggest multiple and even contradictory readings. Just as the inscription "ki" (tree), is supported by a root, which is part of it and yet its subordinate, the inscription "ki" as tree cohabits with other inscriptions of the same utterance of "ki," including those that combine in the name "Kishū" to form radically different compounds, including the "ki" of writing, of narrative or annals, the "ki" of a sort of "spirit," the "ki" of nobility, and even the "ki" of devilry or mischievousness.[18] Nakagami does not, however, just reverse the terms and elevate the authenticity of speech at the expense of writing. His project is to render legible the polyvalence and open-ended nature of meaning in acoustic signifiers as they appear in writing such as the highly overdetermined syllable of "ki." This technique of substitution and scaling is the cornerstone of open-source narration.

The kinds of associations opened up by the *différance* of "ki" are important in revising national literature because they introduce another narrative about the anarchists put to death for allegedly conspiring to kill the emperor in 1910. Always with an eye to the structure of imperial syntax, Nakagami visits many foundational or generative points in Japanese written narrative, beginning with the *Kojiki*. He visits sites where literature is housed in libraries (Ise), as well as places where authors had famous disputes or were born (Matsusaka). He notes places that feature in oral texts, like the *sekkyō-bushi* narrative Buddhist song *Oguri hangan*.

Each specific place offers the pretext to meditate on the relation between language and social formation in the realm of imperial syntax. In chapter 16, Nakagami is caught in a rainstorm in the town of Ise. The town is the site of an imposing Shintō shrine complex dedicated to the goddess Amaterasu, the mythical deity connected both to the gods and to the emperor. He muses: "the substance of grass is not the thing, but the thing called grass ... if what they say is true, that the integrating words (*kotoba*) is the work of the '*tennō*,' and that is the work of a sacred being, calling it 'grass and writing it down as 'grass' is carrying out domination and syntax (*shintakusu/tōkatsu*) in the name of the *tennō*. Given that, what could be grass that if you separated it out from the syntax of the *tennō* (emperor)?"[19] What could identity *be,* and how might value be assessed outside of that attributed in language by the emperor? This is the dilemma that attracted Nakagami to poststructural analysis, or analyzing figural language to undo what seem to be intransigent linguistic, and by extension cultural, structures.

By repeating the listening process, assuming the narrating voice of both Jimmu and Hieda no Are that inaugurated written narrative in Japanese, and "stripping off the kanji" to allow new meanings to emerge, Nakagami aims to unfix the signifier and signified whose lock is the building block for imperial syntax. The remainder of this chapter reads these essays as attempts through fieldwork to place a concerted focus on the terms *monogatari* (story, narrative) and exchange (*kōtsū*), to find a replacement for imperial syntax.

Roots: A Model for *Monogatari*

Immediately after the 1977 roundtable Nakagami conducted with Yasuoka and Noma, editor Senbon Ken'ichirō of the *Asahi Journal* commissioned Nakagami to write a series of essays. Nakagami had complained to Senbon about the "half-hearted" participation of Noma and Yasuoka in the roundtable.[20] During a three-hour nighttime ramble from Ginza to Shinjuku, Senbon and Nakagami agreed on a title, *Kishū: Stories of the Country of Trees, Country of Roots* (*Kishū: ki no kuni, ne no kuni monogatari*), and a genre, reportage, or interpretive documentary based on fieldwork.[21] Senbon proposed that Nakagami model his essays on Alex Haley's *Roots* while leaving the exact specs of the model open. In his mind, *Roots* provided a contemporary format through which Nakagami could return to some of the concerns about discrimination that were introduced in the roundtable. *Roots* had been a big hit and narrated two hundred years of Haley's ancestors, from the family's beginning in West Africa through their abduction and forced relocation, sale into slavery, the Middle Passage, and the lived experience of their lives as objects of exchange in the New World.[22] Senbon suggested that doing fieldwork as Haley recounts doing would set Nakagami up to "face the truth" of his own upbringing and tell a public story about *buraku* life.[23]

The trope of the root as concealed family history with a hidden relation to national history also resonated strongly with contemporary Japanese fiction. Ōe Kenzaburō's magisterial 1967 novel *The Silent Cry* (*Man'en gannen no futtobōru*, literally football in the first year of Man'en) told the story of two brothers Nedokoro (root dwelling place) who return to their rural hometown when one brother moves to sell some family land to a Korean "Emperor of the supermarket."[24] The storeowner has turned the tables on his former oppressors by furnishing them with unlimited and absurd consumer items in his own kind of storehouse, one connected to larger networks of modernity rather than being local and rooted in family history. At the same time, the brothers compete to unravel the story of how their great-grandfather had been involved in an 1860 rebellion and thus compete to understand the family's triumph or disgrace in terms of the Meiji Restoration and new nation. Ōe's emphasis on personal historiography and local oral history drew attention to the important role of narrative in constructing national history. And *The Silent Cry*'s connection of local peripheries to centralizing imperial symbolics established roots as a trope that challenged what appear to be organic relationships by showing their dependence on the operations of narrative.

Haley's project also provided a counternarrative to mainstream nationalism that uncritically celebrated the present. Publishing *Roots* during the 1976 U.S. bicentennial celebration challenged the history of the United States to be told not only more "inclusively," but also according to different terms. *Roots* used archival research about the slave trade to narrate the foundational violence that underwrote the message of freedom, liberty, and self-determination that applied unequally during most of those two hundred years. Although *Roots* was not published until September 1977 in Japan, it was a genuine event. At the same time it appeared in Japanese translation, *Roots* was broadcast on eight consecutive nights on TV Asahi from October 2 through 9, 1977. The "movie" earned extremely high ratings of 30 percent in the Tokyo/Kantō region, and 41 percent in the Osaka/Kyoto/Kansai region.[25] Articles beginning in 1976 noted the "explosive popularity" of the book. Even before its translation into Japanese, critics and journalists called it a *taiga yomimono* or *taiga shōsetsu*.[26] *Taiga*, or "large river," is a term first applied to French writer Romain Rolland's genre of sweeping historical novel. A Rolland novel, a *roman fleuve* like *Jean-Christophe*, was noted for the synthesizing, omniscient narration that arced over several generations of characters, and placed people in the large macroflow of history. Today, *taiga* is most commonly used to describe NHK television's celebrated period dramas. These lushly produced miniseries are costume dramas that chronicle the sagas of epic historical figures, especially those who have played a role in Japanese state formation. When *Roots* is characterized with reference to *taiga* dramas, it underscores how the book and

TV series were received as epic narratives based on historically significant characters, using realistic artifacts and dialogue to attract a mass audience and convey historical texture.

Roots provides a precedent for insisting that race and ethnicity are fundamental constituents of a national narrative, elements that tended to drop out of the "roots boom" in Japan. Following Expo '70 in Osaka, local museums had undergone a "high-speed economic growth" that paralleled the national economic boom.[27] Local history museums had tripled in a "hometown/roots boom" since Expo-based campaigns were formulated to encourage individual travelers to break away independently from group tours and seek a personal relation to history. This approach resembled what anthropologists had begun to refer to as "salvage ethnography," typically conducted on a frontier or in a rapidly disappearing civilization. Salvage ethnography observes from the point of view of an eroded society and documents what is disappearing in a not-yet-eroded society, even as it does not intervene to stop the cause of disappearance. In the words of Jacob Gruber, who coined the term in 1970, this stance of ethnography commenced as people "began to sense the urgency of collection for the sake of preserving data whose extinction was feared."[28] *Roots* was received in Japan just as a focus on personal genealogy was promoted by the tourist industry, as well as a new set of local history museums. By the late 1970s, Marilyn Ivy writes, the notion of a hometown, or "*furusato*," had become a "generalized ideal."[29] Residing "in the memory, but linked to tangible reminders of the past," gauzy with nostalgia and in danger of disappearing.

Roots was the number-two best-selling book in Japan in 1977. The word "*rūtsu*" became a "fashionable word" (*ryūkō-go*) that same year. As it became popularized, "*rūtsu*" was sentimentalized and removed from its status as a counternarrative to official U.S. bicentennial history. It was even applied to Prime Minister Fukuda's attempt to seek out a former landlady while on a state visit to London.[30] But it was viewed skeptically by Morikawa Masamichi, writing in the BLL's magazine, *Buraku Liberation* (*Buraku kaihō*). Morikawa criticized Haley's book as an example of "feudal ressentiment." He felt that *Roots* dangerously romanticized Haley's family genealogy because its origins could be found in a kind of aristocracy.[31] This ideology contradicted the anti-imperial mandate of the BLL, particularly the agenda set by Diet member and BLL leader Matsumoto Ji'ichirō. Matsumoto was well-known because he refused to contort himself into the ritual "crab-walk" stride to approach the emperor in official audiences. He approached the emperor face-to-face, in what he considered a more democratic manner. He also called for leveling of the aristocracy beyond the terms of the 1947 Constitution and the Human Rights clause of Article 11. He wanted the emperor removed entirely, not merely relegated to a "symbolic" position: "if there are aristocrats, there are outcasts" ("*kizoku areba senzoku nari*").[32] The use Nakagami made of *Roots*, however, had little to do with celebrating an imperial origin or a disappearing rural identity. Nakagami uses *Roots* as a template for excavating and reporting untold stories that are important to writing a national history: "What I want to know is, the things that people don't say in a loud voice, the things they shut up about to outsiders."[32] To this end, Nakagami had the aid of many local residents, including members of BLL branches and their youth groups, some of whom would later participate in his lecture series in Shingū.

The reportage style in which *Kishū* is based is typically seen to emerge in late Meiji-era newspaper journalism that researches poverty. Writers sought to bring awareness of local living and working conditions to a wider national audience. Reportage refers to an essayistic style of documentary writing, and often creates a historical narrative of the disenchantments created by capitalism. This narrative is also the backbone of proletariat literature and has obvious resonance with *buraku* historiography.[34] But despite the apparent common concerns, according to Yamagishi Takashi, only two works of the proletariat movement addressed *buraku* issues.[35] Again after 1945, issues of class and ethnicity rose to public debate because of reportage, but focused on indigenous struggles in which a state committed violence against an ethnically different group.

Nakagami explained the method of his nonfiction reportage essays by rejecting mythic literary models of fieldwork and embracing Faulkner's:

I have the feeling that now the Kii peninsula, Kishū is a singular country.

It is without a doubt a country that has sunken into the darkness of those who have been beaten down time and time again, ever since Jimmu. Kumano and Komuriku overlap on this country sunken into darkness. Making the rounds of the cities and towns of this Komoriku, this place and that, and writing down, for instance, the name of Shingū, writing down stories so as to call up the spirits of the land, is, in other words, the method of the *Kojiki* and the *Nihon shoki*. I'll say it over and over again, but this is no simple tourist trip, nor is it a *fudoki*. Rather it's the method of the American writer William Faulkner, when he made up a map of Jefferson in Mississippi's Yoknapatawpha county, and named himself the proprietor.[36]

Nakagami returns to some of the foundational metaphors of Meiji-era reportage and excavates some of the roots of ethnicity that had been obscured. His use of the conventional ethnographic metaphor of the dark continent to describe Kumano is the most clear-cut example. This metaphor is typically used to imply that Africa is unenlightened, a space without culture. It had initially been employed by late Meiji-era writers who drew on a book by the founder of the Salvation Army. In 1893, Japanese social reformer Matsubara Iwagorō described Tokyo as "unknown territory waiting to be discovered by explorers on an expedition in search of the depths of poverty."[37] He drew from William Booth's 1890 *In Darkest England and the Way Out*. This exposé described some denizens of the London of Booth's day as "heathens and savages in the heart of our capital," forced to inhabit "innumerable adverse conditions which doom the dweller in Darkest England to eternal and immutable misery."[38] Booth's description of "the sinking classes" in turn transposed the rhetoric of Henry Stanley's account of his 1887–89 expedition to the Congo, *In Darkest Africa*.[39] Nakagami transposes the terms of light and dark, Christian and barbaric, from an assessment of urban or Victorian African uncivilized nature. Its new purpose is critique of the imperial syntax that places the Kishū periphery of Japan in a similar position. His transformation of the metaphor works because he positions himself as a scribe, committing oral contents he hears to paper like the writers of early Nara writings like the *Kojiki* and *Nihon shoki*.[40]

The section of the *Kojiki* where Kumano appears is pivotal in connecting myth to history through the effort of a scribe. It appears as the site where Emperor Jimmu achieves his first victory in the second book of the text. This is the portion that unfolds the age of men or a historiography rather than the myth narrated by Book 1, which chronicles the age of the gods. This section narrates Jimmu's eastern expedition as he scouts locations for a potential capital and subdues various local residents and deities. The third textual model, *fudoki* gazetteers, was initiated in 713 CE in order to assimilate outlier residents, especially in the eastern provinces, into the symbolic and administrative dominion of the Yamato Court to enable taxation and land distribution. The Empress Genmei decreed her intention that "the local myths and histories of the provinces" as well as things like metals, plants and trees, and soil quality be recorded.[41] Along with genealogies, land features, and inventories of plants, *fudoki* compiled at roughly the same time as the *Kojiki* and *Nihon shoki* tied local histories to the imperial through "stories related by the elders."[42] These stories often narrate the origins of particular toponyms to establish connections and belonging to an imperial center. *Hitachi no kuni fudoki*, written around 720 CE, for example, relates how the mythical Emperor Yamato Takeru (late fourth century) gave the province of Hitachi (present-day Ibaraki prefecture) its name:

> According to another story related by the elders, the name Hitachi derives from a royal prince's tour of the area. While traveling in the Nihihari area on an inspection tour of the Azuma barbarian land, Prince Yamato Takeru (Yamato the Brave) ordered Hinarasu, the *kuni no miyatsuko* [official of the provincial government] of this area, to dig a well. The fresh water in the well was clear and prized for drinking. The prince felt that such delightful water deserved the princely blessing, so he stopped his palanquin. As he ladled out some water with his hand, the sleeve of his garment got wet. From this occurrence [incident] the place acquired the name Hitachi [*hitasu*, soaking in water]. The episode gave rise to the following folk song:

> Dark cloud
> Hanging round Mount Tsukuha
> In the land of sleeve-soaking
> Hitachi.[43]

Although Nakagami does not trace the itinerary of the *fudoki* in his travels, he challenges and provides an alternative to their practice of linking local to Yamato rule through stories that fix meaning to places. He gives roots equal weight in the frame of the *monogatari* (story). He pursues this in the way that he conducts fieldwork in what he has called "calling up the spirits of the land" and commits those conversations to writing. The use of carefully selected language to pacify spirits is a well-grounded trope in Japanese literature and folklore. Nakagami's fieldwork, however, deals with living people as the mediums through which this landscape can be accessed and listened to.

Fieldwork allows him to formulate two further concepts, exchange and *monogatari*, as alternate ways to describe a syntax, set of relations, between Kumano and center—the capital, the metropole, the "civilized" side of culture from which he writes. A 1980 roundtable between Ōe and Naka-gami clarifies how fieldwork is an important dimension of this reportage:

> From my point of view, I don't really make a distinction between the "civilized mind" and the "savage mind" as categories. For instance, there are *hisabetsu-min*, right. And comparing them from the point of view of people who have until now been touting human rights, comparing them with people who are living in the midst of all that, really a completely different civilization or a larger socio-culture sphere, I don't actually think that they're at all lagging in terms of culture. It's just as structuralist theory argues, which is to say that they're far from lagging behind culture or lacking it. Rather, it's the discovery that they have an even greater abundance of culture and daily life. That itself is an amazing thing. Let's say, there is one *hisabetsu buraku*, where I could do some fieldwork from the side of "civilization," to write a novel, and I think what exists is really different than our assumption that these people are constantly laboring under the weight of cultural inferiority.
>
> The fact is that, for whatever reason, it just happens that the grammar of their culture has a different form than the rest of soci-ety, civil society. By doing fieldwork in the way that Lévi-Strauss is now doing, I think you come to understand this well. When I think about this, inside my own self, I just think in terms of *having* that kind of thing. It's not that I am on the side of culture, it's like I am the object of my own fieldwork, too, the civilized and the other side, working in tune with each other.[44]

While the parallax of writing two "sides" is Nakagami's particular perspective, the idea of fieldwork presented here recalls that of Claude Lévi-Strauss, especially ideas from *The Savage Mind* and *Tristes tropiques*. *The Savage Mind* argued that "primitive societies" were governed by rules just as complex as those identified as modern; even if the two kinds of society were different, there was no hierarchy. The word "abundant" (*yutakana*) recalls the efforts of cultural historians like Okiura Kazuteru to shift from understanding *buraku* as relics of the "dark ages" to seeing it as a place of production, largely by reevaluation of the term of culture to include popular performing arts and material culture.[45]

Nakagami's association of writing with domination and exploitation resonates strongly with a chapter called "A Writing Lesson" from *Tristes tropiques,* an elegiac trip to observe Nanbikwara Indians living in a Brazilian rainforest, whom Lévi-Strauss fancies to be among the last uncontacted cultures on earth. He tells the story of handing out pencils to several people who scribbled and drew, whereas the chief had "further ambitions" and delivered a reading of his own scribbling "to astonish his companions, to convince them he was acting as an intermediary agent for the exchange of goods."[46] The chief, in short, hoarded his knowledge and used it to reinforce his rule. Lévi-Strauss concludes that scribes in general have "a hold over others," and his hypothesis, "if correct, would oblige us to recognize the fact that the primary function of written communication is to facilitate slavery."[47] Nakagami's fieldwork taught him that there were ways of using language that were different than imperial syntax.

His point here is not only that the "voiceless" have been excised from the archive of *kokubungaku,* although this effacement is highlighted. Philosophically, his point also concerns how otherness is produced in language; practically, it motivates specific questions when he does have the chance to stir up voices. Nakagami is calling particular attention to how a mode of writing has been formalized to exclude traces of alterity not compatible with the building of a literary national imaginary at each particular instance of the conceptual transplanting from oral to written. If the stories he hears from his informants are similar in their structure—namely, a structure of exploitation, neglect, and forced mobility—the varieties seem infinite and proliferate like kanji when the lid is "stripped off," adding to the possibilities of open-source narration. The questions he asks elicit chronicles of what it is like to suffer anti*buraku* discrimination and how that happens in public health, education, work, and religion.

Yoshi Tarō tells the story of being displaced by a tsunami in 1935. Because his family lived on the "other side" of town, no one came to warn or rescue their neighborhood.[48] Kinoshita Yukie describes the local Buddhist rituals conducted by a priest from not the *tera* (寺, temple) but from the uncredentialed *tera* (テラ, temple).[49] Kawagami-san, a construction subcontract worker, travels long distances to work on crews with Chinese and Korean workers.[50] Yanagioka Shijirō describes fall festivals that took place before the Suiheisha era when *buraku-min* were forced to participate in "after-festivals" rather than as real Shinto parishioners (*ujiko*) on the day itself.[51] K-san was caught in Hiroshima when the atomic bomb dropped. His spinal cord became so damaged he had to quit his peddler work and go on welfare. When his wife became pregnant, she was told by the state clinic to abort the child because it would never be normal.[52] That child was born healthy and came to run a sweets shop.

Like the kanji characters when you strip the lid off, each iteration of this story is different, but the structure remains the same. The North/South paradigm corresponds to the idea of structure that is manifested in formulations of center/periphery and Kumano/Kyoto. In an essay on the Shingū writer Satō Haruo, Nakagami writes that, in his estimation, the formative political event of the modern era in Japan was the late Meiji-era scandal of the 1910 Great Treason Incident (*Taigyaku jiken*).[53] Twelve people, including the doctor Ōishi Seinosuke and the Buddhist priest Takagi Kenmyō, collectively known as the Kishū group, as well as the socialist-anarchist thinker Kōtoku Shusui and anarchist Kannō Sugako, were executed because they allegedly conspired in a plot to assassinate the Meiji emperor with a bomb. For Nakagami, the mass execution signaled that even prior to defending itself against a national enemy, the imperial government considered its own citizens (cosmopolitan Southern citizens from within) to be a threat. While much about the resulting trial is lost or shrouded in conspiratorial mystery as in the Sayama trial, most of the young *buraku* men who were prosecuted remained "totally oblivious to the seriousness of the nature of the charges" because press restrictions were issued on trial coverage.[54] These events consolidated the relation of Buddhism with the state and precipitated a time called "the winter years," a chill placed on public assembly and on anarchist, socialist, and other anti-imperial ideas.[55]

The doctor Ōishi, Nakagami's focus among the Kishū group members, was well connected in socialist circles in Shingū and was the subject of a famous poem by Satō Haruo, "The Death of an Idiot" (*Gusha no shi*). Nakagami analyzes this poem at length in his most systematic writing on *monogatari* and Japanese literary history. The *monogatari* that he critiques is a literary history of exclusion that connects the South to ideas, ethnicity, and imperial critique. The essay's main point is that, according to criteria established by the state, Ōishi is not "Japanese," and Satō identifies with this position. By implication, Nakagami, too, identifies with this parallax identity:

> On January 23, 1911,
> Ōishi Seinosuke was killed.
> Indeed those who break the solemn rules of the majority
> Have to be killed.
> Thinking it's play when it's really staking your life
> not knowing the history of the folk rules (*minzoku*),
> Not being Japanese
> such fools have to be killed.
> You say "truth springs from lies"
> but this phrase spoken from the gallows is the height of folly.
> My hometown is Kishū Shingū.
> His hometown is my hometown.
> Listen, they say that his hometown, my hometown,
> that the town of Kishū Shingū is shaking in fear.
> How this prosperous merchant town is grieving.
> —Calm yourselves, townspeople.
> Teachers, preach the country's history again and better.[56]

The lines "My hometown is Kishū Shingū / His hometown is my hometown" are especially powerful to Nakagami. They serve as a way to write himself into literary history as a resident of Shingū, to claim the same "hometown" as both Ōishi and Haruo, and by using the word "*kuni*" (country) to mean its old sense of region, as well as its modern sense of nation to link the two and suggest a counterhistory violently excised from mainstream Japan. "Hometown" is not only a literal referent but also a structure: peripheral, Southern, and defeated. These particular lines "have exerted an immeasurable influence on many people from Shingū," and, "moreover, it is the same as the influence that the Civil War has had on people in the American South." He concludes that, "It is the same for me."[57] Nakagami interprets "those who betray the rules of the majority" to mean something broader than "anarchists plotting to assassinate the emperor with the phrases of Kropotkin and Bakunin on their lips."[58] Rather, it is "Shingū in every sense of the word."[59] More broadly, he extends the topos of hometown to connect it to a narrative of the literary history of Kumano as it appears at the beginnings of written narrative in Japan. Haruo saw the "rules of many serious people" as a kind of "war," and the scorching mark of the slain bear again links writing to death: "on his fore-head just like the ID number on the arms of Jews rounded up into con-centration camps."[60] He concludes by affirming his link to the Southern traitors of the Kishū group because "*monogatari* itself is a kind of bomb."[61] His outline is as chronological as any Meiji-era literary anthology, travers-ing Jimmu's eastern expedition; triangulated imperial ties among Yoshino, Nara, and Kyoto; the Tokugawa Shingū han's appearances in Edo-period kabuki dramas; and new thought that stirred Shingū locals and led to the Great Treason Incident. In this chronicle of exclusion, each case reaffirms a structure of exile from imperial syntax.

The equation between Ōishi and the South recurs in 1978 in an essay entirely on Ōishi. Where he writes "Doctor Ōishi," the original reads "Ōishi Dokutoru" (doctor poison-taker), troping heterophonically on several local registers. Ōishi was indeed a medical doctor. Part of his job was to assuage illness, or "take poison" away (*doku o toru*). But in the larger metaphorics, *doku* is also a homonym for both reading and inde-pendence as well as poison (and is highly reminiscent of Derrida's notion of the *pharmakon*). It identified Ōishi as part of the constellation of the supplement in terms of center-periphery social relations. The nation needs people like Ōishi to survive, but to survive cannot stand to retain him within its borders:

> The capture and execution of Doctor Ōishi was a great shock to the people of Shingū. From the point of view of townspeople of the time, treason was just an idea that did not compute. They had no idea what Marxism meant, what anarchism meant. What they knew was that the authority took someone who did something extravagant. He knew that poor people who couldn't pay medical fees were too embarrassed to say "I don't have any money," so he told them to make themselves known by knocking on the window three times, and he would look at them for free.
>
> The reason I describe Ōishi of the Great Treason Incident not as a person of "history," but as someone who had live blood running through his veins is through an anecdote about one of those "knock knock" cases. My stepfather's mother, or say my step-grandmother, knocked on the glass in this way, and was seen by him.

This doctor was a complete "idiot."

Even now, more than sixty years after the "death of an idiot," there are still people who talk about the doctor. Local historians have written up accounts of Ōishi Seinosuke. It's probably fair to say that Ōishi Seinosuke has, in a person, come to embody Kishū, Kumano. Since Ōishi Seinosuke was arrested on cause of the Great Treason Incident, time has stopped flowing. Looking at this Doctor Ōishi, as a novelist, for whatever reason it seems to me that it like a fictional version of a North-South Civil War broke out in Japan, *as if I were reading a novel by William Faulkner.* In sum, the Great Treason Incident is a frame-up by the bureaucracy. And in order to make the dirty name of "treason" stick on the scapegoated people, it was necessary to recall a particular form of "Japan." It's one kind of principle (*rinen*). And standing 180-degrees in opposition to that principle were the Shingū group, with Ōishi Seinosuke at its center—no, opposing it is a principle represented by another country called Kishū . . . Ōishi's brand of "anarchism" was the knock knock sound on the glass, hearing it, and opening the door.[62]

Nakagami compares the Great Treason Incident and the U.S. Civil War in terms of pivotal political moments that address internal dissent: two links to Faulkner stand out in this interpretation. One is the idea of an enemy within, or a war on the periphery undertaken by the center; the second is a sense that "time stopped moving" in a structure so that events cannot transform.[63] (As I explore in chapter 5, this sense of vital or kinetic time is what Nakagami seeks in Korea and is a benchmark of how connected Korean popular culture and literature are to politics where Japan is not, due to this foundational oppression.) The key dynamic, or *monogatari*, that the execution of the Kishū group put in place was to scapegoat the Southern political threat and reassert imperial force, relying on the potential resistor to turn traitor.

But at the same time, Nakagami suggests that structures, even literal edifices of architecture that comprise imperial syntax, are powerful only because of their connection to Kumano; by analogy, Japanese literature is powerful only because of its (supplemental) relation to *buraku* cultural forms. He describes this relation in a set-piece passage on the Sanjūsangendō temple complex in the former imperial capital of Kyoto. It was built by the late-Heian general Taira no Kiyomori for the retired emperor Goshi-rakawa (1127–92 CE) in 1164. During his reign, Goshirakawa had been a great patron of the Kumano shrines, to which he conducted thirty-three pilgrimages. The temple is named for its thirty-three bays, which together hold 1001 Kannon statues surrounding a large statue. Each bay represents one of the thirty-three disguises Kannon might assume in the course of granting mercy. For Nakagami it is significant because:

What draws your gaze here is the connection between the imperial capital and Kumano. At the source of the state of ghostly posses-sion that characterizes the Sanjūsangendō temple of Kyōto, the imperial capital, and the land of power by means of which power consolidated culture is Kumano. Kumano: I'm going to write it without the matching *kanji* and only with sounds. Komoriku, Komorino, Kumano. It is a profound thing that the ever-shifting light and dark that reach the same Kyōto whose every and all ele-ment is like a delicate, refined miniature garden become profound indeed as the light and dark of Kumano reaches it. [64]

In this passage, Nakagami argues that Goshirakawa's power is enabled only because of his movement back and forth to Kumano. The role attributed to Kumano resembles that of the "supplement" as also con-ceived by Jacques Derrida. This idea is presented to establish the relation of speech and writing. The use of the phonetic writing system to write the multiple place names strips off the kanji that would fix meaning of each character and locate it in an imperial context. Each phoneme, in Nakagami's reading, can sustain multiple interpretations, even contra-dictory meanings. His point is that Goshirakawa acts as a point of transit or exchange for both rituals and objects between Kumano's layered or simultaneous quality and the centralized imperial power of Kyōto. The chiaroscuro of Kumano is due to its multiple nature as apparent/visible and hidden/invisible elements. It contains elements that are opposed but do not negate each other, and can only be viewed through paral-lax. These multiplicities are violently rubbed out in the appropriation by Goshirakawa, and refigured as the glistening light and dark of the Sanjūsangendō statues.

A 1977 essay, "The Codes/Chords of the Land" ("*Tsuchi no kōdo*") explains the formal workings of *sekkyō-bushi*, an important and neglected genre of oral culture comprising open-source narratives. The homonym of "codes/chords" has two meanings: "codes" as "operational rules," and "chords," or the repertoire of elements that make up the musical accompaniment of *sekkyō-bushi*. The "codes/chords" model is founded on a local scale and uses the paradigmatic dimension of language as the basis of its operations. In other words, each semantic unit is substitutable by any of a number of others. "Each and every *sekkyō-bushi* works by pursuing something we could call 'relations' (*kankei*). They unravel genealogical legends (*engi*), forced to drift about and read in place names, and narrate all kinds of human relations like you would make up a new kind of myth (*shinwa*). I want to call these things, up to and including the scale of human relations, the codes/chords of the land."[65] In Nakagami's work and the folk materials he includes, openness that is available for contributions by the "users" of this code, or those who draw on a common repertoire of oral histories, is particularly weighted to place names. This framework allows him to see a counternarrative to imperial syntax.

An example of this kind of exchange also occurs in secular songs about a ship that runs continually between rival towns, Ōshima and Kushimoto.[66] There is no set origin for the song, as both towns claim it, and it is fundamentally about the movement between the two. The songs composed in a 7–7–7–5 (*do-do-do-itsu*) rhythm linked by a chorus. The chorus repeats "This is Ōshima/the other side is Kushimoto//The ship that/is on a constant round trip" after each verse. All three verses describe states of longing or trappedness, and play off the paradox of having little room to move in the ship or one's station in life, all the while moving in the limitless open seas. The first example describes someone's view being blocked from the sight he seeks. "Even though I can see ōshima right there from my window, opening my *shoji*//I cannot see Sakichi (a brothel) because it is under a pine tree." In the second example, someone is longing to see a prostitute at a brothel, at the same time he realizes her sorrow, which comes out when it rains. He pleads, "Please do not rain in the harbor at sunset because/ Oaki, or Tako [her nickname] will cry and ruin her make-up."

For Nakagami these songs are significant because they contain the same themes and pathos as now-recognized genres, but have been unfairly neglected: "when you read this *Ōshima–bushi*, with its harbor and ships, prostitutes and walking peddlers, you see that all the elements that go to build the literature of Chikamatsu and Saigyō are lined up in the land called *Ōshima*."[67] In other words, the more recognized *jōruri* narration of

Edo-period playwright Chikamatsu displaced local song and oral forms when the canon of national literature was assembled in the Meiji era. These insights are enabled by going out into the field and listening, to see how relations of exchange operate. Having looked at the significance of fieldwork, we are now in a position to revisit the context of South that Nakagami's interpretation challenged.

Another Country: Faulkner Reception in Japan

Karatani Kōjin remarks that Nakagami took his primary Faulkner hint from an Americanist who viewed literature through the lens of political economy:

> Ari Jirō's interpretation was probably viewed by English literature scholars of the time as eccentric; and it probably was. In fact, as is true elsewhere outside of America, Faulkner's literature, and the South writ large, was received through a postcolonial critique of dependency economics (*izon-ron*) and its effects on society. In Latin America, Africa, India. Ari Jirō felt this at a gut level, and gave Nakagami a very important hint. So rather than Faulkner putting his roots down in Japanese literature, Japanese literature used Faulkner as a mediation to leap to a different level.[68]

Faulkner's exploration of past-present relations in the context of new social mobilities after his characters "los[e] to the Yankees" provided a way for Japanese intellectuals to question important issues about postwar history and identity. Faulkner's visit strengthened the place of literature *as* history in the conceptual link between Japan and the Southern United States. In 1955, the rebound of Japan's economy led to announcements heralding that the "postwar era was over" (*mohaya sengo de wa nai*) because its GDP had rebounded to prewar levels.[69] Faulkner gave a series of speeches and attended meetings sponsored by scholars of American literature. These scholars were aware that even if the GDP had overcome its "past," that political, cultural and social forms had not.

A key scholar in the canonization of Faulkner in Japanese literary contexts was Ōhashi Kenzaburō, then a young professor at Tokyo University, and later a correspondent of Nakagami's. Today, Tokyo University is still an influential center of American literary studies in Japan. Its alumni include Karatani Kōjin, who read Faulkner in Ōhashi's seminar and passed it on to Nakagami, who soon announced that he would become "the Japanese Faulkner."[70] Even earlier, Tokyo University had played host to historians of the U.S. South. C. Vann Woodward was invited to give a summer course in Tokyo in 1953, the year after the U.S. occupation ended.[71] He was explicitly asked to address Reconstruction, the ten-year interval that immediately followed the Civil War.

Woodward's 1951 book on Reconstruction, *The Origins of the New South*, had argued that it was not merely carpetbaggers and scalawags descending from the North who were responsible for the new inequalities of the postbellum era. He argued that politicians, businessmen and editorial-writers all depicted attachment to local practices and economies as parochial and urged attachment to Northern capital as a way forward. These new entrepreneurs advocated a "hopeful nationalism that the lately disaffected south was at last one in faith with the country—or would be as soon as a few more bonds were sold."[72] This had the effect of further disabling the economic capacities of black and poor white residents. At the same time as transcending parochialism by forging economic alliances with the North, new institutions sought to "identify themselves with the Romantic cult of the confederacy."[73]

Woodward's argument seemed to fit some paradigms of post-Occupation life in Japan. In the United States, romantic attachment to an invented "old South" had emerged at the same time that a new South had subordinated recovery and self-sufficiency to Northern-led mercantile policies, in which southerners were merely "branch officials" for big capital. Similarly, in Japan, economic recovery was narrated by myths of *Nihonjinron*, nostalgic and essentialist claims about the fundaments of Japanese cultural identity that underwrote economic success. The cult of the past seemed to go hand in hand with economic growth that linked to "Northern" capital as Japan sought to invest overseas. Literary criticism sometimes dwelled on the myth of a prewar organic Japan. But its main attention was directed to understanding how history, memory and textuality mingled in a postwar Japan with a newly emerging industrial class that itself produced the invented tradition of prewar organicism.

Ōhashi's Kenzaburō's first Faulkner work consisted of editing a short story collection in 1956. His first critical writings on Faulkner appeared in his 1957 survey of American literature from the 1930s, and he was in charge of the massive collected works of Faulkner. Japanese writers and scholars, including novelists Kojima Nobuo, Ogawa Kunio, and Ikezawa Natsuki as well as American literature scholar Saeki Shōichi and critic Isoda Kōichi, wrote essays for each volume. In 1964, Ōhashi cast back to the immediate postwar era to give a historical frame for the reception of Faulkner. His article on John Ford's film *The Sun Shines Bright* (1953) placed it in the context of the "splendor and tragedy of the American South." He likens the reconstruction of the U.S. South and postwar Japan while echoing Faulkner's strategically empathetic remark that "we both lost to the Yankees."

> The pure idealism that surfaced when the North flew the flag
> of slave liberation after the war began to flow into the South. At
> the same time, it cruelly destroyed the humanistic, rich commu-
> nal emotional life that had put nature and humans at its center.
> Moreover, modern industrialism also flooded in from the North.
> *No, the state of the South after the war rather resembled the state of our*
> *own country after the last World War,* and the efforts toward an ideal
> Reconstruction got left behind in messy, halfway fashion, while
> the old order was completely broken down by means of the new
> industrialism running rampant.[74]

I read Ōhashi's description as a critique of the linearity of postwar development, one that lacks reflection about how the precipitates of past might inhabit the present. When Japan is interpreted as a national South, it is easy to overlook that the South of the United States was not only a periphery of the industrial "North" brought into the nation by industry where agriculture failed. Though distinct in many ways from the economic industrial north, it too possessed a hegemonic system of its own that had been co-produced along with the modernity of the nation-state: slavery. When Faulkner visited Japan, however, he was more interested in situating Japan as a mythic victim of history, not an active agent.

Faulkner's most important speech delivered during his trip to Japan was titled "To the Youth of Japan." He analogized Japan's future to post–Civil War history: "I believe that something very like [what happened in the American South] will happen here in Japan within the next few years— that out of your disaster and despair will come a group of Japanese writers whom all the world will want to listen to, who will speak not a Japanese truth, but a universal truth."[75] The universalizing move to liken the U.S. South and Japan coincided with Faulkner's own vernacular interpretation of modernization theory in his comparison of local contexts. "This is the same rice paddy which I knew back home in Arkansas and Mississippi and Louisiana, where it replaces now and then the cotton. This one is merely a little smaller and a little more fiercely cultivated . . . nature is the same; only the economy is different."[76]

In contrast to the early postwar identification of a national Japan with a regional U.S. South, Nakagami develops his concept of the South by transposing Faulkner's post-Civil War U.S. South to a specific region within Japan. Nakagami used the idea of a "South" to refer to local peripheries as well as Southern locations outside of Japan, making connections between local and regional imaginaries. This "South" links two scales of regional subnational peripheries and national political areas by asserting a common awareness that resources flow from a "periphery" of poor and underdeveloped states to a "core" of wealthy states, enriching the latter at the expense of the former.[77]

Applied to literature, the basic tenets of dependency theory that specify the status of a global South describe a topos that is external *to* but an integral part *of* the center, a place that brims with the origins of traditions written out of the canon of national literature, and is characterized by constant movement between levels of center and periphery, official and popular. This description is a social-theoretical restatement of Nakagami's basic account of literary history in Japan, one that corresponds with his central notion of the cluster of concepts that converge under the heading "Kumano."

Critical Readings of *Monogatari*

From the late 1970s to the mid-1980s, the term *monogatari* took on for Nakagami a weight that exceeded its conventional definition as a premodern genre of writing. He increasingly employs the word *monogatari* to describe the complex relations between "tree" and "root" that compose the narrative operations of Japanese fiction. Between 1978 and 1981, he published a series of essays called "The Genealogy of Monogatari" in *Kokubungaku* (*National Literature*). The writings on fiction writers Satō Haruo, Tanizaki Jun'ichirō, and Enchi Fumiko make more explicit connections between the concrete events that form the narrative of imperial syntax in modern fiction. Each writer illustrates different directions and limitations for using language as a model for culture.

The essays most pointedly focused on national literature center on the "fiction-writer, poet, haiku writer and, of course, scholar" Orikuchi

Shinobu.[78] Nakagami credits Orikuchi with understanding *monogatari* more than almost any other writer, because he has discovered a number of fixed patterns to storytelling. But at the same time, "there is no human being alive who has ignored the fact that *monogatari* are law and system as much as Orikuchi has."[79] He gives credit to Orikuchi's focus on tropes like the outside wanderer (*marebito*) as spiritual entities that periodically visit village communities from the other world—the "everlasting world" (*tokoyo*) across the sea—to bring their residents happiness and good fortune.[80] Structurally, *marebito* operate as outside forces encountered through relations of exchange of any sort. But he criticizes Orikuchi for merely cataloguing *monogatari* and not transferring this knowledge to a critique of structures of exchange, or outside literature.

Nakagami claims that Orikuchi exhibits the same flaw in all thirty-one volumes of his writing, whether it concerns Shintō or folklore, because he treats kanji in a way that accords with imperial syntax. His "luster" comes from the way he looks to fix the meaning of words by peeling off layers in a hunt for the gluing-point (*teiten-sagashi*) of written kanji at the "some point" when they fix meaning. The problem is "some point" doesn't acknowledge that there might be a disconnect between the timing of written and spoken language, or that the written word might exercise "privilege, oppression or regulation" over the spoken word.[81] Despite the fact that he makes the wandering signifier of the *marebito* his main critical term, Orikuchi looks for stable kernels of meaning in the same way that you might think of the middle of a pearl onion.[82] For a flower (*hana*), he disregards the other meanings of the same phoneme, like nose and edge, as well as the encounter of foreign script with (proto)-Japanese referent. These kanji are seen in logocentric, one-to-one isolation from their relation to other signifiers, apart from the relations of "exchange" they should foreground. The significance is on one hand empirical: there are gaps between written and spoken language. The significance also has a politics: privileging the written word excludes cultural forms that are oral, or that are variant, like many oral genres are.

Nakagami's ideas on *monogatari* suppose two parallax meanings of *monogatari*: one drawn from classical literature, such as *Ise monogatari* (*Tales of Ise*), that intersperses poems with narratives and one drawn from the structuralist understanding of the word to refer to narrative and narratology. This work was employed in the idiom of Japanese cultural criticism when it was used to translate "narrative" in works by Roland Barthes,

Gérard Genette, and others who attempted to classify or inventory the narrative operations of literature.[83] Scholars such as classicist and poet Fujii Sadakazu as well as film and French literary scholar Hasumi Shige-hiko agree that *monogatari* as a law and system is Nakagami's most impor-tant critical concept.[84] Nakagami is, however, the only writer to use both these registers of *monogatari* and also include the subtexts of race and eth-nicity that had infused the French writings on structuralism and textual analysis. Nakagami's retrofit of the category of *monogatari* to accommo-date eighth-century chronicles in synch with postwar novellas stretches back to the beginnings of written narrative in Japanese and represent his effort to create a new line of literary criticism.

Karatani was the first critic to attribute a special status to *monogatari* in Nakagami's works in an essay on a short-story collection, *Make-Up* (*Keshō*). He described it as Nakagami's first work to mingle elements of contemporary reality in the mode of I-fiction, and *monogatari*.[85] By this, I take him to mean elements of premodern aesthetics. The stories in *Make-Up* focus on "the big man," a city-dweller who has been kicked out by his family after incidents of domestic violence. The man gravitates back to his birthplace, Kumano. As he reflects and moves through the land-scape, he seems to be released from historical time. Kumano is saturated with folkloric elements, such as healing waters, pilgrim ritual, and mingled Buddhist, Shintō, and local popular religious figures. The world around him transforms, and he encounters ghosts, a mysterious nursing woman, and other fleeting apparitions linked to his psychic past.

Karatani wants to prohibit us from reading Nakagami's stories as tem-poral exoticism or transcendence. He writes that the "hallucinations" (*genkaku*) of the premodern fantastic that the "big man" experiences are in fact ultimately intelligible only by means of phenomenological reduc-tion.[86] This term—first applied to Karatani's own writing by anthropolo-gist Yamaguchi Masao—means that the text brackets for the reader the way in which modern consciousness presents itself to itself, and does so through a restricted set of terms. When Nakagami brackets the word "imperial" in his phrase "'imperial' syntax," it has the same effect. This "bracketed" experience was the innovative concept in Karatani's own *"Ori-gins" of "Modern" "Japanese" "Literature."*[87] In Karatani's reading, the very terms of explanation for the protagonist's experience are produced by the modern, postindustrial effects of stress and overwork (*karō*) that origi-nally drove him to the provinces.[88] For Karatani, the story is an allegory of how the modern imagination sees the premodern as an alienated category separate from itself over a distance that has to be overcome, as it does in his own work on "landscape" in *Origins*. I would like to suggest that we consider that the multiple senses of time might lead us in a different direction than Karatani suggests. Rather than the past/present or inner/outer split that Karatani identifies, I would like to think about what entertaining these elements as simultaneous and dependent—as a kind of parallax, a relation of exchange rather than rupture—might imply.

We can clarify what is distinct about Nakagami's interpretation by looking at some important contemporaries who also aim to revise how *monogatari* are understood. In the late 1960s, critics and writers begin to work toward canon reform and undoing the effects of nationalism on culture. *Monogatari* analysis was acutely aware that cultural nationalism that underwrote the emperor system turned on the idea of a continuous history, one that interpreted even classical texts in realist terms, with coherent narratives. Critics such as Fujii Sadakazu and other members of the *Monogatari kenkyū-kai* (*monogatari* study group) were primarily based in classical literary studies. They worked to contextualize the speaking subject, one of the main elements of how literature is conceived through a realist perspective. Their aim was to detranscendentalize this subject by showing the multiple perspectives necessary to produce narrative. Doing so, they worked to relocate its rhetorics in material and social fields.

To scholars of classical literature, *monogatari* first and foremost implies a stylistic or thematic association with classical, narrative tales. It describes a formal or stylistic set of tendencies, ones that are internal to the text itself. The conventional understanding of *monogatari* defines it as a loose narrative mode, a "tale," used to anchor *waka* poetry and poetic exchanges in classical writing. Haruo Shirane notes that in the Heian era, "the word *monogatari* meant either gibberish, idle talk, or a work of prose fiction in the vernacular, as opposed to the learned language, Chinese."[89] *Monogatari* often center on the court, narrate its events, and incorporate historical figures. On occasions *monogatari* give the impression of orality in their written form; many have a wide array of variants and long traditions of commentaries that establish the contexts for discursive reading. Formally, *monogatari* often become meaningful or aesthetically significant because they are intertextually embedded in other writings that appeared from the Heian to the Kamakura periods.[90]

Nakagami certainly incorporates the stylistics of these classical *monogatari* as a repertoire of forms, figures, and vernaculars into a wide array of his works. In Nina Cornyetz's words, the literary texture is "precisely a weave of language, multilayered with significations and inscribed with narratives and histories" whose project is to "revitalize oral folklore within the confines of a modern written text."[91] *Monogatari*'s loose, unbounded nature is a subtext in his modern retelling of *The Tale of the Hollow Tree* (*Utsuho monogatari*, late tenth century), a sequence of lyrical stories about Muromachi-era artisans. The *Hollow Tree* stories use the motif of the "exile of the wandering noble," a fixture of *monogatari* that Orikuchi's scholarship had raised to prominence. The *Hollow Tree* stories also place the foundational but hollow tree at the center of the story, where its open nature serves as the generative space for a fictional mythic system, but one that is open at its center, like the lidless kanji of Nakagami's Shingū stories.

As a genre, *monogatari* offered the kind of open-ended narrative that seemed most fruitful for understanding how narrative might depart from realist conventions and limits, particularly those that emphasized a transcendental perspective and equated it with subjectivity, freedom, "the self," autonomy, or any of a number of "higher" metacategories that would judge whether Japan had a successfully "modern" literature because it exhibited these universally valued formal traits. *Monogatari* analysis as fueled by structuralism offered the chance to positively reevaluate qualities of *monogatari* that had been viewed as shortcomings when viewed according to transcendental criteria: incoherence and failure to enunciate in a consistent manner, Ted Fowler describes *monogatari* as a mode in which the transparent confession of the speaking subject, "the linear narrative flow . . . is constantly intersected by allusion, polysemy, and discursive meditations, which disrupt the reader's focus on the object of narration and redirect it insistently to the narrating subject and/or the very process of narration."[92] In the 1970s, critics such as Takeoka Masao focused on how narrative voice in *monogatari*, such as *The Tale of the Bamboo-Cutter* (*Taketori monogatari*), "is explicitly discursive . . . without being anchored to a consistent spatio-temporal and thematic coordinate of a singular speaking subject," in Tomiko Yoda's words.[93] Perhaps the most notable critic to carry out this work by analyzing the formal rhetorics of modern literature was Komori Yōichi. Komori's short book on Tanizaki Jun'ichirō's story of fieldwork by an amateur scholar in *Arrowroot* (*Yoshino kuzu*) showed Tanizaki's stealthy emplotment of imperial history as a kind of fakelore.[94]

Nakagami's work on *monogatari* stands out for three reasons. First, he focuses on classical *monogatari* such as the *Kojiki* and *The Tale of the Hollow Tree,* diverging from the focus on *The Tale of Genji* (*Genji mono-gatari*) that distinguished *kokubungaku.* Second, while he shares a desire for canon reform with scholars of classical literature, Nakagami takes the formal analysis of writing, the antifoundational critique of enunciation as something held together by framing contexts, or "the constant re-drawing of communicative context," outside of scholarly settings to other places where he sees the same narrative rules operating.[95] Drawing on our under-standing of "imperial syntax," we could ask of stories like *Make-up:* by what set of sociohistorical criteria does it come to be that this "big man" needs to exist in multiple places and temporalities to account for his character?

The third and perhaps most important element in Nakagami's analy-sis of *monogatari* as a system and not a set of formal characteristics or even a genre, is that we never see *monogatari* without some sort of dif-ference (e.g., racial, *buraku*) that is differential in relation to the (unspo-ken) mainstream subject of a national structure. Nor do we see the discussion of such difference without some relation to *monogatari* after the term first surfaces in a 1968 novella (I treat this work in chapter 4). Nakagami's reception of structuralism and poststructuralism happens in extraliterary as well as literary contexts—namely, in the legal system, and in the ethnographic framings through which *monogatari* channels the "confessing" *buraku* voice as "law and system" traverses from page to courtroom. He applies the analytic tool of imperial syntax to note how fixing meaning has worked to send *buraku* characters and settings into symbolic exile from the imperial domain. He also uses it to show how the written versions of *buraku* cultural forms have been excised from the archive of that national literature.

Exchange

Karatani's placement of *Make-Up* in the analytic of "landscape" is symp-tomatic of a larger current of literary criticism focusing on space since the 1970s. I want to briefly review what this consists of before locating Nak-agami's writing in the context of the discussions of postmodernism and space that happened at the level of public policy beginning in the early 1970s. I want to show how, for him, concepts from structuralist thought were not just epistemologies for abstractly theorizing the world. They also presented a way to locate the spatial turn in postmodern thought in discussions of political economy and public policy.

Maeda Ai's influential writings on urban space present a more temporally layered understanding of Edo literature's precipitates in Meiji literature than Karatani's idea of sudden rupture and alienation.[96] But despite his emphasis on layered modernity, Maeda, too, focuses on the transcendental narrator in his analyses of urban space and literature through his emphasis on subjectivity (*shutaisei*) and perspective as the determinants of textual meaning. Alternatively, Kamei Hideo (1937–) is concerned with the rise of the "non-person narrator." This narrator emerged in new styles of reportage in the 1880s as the precondition that the narrator remain apart from the diegesis to complete a self-reflexive circuit between narrator, characters and reader.[97] Despite the divergent ideas of these approaches to landscape, they are unified by a common investment in visual means of representation to provide formal analogs to schemes of power from which the subject is severed and which act upon it. This particular emphasis on subjectivity and subjectivization in each mode of visuality, moreover, stresses the autonomy of the individual.

Nakagami's work presents a different model, a dynamic interaction between character and landscape in which humans change the landscape; they are not merely acted upon while projecting a psychologized impression of a phenomenal world. In roundtables that theorized how literary history could be told other than emphasizing the self, Nakagami began to use the word *kōtsū*. *Kōtsū* is a key term of political economy that appears in both capitalist and socialist frameworks. In today's colloquial Japanese, the word *kōtsū* means "traffic." It might be seen more abstractly in Lévi-Strauss's or Gayle Rubin's terms of women, objects, and messages.[98] Planners and policy makers in 1970s Japan used exchange to describe the "third industry" of information technologies and communication that would follow the first industrial revolution of natural resource extraction and the second industrial revolution of manufacturing and construction in which ships, railways, and engines were used to put products of the first into motion. Exchange valued communication and information structures over material ones by highlighting ideas of connectivity, information, and immaterial labor.

The salvation of immaterial/postindustrial work was featured in national policy documents on "computopia" and economic growth beginning in 1973, including Masuda Yoneji's *Information Society as Post-Industrial Society*.[99] Nakagami describes exchange at length in his critical essays from the late 1970s. The "desire" to make these exchanges visible in narrative form is something that in his mind sets him apart from the "synchronicity" that journalists cite when they want to group him with writers Ri Kaisei and Murakami Ryū.[100] It appears in his plans for renewing the unfulfilled agenda of "socialized self" that is the key concept of Kobayashi Hideo's I-fiction. And it is a featured term in the lecture series he delivered in his hometown of Shingū in 1978, when he tried out his highly abstract literary criticism to audiences who had lived through frequent stints of migrant or itinerant labor.

These ideas about exchange became connected in popular discussion to the decentralization of economic development proposed in Tanaka Kakuei's 1972 best-selling *Plan for Reconstructing the Japanese Archipelago* (*Nippon rettō kaizō-ron*), published the month before Tanaka became prime minister. Tanaka's goal was to equilibrate and "homogenize" the difference between a resource-heavy *omote* (surface) urban industrial belt and a resource-poor *ura* (underside) agricultural Japan, using info-communications networks. The fact that Tanaka situates the center-periphery model of *omote/ura* within the explicit terms of information culture and communications should convey to us how the local scale is already being imagined, if not yet materialized, as an iteration of a global scale. Ishikawa Hiroyuki links Tanaka's plan especially closely to Nakagami's *The Ends of the Earth, Supreme Time* because that work marks the razing of the *roji*, the building of a large supermarket, and links the city to a larger homogenized network of distribution.[101]

A hundred years earlier, in the cauldron of "second industries," Marx and Engels had used the very same word *verkehr* (*kōtsū*) in their 1845 treatise *German Ideology*. They outline a materialist concept of history in which they attack metaphysical "phantoms." They argued that just as the physical world is regulated by the law of gravity and not divinity, the material world is regulated by material conditions and the actions of men, who enter into political and social relations through exchange.[102] In his ongoing conversation with Nakagami, Karatani focused attention on the concept of *kōtsū* as the basis of a new kind of historiography based on materialist history that tracks not "world history" but "world exchange." The effect is to draw attention to the mediating kinds of relationships that comprise "history" as kinds of interdependence. Needless to say, this concept of exchange is already visible in Nakagami's treatment of circulation between North and South, Kumano and imperial centers.

In a 1979 roundtable with Nakagami, Karatani explains how he sees exchange producing history as an ongoing process of the social relations between people:

> Recently I published an article on Kobayashi Hideo in *Contemporary Thought* (*Gendai shisō*). You know this very well, but in *German Ideology*, Marx uses the concept of *kōtsū/verkehr* along with that of "division of labor," and establishes a really broad meaning that covers exchange, communication, relations of production, war . . . You and I use it so often, it's really irritated certain people (laughs). But to put it simply, in history, there is no "telos" and no "meaning," no "necessity" and no "center," as these are ideologies or metaphysics that are always attributed later . . . this is the position that leads to thinking in terms of "division of labor" or *kōtsū*.[103]

Nakagami's use of exchange extends the materialist conception of social relations to the textual world to make relationality the basis of his writing. His position also revises both Karatani's class analysis and the conventional use of the word by state policy-makers and planners. It adds relations from the specific historical character of *buraku* history, and particular places in the division of labor that *senmin* have occupied. (Here I use *senmin* to correspond to the structural position of outcasts Nakagami refers to, who appear at differing times, from the Muromachi period to the present.) *Kōtsū* emphasizes relations between parts in a fluid system rather than fixed meaning from a detached perspective. This formulation is more useful for understanding how narratives stretch beyond one character, work or author, and how they draw on larger extraliterary kinds of writing and oral culture.

The model of exchange allows us to think differently about one of Nakagami's central characters—Akiyuki, a young construction worker who is the protagonist of the Kishū saga. A common reading of Akiyuki suggests that he is less a character than a vessel who wants most of all to sublimate his own subjectivity into the landscape. In early formulations of Akiyuki, he digs, arranges tools, and pours concrete for hundreds of pages, yet never builds anything. In *The Cape*:[104]

> The lady construction worker got out the portable propane stove and was boiling water for tea. The boss and Suga-san were tying

something off with a rope. Fujino-san was sitting on his haunches like he was working out in the field and was digging up dirt with a hoe. Yasuo jumped up from the hole in the ground he was digging. Tattoos peeked out from his wrists on up to where his shirt sleeves were rolled up. Yasuo radiated a stinky underarm smell. [Akiyuki] breathed in deep. He felt like throwing up. He thought he would keep turning up the dirt until it was time to take a break. He punched the pick down. Amazingly it went in all the way to the handle. Turn it over. The land bulged and turned over. He put the pick aside and changed to a shovel. He put his weight into it, and put his foot on the trowel, and pried loose the dirt. He turned it over and threw it outside. Sweat started to run. It was still all salty. Whenever he was excavating, when he was sweating salty sweat, he had to put his energy even into breathing. When it turned to water, his body felt a lot easier. He got into the rhythm of digging, put his weight into it, and synched his breath with the movement of pulling the shovel out. He particularly loved this work of excavating. More than anything, it felt like what "work" should feel like. He liked that kind of simplicity.[105]

All conversions move fluidly into an exchange that merges with the landscape and is heightened because it goes hand in hand with social detachment. *The Cape* narrates Akiyuki's reflections on his odd and opaque behavior in a free, indirect style that eavesdrops on Akiyuki's consciousness. A tableau that dramatizes Akiyuki's depicts his identification with a scene of nature, a "single tree" set apart from any other object. This scene is potentially lyrical. Taken in the direction of Romantic Naturalism, it could solve his alienation formally and philosophically by yoking his psychic life to the landscape. In fact, it is stripped of any hint of Akiyuki's assimilation to a context or a larger landscape. The thoughts that should clarify the goings-on in Akiyuki's head actually become more distant in proportion to the scrutiny focused on them:

Next to the railroad crossing where the *roji* curved off to the left, a single tree was leisurely shaking its leaves. The tree could have reminded him of himself. Akiyuki didn't know what kind of a tree it was. And he didn't even want to know. The tree had no flowers or fruit. All it did was spread its branches to the sun, tremble in the wind. That's enough, he thought. The tree doesn't need any flowers or fruit. It doesn't need a name. Looking at the tree, Akiyuki felt like he was dreaming.[106]

The remarkable feature of Akiyuki's reverie is the way he extracts the tree from anything that might "root" the organism in meaning, the way he is dispossessed of a context in anything that lies in front of him, but does not transcend it with a larger narrative. His identification with the tree proceeds paradoxically, exclusively by means of dis-identification from a series of attachments, comparisons, and ways of attributing value, only to negate them. The tree produces nothing and attracts nothing, having neither fruit for eating, nor flowers for admiring. It shivers passively in the wind, but responds equally, which is to say, indifferently, to the sun's warmth. Akiyuki does not care to classify the tree and understand it in terms of a context or a kinship. The prose style in the passage works similarly by cutting off all links. No adjectives, similes, or other elements of figural language connect Akiyuki to a pre-existing semiotic context.

Alan Tansman argues that Akiyuki aspires to emptiness during moments of repetitive physical labor. Watanabe Naomi speaks of the "fetishism of grass" in Akiyuki and later characters because their young male characters are so easily "dyed" by the sensations of the natural world that they appear to exchange properties with its elements.[107] Nakagami himself encourages this interpretation but states that he designed the second and third volumes very differently. In my view, changes over the three volumes are often overlooked because critics see the character's consistency as a representation of Nakagami himself. "In *The Sea of Withered Trees,* I cut all the issues of wages," Nakagami says, "to show the pure joy of work when you subtract the pay. Now, six years later [in 1983], what I wanted to write was capital (*shihon*) using Akiyuki as a brother-killer, but also a work-killer. To show Akiyuki as a mediated existence."[108]

The Cape ends by violently showing this existence as Akiyuki manipulates the literal meaning of *kōtsū,* intercourse, through a woman and a message. In the last scenes of the work, Akiyuki purchases the favors of his half sister, a prostitute who is unaware of their kinship. He meets her in a bar called the Yayoi—the overdetermined name of the historical period when settled life, or culture, is generally considered to start on the Japanese archipelago. Akiyuki is poised to consummate this taboo sexual exchange, in a place where culture is not only founded, but bought and sold. Capital is reintroduced in a context that recalls the episode that creates the world in the *Kojiki*. The *Kojiki* begins with the coupling of two sibling gods, Izanagi and Izanami. Their tryst creates the Japanese archipelago, and conceives the goddess who becomes the progenitor of the islands' population. *The Cape* ends as Akiyuki watches his sister, thinks of his father, and imagines reproduction as a form of retribution: "now . . . that man's blood will spill over."[109] Akiyuki's reentry to the world of connected meaning and the foundational violence of state-building certainly come though his oedipal grudge with his father. But they also come thanks to the purchasing power of cold cash and its powers to enable all kinds of exchange.

By *The Ends of the Earth, Supreme Time*, our understanding of Akiyuki as a character has changed almost completely. He is now deeply embedded in the world of exchange. He arrives back in town after a three-year stint in jail, and is stunned to find that a construction boom has taken place. A mountain that loomed large in his personal geography has been razed to make way for the literal engines and currencies of economic development. The results of *kōtsū* are evident in the mentions of money changing hands, the new infrastructures connecting the town to faraway places, and the metaphors of communication that Akiyuki uses. No longer can ideology be contained in a pure subject–object relation, whether it is brother–brother, brother–sister, father–son, or Akiyuki facing the pure landscape of "work" and digging.

> In the three years he had been away, Akiyuki had heard from relatives and their delegates who had come as far as Osaka to visit him that the area around where he grew up had drastically changed. In the new development, Mon, who ran the bar named after herself, had compiled maps and photos with great care that explained how it was decided to build three nuclear plants within a radius of fifty kilometers of the neighborhood, how construction of a freeway making a circuit around the Kii peninsula had started, and how the surrounding land had completely changed face. Both the *roji* and the *shinchi* were wiped out. The mountain that had been between the city center and another land ridge had been completely razed. Land value had undergone an unprecedented boom, and that boom meant that men who before had been pushing wheelbarrows, part of an overflow crew sent to work elsewhere, were now bombing around in Cadillacs, spending money like crazy. (12)

This passage narrates the displacements that Akiyuki confonts when he returns home from jail. Objects that had previously been valuable for their fixity are transformed, their values mobile. New kinds of exchange facilitate new kinds of social mobility along with the diaspora of work, new highways, and power plants. Akiyuki struggles to catch up with this local South's attachments to metropolitan money. My next chapter turns to look at a novella that thematizes work in the metropole through a critique of the particular kinds of exchange found in managed society (*kanri shakai*).

CHAPTER 4

Inaudible Man

Lower Frequencies

In a 1968 novella titled *On the Japanese Language* (*Nihongo ni tsuite*), Nakagami takes received tradition from both African American and *buraku* writings and puts it in the service of a modernist first-person narrative.[1] This chapter focuses on a set of close readings to explore how these allusions are woven into the text of *On the Japanese Language* to bear specific reference to Japan's alignment in the Vietnam War.[2] I explore the role of "nameless-ness" that appears in James Baldwin's 1961 essay collection *Nobody Knows My Name*, the "invisibility" of Ralph Ellison's 1952 novel, and the key rhetorical device from the *buraku* context that appears in *On the Japanese Language*, a 1922 manifesto. The allusions that link *On the Japanese Language* to other works suggest that for Nakagami in 1968, identities through solidarities with minoritarian writers outside of Japan serve as models for text-world relations unavailable in Japan.

The story is set in the turbulent atmosphere of the Zenkyōtō student movement and features a young man whose girlfriend introduces him to a leftist student group. The students hire him for a curious part-time job to convince an African American soldier to desert the army while the soldier is on R and R in Tokyo during the Vietnam War. Without the soldier's knowledge, the student group claims he deserted the army after realizing his ideological solidarity with the students. The student group splashes his photo across the pages of a campus newspaper and trumpets his deser-tion. Their plot to showcase him as a test case for desertion sends the soldier into a suicidal tailspin as he realizes he is being exploited for his symbolic value as a representative member of an anti-imperial solidarity network. Ironically, the photo and accompanying articles land the soldier in the hospital, even more firmly in the grip of the U.S. military.

The photo that provokes the soldier's suicide attempt is a vivid example of how the power of looking has been interrogated for its ability to convey

truth and reality in postwar Japan, especially when harnessed by the photograph and the ethnographic gaze. In another example, Bruce Suttmeier
notes how Oda Makoto's best-selling 1961 travelogue of America, *I'll Give
Anything a Look* (*Nandemo mite yarō*), uses the conceit of looking at "anything" to display the seeming openness of the traveler because it allows the
traveler to "insinuate himself into practically any situation and therefore
adapt to different cultural conditions."[3] But the easy detachment and attachment to foreign places came under critique by contemporary readers who
questioned the consumerist role that even bohemian tourism appeared to
advocate. When Japanese journalists began reporting on Vietnam in the late
1960s, the Teflon gaze of the Japanese traveler sparked a critical commentary in the form of the bystander novel. These works (one of which I will
explore in the final section of this chapter) used irony, shock, or exaggera-
tion to depict Vietnam War atrocities experienced by travelers like Oda who
moved fluidly above their surroundings. Bystander novels critiqued Japan's
consumption of the war from a safe but economically profitable distance.

The transcendental traveler and the bystander novel accuse visuality of
falsifying what should be truth or providing a remote, proxy access to reality.
My reading of *On the Japanese Language* proposes a third way that visibility
and knowing are linked. In contrast, I steer the question to a level of media
literacy and trace the parallels between the two main characters in this
novella, the narrator Boku and the soldier Ludolph, as they occur through
the figural language of visibility that itself builds on allusions, a literary element of style that emphasizes proximity and connection. My aim is to show
how a sustained comparison exists in the allusions through which both
characters express themselves and to show that Nakagami's use of allusion
to traverse oral and written registers differs from other 1968 conversations
about African American literature and its relation to labor. I explore how
the sustained alliance brokered through allusion does not redeem Boku's
betrayal of the soldier, but it does prompt us to think about what is at stake
in the imagined solidarity, even if it does not ultimately surface in the story.

In order to explore how language is freighted with these kinds of meaning in *On the Japanese Language*, this chapter draws on the *Buraku* writing
on Afro-Asian solidarity. The editors of a 2003 issue of the journal *Positions*
note that, "with very few exceptions, the field [of Asian Studies] has been
characterized by a studied failure to consider the question of race in the
constitution of colonial modernities in China, Japan, Korea, and elsewhere
throughout Asia."[4] Historiography of Afro-Asian solidarity begins with the

writings on the 1955 Bandung Conference that, as Adekeye Adebajo writes, "helped to spur the creation of the non-aligned movement (NAM) to challenge Western domination of the globe."[5]

Japan's alignment with world events presented a heady range of choices in the Vietnam era because Japan's defense was essentially outsourced to the U.S. military, which both restricted its sovereignty and promoted economic growth. The government announced it was enforcing eminent domain over farmland to build the New Tokyo International Airport in Narita to make it, as Mark Nornes writes, "a huge aircraft carrier for the Pentagon," staging flights to Vietnam.[6] 1968 was a significant year for leftist student activism in Japan, as the date for renewing the U.S.–Japan Security Treaty (ANPO) approached. I would like to slide the chronology one year closer to us and show how *On the Japanese Language* should instead be read as a work of 1969 fiction. In 1969, a long activist campaign, arguably the most successful such grassroots effort in postwar Japan, culminated in legislation and funding to improve education and living conditions in *buraku* neighborhoods nationwide. We should see this story as an indictment of student movement activists for applying elitist technocratic skills to the characters of Boku and Ludolph through allusions that bring together the contexts of 1968 and 1969.

As Nakagami was writing in 1968, some Japanese scholars of U.S. history and buraku movement leaders too turned to frame their opposition to the 1960 U.S.–Japan Security Treaty (*Nichibei anpō jōyaku*, or ANPO) in ways that do not see the struggle end only in Japanese national liberation from U.S. militarism. Some focused on internal histories, while others looked keenly at possible links between subnational liberation movements in Japan, the United States, and the emerging Third World. They both followed on a connection established by former Buraku Liberation League (BLL) leader Matsumoto Ji'ichirō, who had led a shadow delegation to the 1955 Bandung Conference. Matsumoto's group was separate from the official Japanese delegation that had agreed to play by U.S. Cold War policies and not join other Afro-Asian nonaligned states.[7] In a commentary on the *Kokujin bungaku zenshū* (Anthology of black literature, 1969), historian of U.S. labor Yukiyama Yoshimasa extended this connection and—importantly for Nakagami's novella's focus on labor—remarks on the influence of African-Asian/"A-A" transnational independence movements in U.S. labor organizing.[8] The BLL head who succeeded Matsumoto, Asada Zen'nosuke, takes the opposite, exceptionalist position in a 1968 roundtable with Yukiyama, asserting that "the origins of our discrimination are feudal, where theirs are in the slave system."[9] In that same discussion, Noma interprets Black Power to be a broad movement encompassing older civil rights struggles as well as writers like James Baldwin whose careers date to the early 1960s and idealizes the Black Power movement's strong attachment to culture in movement politics. He contrasts this power to the fledgling role it plays in the *buraku* liberation movement, where a "real cultural movement ought to have come straight from the Suiheisha manifesto" but has not yet arrived.[10]

Noma's treatment of American literature as culturally split echoes Nakagami's sourcing of both Faulkner and African American writers to shape his own vision of national literature but separates them more distinctly. He credits black American writers with updating his sense of African American daily life experiences, but his appreciation is confined to the contents of a social realist vein he attributes to black writers. With its ensemble of characters that "cook, eat, drink and talk," Baldwin's novel *Another Country* allows him for the first time to see "America as it is, as a whole" because it supplies a missing black authenticity.[11] Like many readers, including Nakagami, he had previously derived his understanding of black characters from "the great" (*dai*) Faulkner. While Noma hedges that "it is hard to judge that Baldwin's novels transcend Faulkner," he admits that Baldwin "has a consciousness that is able to capture in a vivid manner the things that white people don't see—the things that Faulkner hides."[12] In short, like Nakagami did, Noma saw writers like Baldwin as the standard-bearers for challenging the belief that a national culture is necessarily monocultural. He did not, however, bring together the registers of public speaking and fiction as Baldwin, Ellison, or Nakagami did. Nor did he see that literature as written or writable in a nonrealist or modernist mode.

In tune with the different relations suggested by this nonaligned work and shifting it to a cultural-literary ground, I explore how *On the Japanese Language* imagines an anticolonial alliance between an African American character and a *buraku* character that overshadows the national domestic agenda of demilitarization. Earlier writers like Ōe Kenzaburō featured black characters in their fiction but on the rare occasion these characters had names, they lacked specificity, and showed little sign of interior life.[13] *On the Japanese Language* attributes the character a name and an identity based in writing, critiquing the way that the student movement reproduces in practical economic terms the managed kind of exploitation that it decries in its ideology and slogans, specifically with respect to labor practices and the historical place of *buraku* workers in demanding and dangerous lines of work.

Figural language emphasizes embodied knowledge rather than imme-diate seeing and suggests through allusion that the narrator is a *buraku* character without openly defining him as such. *On the Japanese Language* uses the interface of language to show that, instead of assuming that "see-ing" takes place, knowledge is made meaningful through contexts. I argue that the power of the story lies in the transformation of the narrator vis-à-vis allusion. He fails to be heroic and to directly resist either the war or the students. But he explains his growing sympathy with the soldier through a series of allusions to other works of fiction, works that call attention to his own status as an "inaudible" man (*kikoenai ningen*), alluding to an invis-ible person racially marked and unseen by the majoritarian leftist politics of the student movement and anti-Vietnam movement.[14] Thematically, the Brotherhood section of *Invisible Man*, where the narrator is framed in a media plot and imagined to betray the solidarity of his fellow party members, is also pertinent. That sequence treats labor, solidarity, and the party's manipulation of people for a universal "historical" cause at the expense of the invisible narrator. Nakagami's narrator changes from being a conduit of orders and information hired for three thousand yen a day to understanding his own situation as a worker through an increasing sympa-thy with the soldier.

After briefly introducing the critical concepts of hidden transcript and hidden polemic, I move to a set of close readings to explore how some ele-ments taken from *buraku* activist rhetoric and African American literature are woven into the text of *On the Japanese Language*. Next, I explore the role of the key rhetorical device from the *buraku* context that appears in the novella, a manifesto. The manifesto has served, in the twentieth cen-tury, as a mode of avant-garde poetics that creates a platform for rising against an oppressive history and imagining a better future. It addresses an audience of individuals through a narrative and symbolic language, an interface that convinces them to think as a collective. In Shalini Puri's words, by reading discourses of hybridity as manifestos—and here we might recall the imagined solidarity between the two characters in this novella—we are allowed "to address them not only as discourses of truth that can be proven or disproven, but as documents of desire."[15]

While they did not link it to fictional rhetoric, postwar *buraku* activists were keenly attuned to the role played by public speaking in the civil rights and Black Power movements. Asada and Noma credit Martin Luther King's April 4, 1967, speech, "Going Beyond Vietnam" (*Betonamu o koete*), with awakening them to the need to disengage from Vietnam. They too realized what King called "a very obvious and almost facile connection between Vietnam and the struggle I and others have been waging in America."[16] In other words, *buraku* activists see King's alliance of civil rights in the United States with liberation in Asia as a cause they can reciprocate with, and they do so primarily by reading his speeches. King's narrative followed a similar narrative as foundational *buraku* liberation documents such as the most famous and rhetorically influential *enzetsu*, the Suiheisha manifesto, did.

Rhetorical echoes can be seen in the figural language of documents from both movements. Both bring preexisting tropes that circulate between oral and written worlds into contact with vernacular contexts in the service of present liberation. King's aim "to speak from the burnings of my own heart," for example, resonates with the consciousness-spreading aims of the Suiheisha periodical *Burning Heart* (*Moeagaru kokoro*).[17] This magazine began publication shortly after the 1922 convention and described the motivation of the Suiheisha as directed by the impulse of "eta ethnic awakening" (*eta minzoku no jikaku*).[18] The writer contrasted the fire of the Suiheisha to the "water"-like character of previous movements. Both documents underscore a conductivity of consciousness that draws on transcription of oral culture to enter the print world without abandoning public speaking: precisely the parallax composition I have been mapping in Nakagami's works.

We need to ask why this specific comparison—of Boku and the African American character—should occur in this place and time, through the specific genre of I-fiction, using the specific kinds of figural language it does.[19] I use the more colloquial term of allusion rather than intertext because allusion accommodates the spoken word, as well as the written text, in ways that are constitutive to the way Nakagami's works as a whole traverse oral and written domains. The allusions and figural language that traverse these works to the 1968 fiction suggest that Boku has suffered some of the same experiences of discrimination as the soldier. By comparing these texts, the novella realigns both our understanding of the text at hand and expands the geopolitical relationship between the United States and Japan to include identification at a subnational level.

Hidden Transcripts / Hidden Polemics

Modernism in Nakagami's work is most often seen as compatible with the realist mandate when it defers to music for its method. Critics compare his writing to free jazz, drawing on links that Nakagami himself made between the "chords" of free jazz breaking away from the "codes" of a mainstream musical repertoire.[20] I argue that *On the Japanese Language* brings modernist style into the story but does so without discarding the "differential" points of reference that advocates of liberation literature might fear would be lost in modernist representation. I show that allusions to the three textual sources I examine carry a weight equal to musical modernism.

Ralph Ellison's 1952 novel, *Invisible Man*, concludes with a direct address to the reader. "Who knows," he intimates, "but that, on the lower frequencies, I speak for you."[21] I take "frequency" to mean not a lesser volume but a broadcast that transmits from an underground interpretive source. Alan Nadel calls *Invisible Man* a sustained work of "invisible criticism."[22] Ellison's narrator is, of course, not literally invisible. Rather, he is not properly seen: "I am invisible, understand, simply because people refuse to see me."[23] I take Nadel to mean that Ellison's story is equally about replying to, reworking, and going beyond the canon of American literature as seen by our *kokubungaku* (national literature). *Invisible Man* responds to preexisting canonical texts by selecting and reworking them to make them yield a different narrative of American literature. When African American storytelling is placed at the center of the work, the novel, in other words, has a critical agenda, and the act of retelling episodes of the literary canon becomes an act of interpretation: literary fiction and literary criticism are mingled and interdependent.

The term "hidden transcript" is used by anthropologist James C. Scott in his work in subaltern studies to describe interactions where communication occurs through subtexts rather than overt statements. It refers to kinds of resistance or communication that are articulated in elliptical ways, "in disguised form."[24] I use the term "transcript" to keep in play the frequent moves between oral and written worlds that Nakagami drew on in the service of creating a distributed "I." This self-identity dispersed across situations, genres, interlocutors, and media was especially crafted in the roundtable, an edited form of a transcribed conversation. I should also note that indirect communications also greatly inform works by Baldwin and Ellison that Nakagami draws on in *On the Japanese Language*, works that in turn draw on prior myth, fiction, and songs.[25] Both *On the Japanese Language* and the African American intertexts it draws on enact Henry Louis Gates's descriptions of double-voiced writing as a "hidden polemic" whereby "one speech act determines the internal structure of another, the second effecting the voice of the first, by absence, by difference."[26] The tropes of invisibility and namelessness characterize the alliance between the two characters. The hidden polemic of the Suiheisha Manifesto derives from moving the protagonist of brothers from a relation between *buraku* men (the long-suffering brothers of the Suiheisha Manifesto that I examined in chapter 2) to the relation between two men of different nations and races that hints to an anticolonial solidarity.

The unheard, not unspoken, yet significant nature of this allusion is stressed in Scott's idea of a hidden transcript. Scott's work is largely anthropological and focuses primarily on how gossip, rumor, and other subtexts have sustained lives as "the fugitive political conduct of subordinate groups that take place offstage, beyond direct observation by power-holders."[27] These subtexts are called transcripts because they are understood to be part of an ongoing record, but the rules and the conventions that make the interaction intelligible may not be recorded. It is this potentiality that interests Scott: the fact that communication may exist precisely in the gaps that appear to be the biggest aporias or digressions in communication. In Nakagami's fiction, these hidden transcripts are made, often cited but not quoted, through allusion, a citation or connection to another work or text, oral or written, from which it draws meaning and which may in turn link it to a broader network of affiliations.

The term "hidden transcript" is relevant in 1968 Japan because, at the time, no writer successful in the literary establishment had yet identified himself in the public record as a *buraku* writer. As we saw in chapter 2, Nakagami literally hid but made elliptically available the roundtable conversation that suggested his *buraku* background through the absence and difference between the two referents "I" and "a young writer I know." The hidden polemic can be read in terms of the confessional voice of the I-fiction that is a heroic protagonist in Japanese literary history but a craven flunky of the political establishment in *On the Japanese Language* who yearns for escape through solidarity with another. These two concepts are useful for understanding the relationships in this novella because the language of allusions is key to establishing the respective national and ethnic alliances of the characters and their relation to each other.

Thinking of allusion as hidden transcript or polemic can help us to understand how the exchanges that the narrator imagines between himself and the soldier might bear on the question of solidarity at the same time they enrich a common Japanese mode of storytelling, adding social contexts to I-fiction or first-person narrative fiction. As I outlined earlier, the "socialized self" appears in Kobayashi Hideo's 1935 essay, "On I-Fiction," which famously scorned Japanese confessional writing of the 1930s because "owing to [its writers'] situation, wherein they had inherited an I-fiction totally innocent of ideological strife, they lacked the power to conceptualize the impasse between the individual and society or the issue of the flight of the self from the instability of life."[28] They failed, in other words, to show how self and society are mediated or to confront "selves" that flee from engagement with life.

Tomi Suzuki, however, sees I-fiction less as a genre defined by its themes or choice of narrator. She sees it as a mode of reading or an encounter between reader and text made possible by strong assumptions about media literacy: "The I-novel is best defined as a mode of reading that assumes that the I-novel is a single-voiced, 'direct' expression of the author's 'self' and that its written language is 'transparent.'"[29] From my point of view, in Nakagami's work, the contract that Suzuki maintains exists between reader and writer is less about divulging insights into a private world and better viewed as a hidden transcript that socializes the narrator by placing him in context through allusion, to make two split levels of reading possible, if not inevitable, if one possesses the requisite media literacy.

Nakagami is outspoken regarding his own effort to connect I-fiction and sociality. A decade after he published *On the Japanese Language*, Nakagami would publish an entire book, an extended roundtable conversation with Karatani Kōjin, on the subject of *Overcoming Kobayashi Hideo* (*Kobayashi Hideo o koete*). In that conversation, Nakagami explains that he is trying to resocialize prose fiction by introducing it to *monogatari* (literally, narrative) or the elements of alienation, division of labor, and exchange (*verkehr, kōtsū*) that feature in a key text he read in this period, *The German Ideology* (1842–43), one of Marx's essays that had been largely eclipsed in Japan by his monumental *Capital*. For Nakagami, exchange (*kōtsū*) and division of labor (*bungyō*) are the two concepts that he uses to write fiction that analyzes systems, without teleology or metaphysics.[30]

Exchange and division of labor are also the two concepts that dramatize the relations of characters in *On the Japanese Language*.

The hidden transcript in *On the Japanese Language* socializes the narrator through two specific conventions that it draws from I-fiction. First, embedded in the work is a doubled diary structure. Like the exemplary novel of Kobayashi's essay, André Gide's *The Counterfeiters* (1926), the story contains a self-reflexive story of its own composition, a "running criticism of [the] novel."[31] But unlike Gide's novel, *On the Japanese Language* contains a running criticism that is written by the secondary character, the soldier, although it is excerpted and intercut into the main story by the narrator, Boku. It contains sections of a diary where the soldier, Ludolph, keeps his field notes on the "youth awakened to fascism in the postwar era" that he makes as part of his training to be a social scientist, unbeknownst to them.[32] The story, in my reading, offers an "out" or at least outside to the pressure of authenticity that the Boku character places on Ludolph by making the soldier someone possessed of dual identities, at least one of which is highly invested in writing or, as he calls it, "observing." This kind of experimentation is a license he embraces, even as he does not allow the soldier to use language to change the stuckness of his situation. Our view of Boku, then, is qualified by the external opinions written in Ludolph's diary. The fabled mirror of socialization that Kobayashi admires in Gide takes place in Nakagami's work not through self-reflection but through the diary kept by Ludolph, who wants to be a sociologist when the war is over. Socialization requires the contribution of another person, a perspective unavailable to the self.

The second mode of hidden transcript is found in Boku's narration. He uses tropes and narrative operations taken directly from two sources that write him into ongoing conversations on open versus fugitive resistance: writings by postwar African American male writers. These are most centrally Ralph Ellison's *Invisible Man*, James Baldwin's essay collection *Nobody Knows My Name*, and the founding document of the *buraku* liberation movement, the Suiheisha Manifesto of 1922 that I introduced in chapter 2. The transcripts that remain hidden in the novella scheme are like the invisible parts of the invisible man or the inaudible parts of the narrator in *On the Japanese Language*. They are present but not necessarily grasped by us unless we read for them, simply because we do not see them, not because they fail to be there. These transcripts between the invisible or inaudible character and an attentive reader add a socialized dimension to the conventional framework of I-fiction.

Like the Japanese translation of *Invisible Man,* the narrator identifies himself only as "I," or Boku. His near-namelessness suggests that socially he is not known or is unintelligible. Recalling "Nobody Knows My Name," the title of Baldwin's essay collection, Boku is only called once by his proper name, Saitō. He is explicitly instructed by the students that the soldier is a "test case" and that he should not indulge a sentimental approach (*kanjō-ron*) to the antiwar, antinuclear effort but act in the ideological service of South Vietnamese liberation and support of North Vietnamese efforts against imperial invasion.[33] But during this time, the narrator's initially clinical distance from his subject who he treats as a "commodity form" (*shōhin*) shrinks, and he starts to imagine that he and the soldier share similar experiences and points of view.[34] He departs from the leftist vocabulary of the students and comes to think that he is the sole person to have a clear understanding of the soldier. He expresses this understanding by projecting his state of mind onto the soldier and interpreting the soldier's behavior to confirm the accord with his own motivations and feelings.

The seed of this story was planted in 1966, when Nakagami met an American infantryman returning to Vietnam. In 1967 he published a sketch in a local magazine based in his hometown of Shingū, the *Sunday Journal,* titled "The Black Soldier and the Japanese Youth" (*Kokujin-hei to Nihon no wakamono*). The essay is narrated from the point of view of a young man who accidentally meets a black soldier and thinks "of mounting an argument against sending him (or any other soldier, really) to Vietnam."[35] The soldier in this early sketch is written entirely in a detached voice, in broad strokes that reprise fairly boilerplate stereotypes of impulsive personality and primitive emotionality in the black artist character. He confesses to being a gang member, plays the tabletop like Thelonious Monk, "attacks" the piano keys, thinks the Vietnamese are "evil," and "hates" China.[36] After the narrator parts from the soldier, he is dejected and angry both at the soldier's presumed fate on the front lines and at his own failure to intervene. The narrator mourns but displaces his anger onto the American war machine: "If at this moment Ludolph is lying dead on the ground, this is not because he was killed by the Viet Cong, it's a murder committed by the affluent US of A."[37] The first version of the sketch clearly sees the soldier as a sacrifice to U.S. imperialism and heightens his tragedy because his race allows him to be killed by his own citizens.

Two years after this sketch was published, an expanded version appeared as *On the Japanese Language*. This work, with its clearer focus on the powers of language to create relationships and exercise power between people, was the first of Nakagami's works to get national attention. As the sketch was amplified into a novella, it featured a main character who was more fully developed. The soldier has the same name, Ludolph L. Witt, and arrives in Japan for a five-day period of R and R, rather than a brief viewing by the narrator. In a 1983 conversation with Murakami Ryū, Nakagami remarks that the actual soldier he met was white. However, the relations established among the narrator, the character Ludolph, and the reader in the novella take on a magnified importance through the alliances made because Ludolph is black.[38] The novella was published in *Literary Metropole* in 1968 and subsequently won a prize from a Nagoya magazine called *The Writer* (*Sakka*), where it caught the eye of Suzuki Yōichi, an editor who would facilitate Nakagami's debut in the Tokyo literary scene.[39]

Established critics assessed *On the Japanese Language* in 1968 as a work of realism. The jury was split on three criteria: originality of its plot, innovative style, and fidelity to the craft of realistic Japanese prose. They did not see it as a particularly intertextual story, much less in relation to writing from outside Japan. Inagaki Taruho, a writer of modernist fantastic fiction, derided the author as an "epigone of Ōe Kenzaburo."[40] In his opinion, the novella reprised two features often seen in early stories of Ōe's that critique *kanri shakai* (managed society), a term that described the highly rationalized nature of everyday life in the prosperous postwar era.[41]

Managed society referred, on one hand, to a stage of economic development, an advanced stage of industrial society that predated and shaped the information society that would emerge in the early 1970s. More broadly, it referred to social auxiliaries that supported the corporate life in which management was a key feature as well the kinds of personal techniques that emerged to treat personal interactions as places to exercise and evaluate experience through techniques of business culture. One link to Ōe was the detached but deadpan voice of first-person narration used to describe morbid or grotesque events, a gap that heightened the irony of irrational events that unfold in an orderly fashion characteristic of managed society. The second of Ōe's links of grotesquerie and routine was the odd jobs of the protagonist, such as killing masses of dogs in an assembly line formation in "A Curious Job" (*Kimyōna shigoto*; 1957) or washing the corpses of the dead in "Lavish Are the Dead" (*Shisha no ogori*; 1957), kinds of work that exaggerated the rational, administrative ways in which managed society was organized.

A second judge, postwar leftist Shiina Rinzō, did not see the novella as derivative but panned it for other reasons. He describes the very premise of the soldier's desertion as *"nansensu."*[42] This favorite phrase of hecklers at student-movement demonstrations was typically used to suggest that an opponent's position was completely unrealistic and probably masking an ideological function. Here it suggests that Shiina found it highly unrealistic that a soldier would desert the U.S. military.[43] Sugimori Hisahide, in contrast, praised the "volumetric" subjectivity of the narrator as a gauge of realism.[44] This term, while it sounds abstract in English, refers to a basic mandate of the naturalist novel to describe things as they are. It means that a character seems to be fully rendered or have a three-dimensional inner life. By singling out the narrator's way of looking for special notice, Sugimori applies a realist standard to claim that the narrator is psychologically credible. Overall, critics saw the novella in terms of how its style situated Nakagami in historical relation with other Japanese writers, not in terms of the text's lateral relations with contemporary historical and literary movements, much less those outside Japan.

However, close examination of the story shows that it is quite aware of how writers outside Japan—specifically African American writers—used the "I" persona to address social issues. That context is made apparent through allusions that develop its main characters and emphasize the narrator's growing identification with the highly reflexive black character. The story is primarily told through the narrator's five-day stint with the soldier, with occasional flashbacks that illuminate particular moments. Whatever compels the narrator to identify with the soldier and to project his own desires and emotions so freely onto him is unspoken apart from the allusions brought in. One key example occurs when the soldier refuses to communicate. The narrator states that just as Ludolph is an unvisible man he has become an inaudible man (*kikoenai ningen*), someone who is not heard because people do not listen or are not attuned to his speaking.[45]

Ellison's use of the hidden transcript is one model for how Nakagami is trying to revise the terms of *kokubungaku* by showing its dependence on vernacular *buraku* cultural forms. One of Ellison's main transcripts in *Invisible Man* was the first generation of literary critics to put American literature on the map. Until World War II, critics aimed to build a canon and escort the dowdy repertoire of American literature into curricula and histories as something beyond "English studies" from the Old World.[46] Before the war, critics such as Lewis Mumford and F. O. Matthiessen had pioneered the discipline by singling out a small group of overlooked writers (Melville, Twain, Howells, Hawthorne, Whitman, Emerson, and Thoreau) and putting them at the center of their pantheon.[47] These critics saw a heroic flourishing of novels and prose poems composed in the mid-nineteenth century and called this high point the American Renaissance. But this canon was founded on a very significant oversight. Excluded in the rebirthing of the renaissance and in the creation of the pastoral myth that underwrote the agrarianist canon of American literature were black writers and any mention of slavery at all.

Writing in the postwar era and drawing on African American folk, oral, and experimental cultures, Ellison of course had a very different view of received tradition than earlier literary canonizers. Ellison was working at just the same time American studies was being institutionalized in Japan through canonizing Faulkner as a writer of the defeated South. *Invisible Man* uses set-piece scenes from American Renaissance works and puts them into relation with formal elements and tropes from jazz, oral, and vernacular forms of storytelling set to a modernist spin. This set of allusions demands that readers—the "you" of the epigraph—reinterpret tradition in light of the new work. *Invisible Man* gives an ongoing response in fictional form to specific texts that were revered and held up as exemplary of the American Renaissance—and engaging these works, it rewrites them. I now turn to look at similar kinds of exchanges in *On the Japanese Language*.

First-Person Lyrical

On the Japanese Language begins with a plaintive question that directly asks the reader to imagine or even participate in the narrator's effort to communicate with the soldier:

> If you met a foreigner who understood virtually no Japanese, and it were you, what in the world is the first word you would begin to teach him with?
>
> Sayonara, hello, booze, girls, or maybe you would show him one of those over-intensely tinted postcards, and explain to him

that this is the famous MOUNT FUJI, and that Japan and Japanese people are colored with the same wonderful lyric nature.

Courage, that's what I would start with[48]

Boku thinks of communicating with a series of items exchanged in the lingua franca of GI talk ("sayonara" and "girls"). He rejects these in favor of lyrical visual cliches, such simulacra as the postcard of Japan's most famous mountain. The first graphic representation of viewing, "MOUNT FUJI," is rendered in capital letters using the type in a modernist fashion to show the mountain's scale and magnitude as if it were focused through a viewer's perspective. Showing a similar fusion of perspective and interpretation, the intensity and blackness of type marking "**courage**" (*yūki* or, in Japanese kanji characters, 勇気) seem to literally convey Boku's experience of viewing the soldier.

The use of experimental typography is common in Japanese modernist poetry and advertising and more belletristic concrete poetry. This accord between high art and commercial culture employs new media forms to put readers in contact with the new kinds of perception available in the modern city.[49] What I call typographical modernism is also characteristic of the manifesto form, with its shouting and its attempts to get attention with avant-garde tactics of shock and beauty and link them to a new narrative. In *On the Japanese Language* typographical modernism sometimes indicates that the narrator's perceptions are filtered and magnified through the intense personalism of psychedelic drugs, as in "**LSD, or in other words reality**."[50] Such experimentation is much less frequent in postwar prose fiction than in earlier avant-garde moments. To contextualize its use here, I follow Jennifer DeVere Brody, who writes of the capacity of graphics to convey impressions beyond semantics. Citing how punctuation translates into the pacing of oral speech and the "blackness of blackness" in *Invisible Man,* she asks that we "re-cognize the role typography plays in our perception of things and concepts" by remembering its ability to interpret in graphic terms and not just convey meaning.[51]

The word that Boku settles on, "**courage**," appears in type that combines the impression of the soldier's hypervisibility with the intensity of his encounter. From the narrator's point of view, the soldier is quite literally a bold-faced character. I read the hypervisible nature of the exchange as the first instance in the unfolding narrative of Boku's feelings of fusion with the black soldier. Semioticians would call this experience of the scale of "MOUNT FUJI" or the intensity and darkness of "**courage**" an indexical representation, "an existential connection between a specific referent and the signifier" that gives "credibility" to "subjective obsession."[52] Boku develops this subjective obsession throughout the novella with allusions that imply that he has a special insight into the soldier's experience.

We find out the context for the exchange of words in the next paragraph. Boku ignores context altogether and imagines the soldier to be contemplating language while lying in a thicket on the battlefront—not dodging bullets or worrying about his safety in a thicket of grass where being hypervisible is a less than desirable quality. Boku proceeds to appropriate shared language and images into his own narrative. He then projects that narrative onto an imagining of the soldier's mind and actions into the future. At the end of the reverie, the word "**courage**" is a talismanic reminder of Boku's perception of the soldier:

> This is what I wrote in his notebook. I don't really think that this twenty-year-old foreign man, in despair because he can't make out the difference between Japanese and Swahili or Vietnamese, was able to make out the word **courage** that I wrote down in his notebook. Even now I still think about the meaning of the Japanese word courage that I taught him. Even though I don't properly understand this word courage, here talking to you in Japanese, can you picture the image of the twenty-year-old young man sent off to the front, lying in a thicket of grass muttering the only Japanese word he managed to remember?
>
> What I want to know is, if it were you, what Japanese word would you start to teach him with?[53]

This paragraph addresses the reader just as directly as the narrator of *Invisible Man*. But the contract between narrator and reader is more restricted.[54] It is not clear whether "**courage**" will accompany the soldier into a tragic death or be the magic element that helps him to stay alive. Two things, however, are clear. First, that this single heavily freighted noun "**courage**" is the bond that seals their relation in Boku's view (a feat of communication that is, of course, likely mistaken). And second, while Boku supplies the form of the word, the soldier is imagined to grasp and perform the content of courage far better than the strangely detached narrator. In short, while the soldier is literally hypervisible because Boku has a heightened response to him, he is invisible in the sense that he has no independent subjectivity that is intelligible to Boku. This story dramatizes at a metalevel exactly how parallax reading works by making explicit the two levels of meaning production. The irony of the story made clear in the distinction between the retrospective narrator and the craven character Boku (that doubled reading does not necessarily produce resistance) only underscores how much weight is placed on the discursive reader to complete the work as she or he sees fit.

The distanced observation of the soldier brings us closer to the soldier's inner life but only as Boku imagines him. The soldier's consciousness is materialized in specific, organized ways. While the selection of the heroic word "**courage**" is indeed strange, perhaps even odder is the leap of consciousness itself that the narrator makes. Boku performs a leap of literary style from the bounded first-person discourse characteristic of I-fiction seen in phrases such as "I still think" and "I don't really understand." The leap also shifts from a descriptive place—what *is* there—to a prescriptive place—what *should* be there, in the line of a manifesto. The soldier, in the languages the narrator imagines to jumble together in his hearing, is equidistant from Japanese, Swahili, and Vietnamese. Moreover, this distance remains unspoken.

Two things interest me about the way this story asserts that language and national liberation projects work in parallel ways between the off-screen Vietnamese and other protagonists of decolonization. First is the combination of distance and proximity as Boku shifts from observing to imagining. The second element is the terms of imagination that the narrator latches onto, terms that align the languages of postcolonial Swahili or anticolonial Vietnamese with Japanese. In the paratactic sequence, the series seems to leave an unfilled blank, to ask the reader to answer what sort of language might be appropriate to a Japanese speaker committed to an unspoken project of decolonization if this story is, indeed, a meditation on the Japanese language. Or, in other words, given the parallelism, what might tie the sequence together? If Swahili is spoken by residents of decolonizing states such as Tanzania or Kenya, and Vietnamese is spoken by residents of anticolonial Vietnam, what sort of language might be both imagined and communicated from the point of view of Boku? Answering this question requires a rather intricate trip through figural language that transforms the story; shifts the relation between Ludolph and Boku; and, in consequence, reconceptualizes Japan's position in a global era during wartime.

The opening of the novel leaves readers at a vast distance from the most important part of the plot: we can only imagine the soldier's fate through the eyes of the narrator. While Boku in fact is complicit in the circumstances that send the soldier back to the front, he seems to redeem his own betrayal by monumentalizing Ludolph in bold type. The emphasis on modernist style and allusion we see in *On the Japanese Language* departs from the dominant critical approach to *buraku* literature via liberation literature that we saw in chapter 1. In readings of *buraku* literature, critics have usually privileged realism at the expense of modernism because realism carries a mandate to convey textures of lived reality in *buraku* characters and settings and to correct distortions that many activist critics feel are all too present in writings from outside the *buraku*.

On the Japanese Language attacks a certain conception of realism I call ethnographic because Boku's technique is described using the verb *kansatsu suru* (観察する, to observe). *Kansatsu* has a long history in the transcriptive styles of I-fiction. It can be traced back to Meiji-era debates that disapprove of artistry and figural language because these kinds of modernist style muddy the expression of a self trying to communicate to a reader through a contract that ought to be transparent. *Kansatsu suru* indicates a detached, observational stance in which the observer is not a participant in the system, though he conveys his perceptions of that system. The verb is often employed in a positive way by social scientific writers, such as the ethnographer Yanagita Kunio, who strive for a style that reports what they hear from informants "without adding a word or phrase."[55] The perceiver is supposed to transcribe his data into language in an unmediated fashion with as little intervening subjectivity as possible, letting the facts speak for themselves.

Tayama Katai uses *kansatsu* when describing his experiences as an embedded reporter on the fighting front of the Russo-Japanese War. The verb *kansatsu suru* appears with special regularity in literary criticism on *buraku*-related fiction to refer to fieldwork that twentieth-century writers conducted in or around *buraku* areas to which they were themselves strangers.[56] Iwano Hōmei conducted fieldwork excursions (*kansatsu*) to a "shin heimin buraku" on Saturdays and Sundays during the years 1900–1903 for his story, "Young Lady of the Buraku" (*Buraku no musume*).[57] And after the war, Ishikawa Jun uses *kansatsu* to describe his tour of a "certain neighborhood" (*chiku*) in "Early October" (*Kanro*).[58] In contrast, Boku's act of interpretation is foregrounded through graphic mediation as he responds to and interacts with the soldier. Clearly, given the interpretation through typographical modernism that we just examined, Boku acknowledges that he has performed an act of interpretation as he responds to and interacts with the soldier. Our job is now to figure out what that interpretation was.

We will recall that Boku has been employed to co-opt the soldier. He is ordered to carry out the students' commands without adding input of his own. He takes field notes of Ludolph's reactions and phones in daily reports to his managers. The novella casts the students as both ideologues and technocrats in the manner of *kanri shakai*, or managed society. They view Ludolph as a test case and suggest that the operation of psychological influence may be carried out on a larger scale if this sample proves to be effective. Boku is quite aware that the students' pose puts the soldier at risk, but he continues to carry out his duties. Here, he disavows any complicity in the mission by ascribing its outcome to laws of chance:

> This part-time job is one sort of wager. It's just like gambling.
> The gambling operation that these students have plotted is that
> four days from now, the Black soldier will either desert the army
> after taking in the dangerous poison spit up by optimistic young
> people like us who live in this peaceful Japan and in by anti-war
> sentiments—or he will go back to camp and on to the war, feeling
> that poison in the way his skin flames up or he feels this poison at a
> visceral level.[59]

But after only a day, Boku stops doing his job as a worker of chance. The distance collapses, and Boku not only acknowledges the soldier as a singular being; he even surprisingly finds himself identifying with the soldier and wants to stop using him as a study in psychological influence (*seishinteki eikyō*).[60] This transformation from subcontractor to saboteur occurs because Boku feels he is able to understand (*wakaru*) Ludolph. As he delinks from the students' business plan to assert his own independent viewing stance, Boku attributes a subjectivity to the soldier and also limits it so that he is the only one who truly sees Ludolph as visible: "He is completely effaced from the image etched into [the students'] brains. In that way he is literally an unvisible [*sic*] man (*fukashi ningen*)."[61] The special link between the two characters is maintained through the rest of the story by the connection Boku establishes between his own independence as an exploited worker who seeks recognition and Ludolph's "unvisible" appearance to the students.

The soldier's subjectivity continues to deepen by means of allusions to African American writers, no doubt contributing by association to the volumetric impression that critics have of the narrator. Later in the story, an entry scribbled in Ludolph's diary cites "Nobody knows my name," the title of James Baldwin's 1961 essay collection.[62] The diary attributes Boku's exploitation to the students, not to Boku himself:

> Sunday. Meeting with the Japanese students.
> 1:00 p.m.
> What the hell do they want me to remember? Things about Ken, or Jimmy, or Jackie, who died screaming? It makes me furious, what did the Japanese chickens do? This is a matter between the VC and us. You're from California so tell me about your brothers and sisters and mother back there, they say. They have no idea about why people with no feelings have died.
> Nobody knows my name.[63]

The diary entry certainly does not deepen our understanding of Boku's inner world or spark sympathy for him. But it *does* socialize his story and render it with complexity by showing how Boku's narrative is important but qualified in the context of the exchange with Ludolph, an insight available only from the soldier's point of view. In this context, "Nobody knows my name" does not suggest a welcome relief from oppressive U.S. history as it does in Baldwin's collection, written partly when he lived in Europe. It seems to stand in for being misunderstood and overobserved for his value as an informant or ally. Later, the title is even interchanged with the concept of the invisible man, such that Boku seems to reproduce the invisibility he attributes to the soldier by using both these texts as metaphors for his own personal alienation. Boku writes, "It would be better to say now I was sick-drunk not on the whisky, but on that part-time job of getting the soldier to desert. At the time I thought I understood that shaky, trapped feeling that enwrapped the black soldier. If I could change the name of Ludolph L. Witt into the title of that novel by the black writer, *Nobody Knows My Name!* I am the only one who knows who you are!"[64]

Boku later cites Baldwin's title to refer to his own experience. The allusion captures the sense of anonymity he felt in the hotspot frequented by the students when he arrived from the provinces, a jazz *kissaten* coffee shop.[65] This space provides a point of entry for making Boku's alienation concrete. When the relation to urban alienation suggested by the allusion is factored in, however, the attention to Ludolph's exploitation by an overeager Japanese bystander shifts to Boku's treatment by an instrumentalizing boss. The near-nameless Saitō typically goes by a number of other impersonal pronouns. His employers most typically address him as *kimi* (you), a pronoun that reinforces the precarious and interchangeable nature of his status, using the snippy tone of boss to underling. This tone and anonymity reinforce the atmosphere of *kanri shakai*. Ironically, this structure is present in the revolutionary organization that is supposed to be most opposed to corporate rationalization of daily life.

As we read further, we find that the allusion to Baldwin indeed socializes Boku yet further vis-à-vis his relation to the soldier, in a relation of exploitation specific to 1968 Tokyo. The information he gathers from the diary gives Boku a new insight. Boku is shocked to discover that the budding sociologist Ludolph has observed him all along. The diary suggests that there is a way of looking that is not *kansatsu* but a thinking of one's self by way of seeing the other. Not only does the ethnographic gaze look straight back upon him while taking meticulous notes, but Ludolph's scholarly capacities show that he is far from being, in the primitivist words the narrator employs to report to the students, "like a bear caught in the cage of your plot."[66] Unlike Boku, invested in the project as a gamble, a detached form of speculation from which he can earn a living, the soldier shows an interest in manipulating the symbolic structures of the social sciences: "He first approached the students with the goal of observing them" ("observing" in English in the original).[67] Despite his claim of psychological intimacy, the narrator ultimately betrays the soldier by failing to anticipate how the students will manipulate him. The novella ends, like *Invisible Man,* with an apostrophe to the reader that is the exact same question the story opened with. But rather than anticipating solidarity, *On the Japanese Language.* Boku laments his own failure at length, addressing himself, the policeman, and the reader and calling attention to the superimposition of identities that has transpired.

I sat in the small, hot interrogation room and asked the policeman, who was looking at me with contempt, and a wry smile.

I want to know, "if it were you, and you met a foreigner who understood virtually no Japanese, what in the world is the first word you would begin to teach him with?" I want to know, if it were you, what Japanese word *could* you start to teach him with?

The policeman listening to faltering, trailed-off words gave a wry smile as if he were listening to words used somewhere near Thailand or Burma, not Japan. If you met a foreigner who understood virtually no Japanese, and it were you, what in the world is the first word you would begin to teach him with?

I saw the policeman's wry smile devour my words in the middle of the room, and felt a fear that seemed like it might melt into my body and twist itself into me. I felt the words that could barely muster up any sound rumble around in the depths of my body. What I want to know is, if it were you, what Japanese word would you start to teach him with?[68]

As the last monologue of the narrator fades away, he is still stuck on a single word as the key to enabling him to communicate with the foreigner. The novella opens with a question about what the speaker intends to say but closes with a query about what could potentially brook the gap between two people. The common project of the two characters is never resolved in the novella, and any alliance stays in the realm of thought rather than thought transformed into action. As I explore in the next section, one alliance between the two characters is suggested by means of allusion that any discursive reader schooled in *buraku* activist rhetoric would pick up. The figures that establish a parallel between Boku and Ludolph depart from the realist ethnographic stance and make allusions to a prominent manifesto whose mandate is to transform the personal "I" into a collective, active "we," a document of desire for connection and solidarity.

Manifesto Destiny

Allusions to texts by African American writers and extraliterary documents guide Boku's transformation from clinical detachment to engaged member of a group, one that contests and challenges the norms of invisibility. The narrator of *On the Japanese Language* is intelligible to readers primarily through bodily perceptions of vision, sound, and touch, which tend to overshadow psychonarration. Accordingly, the alliances between narrator and soldier are solidified by likening experiences of sensation, the most prominent of which is how skin is imagined to link visible and invisible realities. We saw how the soldier's blackness is illustrated through Boku's perspective primarily by means of his skin. Skin as an interface between world and socialized self is a well trodden line of inquiry in Naka-gami criticism. Watanabe Naomi has surveyed the trope of skin as surface of inscription in Nakagami's works. He argues that the skin's potential as an interface is key to the heightened sense of contact that Nakagami's characters experience between internal and external worlds.[69] The alliance that *On the Japanese Language* suggests is meaningful beyond the repro-duction of hypervisibility that I explored earlier because it overlaps with a set of figures that structures the document I examine in this section that feature skin and connect somatic pain to discursive pain in ways that ally the two characters figurally.

The Suiheisha Manifesto was presented as a foundational document of the first nationwide *buraku* movement along with a flag emblazoned with a Christological crown of red thorns on a black anarchist background, held up by a bamboo spear, a referent to the militant tactics of peasant protests during the Tokugawa era. Since it was first read aloud at the inau-gural Suiheisha gathering, the manifesto has become known in *buraku* his-toriography as a forceful and impassioned oration that conjured a sense of community as it was read. Figures from this document create a sense of rhetorical community as references to this hidden transcript when they appear in off-the-cuff remarks by writers and partisans affiliated with the liberation movement as well as official speeches. It is therefore an ideal document to use as an allusion to a social collectivity galvanized by a text and for transforming individual listeners to members of a self-defined col-lective, as Boku imagines himself doing with Ludolph.

This document shares many of the structural features and rhetorics that make the manifesto a genre of public declaration, in Janet Lyon's words.[70] Although the manifesto may be read by a single person, he speaks in plural to claim a foundational status, exhibits a strident tone, includes discourses of prophecy and persuasion, speaks directly, and emphasizes transparent communication between citizens in the interest of articulat-ing a not yet formed community that challenges a prior historical account. The collective, direct nature of the Suiheisha Manifesto contrasts to both official rescripts like the Imperial Rescript on Education, issued in the name of the emperor, which, as Sumii Sue notes, "no one has any sympathy for," and to the mass media "rhetoric" (*yūben*) campaigns that aimed to educate bourgeois households in the use of rhetoric by gathering people around the radio beginning in 1925.[71] In contrast to these one-way modes of transmission, the manifesto encourages the listener to join in, to complete the task the speaker outlines. The apostrophes in Nakagami's novella recall this direct mode of address.

Three rhetorical features typical of the modern manifesto as a genre are visible in the Suiheisha narrative. It begins with a foreshortened, impassioned, and highly selective chronicle of oppression against "our ancestors" that leads to the present moment of crisis, of "no appreciable results." Then, it recounts a list of grievances that cast oppression as a struggle between the empowered and the disempowered, which Lyon reminds us often appear in the form of parataxis, as we see in the list of wrongs and injuries (being skinned alive and spat at and having hearts torn out).[72] Finally, it issues a challenge to the oppressor while issuing an exhortation to action to "throw off the brand of martyrdom" while pursuing "human rights."

The critique of injustice is directed at the ways that labor sets the terms for identity and alliance. This set of terms includes a common rhetorical feature of *buraku* activism, an exposé of how natural-seeming orders of history and order are actually unjust and cruel—in other words, highly unnatural. In the above lines, the symbolic domain is referenced in terms of the unfair exchange of labor, referring to the common association of animal slaughter and butchery with *buraku* labor. This occupation works metonymically to stand in for the whole of *buraku* experience, modeling it on a painful and wrong relation to labor. The acts of "skinning animals" and "tearing out animals' hearts" have turned "our ancestors" themselves into beasts.[73] Instead of being humanized, the manifesto asserts, *burakumin* are still susceptible to being rendered just like the very beasts their representative occupation associates them with. The manifesto describes "our ancestors" as humans who were sacrificed in exchange for their work, fifty years after the status system that consigned members of outcaste classes to subordinate positions was abolished in 1871.

The collective subject formed to right the inverted, unjust structure is a rhetorical community of brothers. The manifesto exhorts this collective that the "time has come" to organize as *eta-zoku* (tribe of *eta* outcasts) and to turn the tables on their oppressors. As they step out of the dialectic of master-slave relations, they take on the job of self-determination. The manifesto performs this very goal in a language that says that the claim of subjectivity is prefigured on breaking with a history in which discursive violence and somatic pain are connected. The rhetoric of somatic pain is superimposed on a critique of the division of labor: discrimination has "stripped [them] of their own living flesh in recompense for skinning animals," and so the manifesto's readers and listeners are encouraged to "throw off their stigma."[74] It is easy enough to read the passage of the dehumanized human as a description of the painful rending of attachments; just as the skin of the horse is flayed from its whole, the attachments of the nonhuman humans are torn from the body to which they might otherwise belong. How, then, do these elements of genre and figure connect the 1968 story to this liberation history? In the novella, the narrator applies figural language highly reminiscent of the Suiheisha Manifesto to his imagination of his effect on the soldier's actions. This hidden transcript establishes a series of suggestive connections and polemics.

Three elements of this modernist manifesto are especially pertinent to the use of hidden transcript and polemic in Nakagami's work, especially in *On the Japanese Language*. These elements of allusion connect Nakagami's novella to a received tradition of narrative that expands the canon of national literature in important ways: through introducing materials from literature outside Japan and through drawing on materials that exist in both written and orally communicated forms. First is the emphasis on ethnic self-determination "through which we shall liberate ourselves." In the novella, in contrast, self-determination occurs through alliance, not autonomy. The black character and the alliances, aesthetics, and intertexts he uses and prompts to narrator to use have something to offer that *buraku* movement politics does not. Second is the position of the *eta* as a quasi-ethnic group based on lineage ("our ancestors") as well as occupation. Nakagami's works and their reception have often been criticized for overemphasizing blood kinship as an exclusive guarantee of ethnic identity. But this novella envisions brotherhood across racial lines. The third and most important element is that like *Rhizome*, the novel we examined in chapter 1; this suffering takes place in both a somatic realm and in a psychic realm ("their own hearts were ripped out"). The figure of blood does not limit the alliance to lineage but refers to suffering due to the unfulfilled rights of man that modernity should provide (liberty, equality) and the persistence of humanness and vital connectivity even in the absence of these rights ("human blood has kept flowing"). The parallel nature of the tropes of flaying, suffering, and other kinds of somatic pain that the narrator imagines in the soldier liken Boku's own desire for anti-imperial liberation to the soldier's presumed longing to be rid of the pain caused by oppression based on the nature of his skin.

As in the Suiheisha Manifesto, suffering from discrimination is dramatized through the correspondence between discursive and physical violence. In *On the Japanese Language*, figures of thorns, poison, and irritation to the skin dramatize the suffering that Boku imagines Ludolph feels when his abilities to make decisions and communicate are exploited for ends that do him a disservice. Boku imagines that his pointed questions about civil rights movements and antiwar sentiment will injure Ludolph's conscience like "a thorn of poison that works without fail." He later repeats the image: "I turned to the black soldier and wracked my brains to pick out the English words like thorns that would stab him like sure-fire poison" (50).

As he gets closer to understanding the soldier—or sympathizing with him through a common figural language he has devised—Boku's sensations and perceptions are filtered through an interface of figures attached to the skin. As in the opening paragraph, this encounter is shown in typography that registers an indexical relation to the encounter. The interface of perception is different than the series of visual metaphors employed by narratology, which commonly uses the term "focalize" to indicate how perceptions are made cognitive through a metaphor of sight. Here, sight is transposed instead into perception registered on the skin, as it was in the assertion of "**courage**" in the novella's opening passage. The same types of figures appear in the descriptive language that introduces us to Boku. The story begins by likening Boku's barrier against the world to a crayfish's armor because both are shields that stave off the world and shelter the delicate life within (8). When Boku moves between his home bases of the jazz coffee shop and the students' venue and sees a swag of branches swaying in the wind, he describes himself as a human who has lost his sense of touch (10). In short, terms of alienation are articulated in terms of sensations, and sensations of relationality are based on the skin and its relation to the world. Indeed, the final blow of betrayal by the students comes when "As I read the puffed-up prose of the newspaper galley that the student brought, I read with all my sensors alert, like a hedgehog bristles its needles" (81).

The figural language that the narrator imagines the soldier expresses his pain with, assigning somatic pain to discursive violence, is a projection of Boku's free indirect style, his narration of the soldier's presumed interior life. But the first-person basis of experience also allows us to see how the conventions of I-fiction are brought close to the manifesto, providing it with a socialized dimension that would seem to counter Kobayashi's melancholic claim of I-fiction's failure. The figural language, affiliations, and narrative operations bring the weight of the manifesto's rhetorical tradition to bear, as a series of precedents that suggest how social abjection and somatic pain are allied, through a new collectivity of brothers in a genre that is all about being heard, creating a shared sense of imagination about what it would mean to be heard. If Boku and the soldier are, indeed, "long-suffering brothers," it is not exclusively because Ludolph is imagined to correspond to Boku's liberation narrative in the manifesto.[75] In the post-Enlightenment tradition of rights cited by the manifesto, brotherhood, after all, typically demands some reciprocity. Ludolph's experience is textualized as a narrative of liberation. But when Boku's experience is also textualized, the reciprocity is imagined to happen as he transposes the trope of invisibility from the presumed narrative of the soldier's experience onto his own increasingly plaintive alienation as the "unaudible man."

The correspondence between the figural language of the 1922 manifesto and the exploitation of Boku's subcontractor job compel me to associate it with the narrative of *buraku* liberation. I see *On the Japanese Language* as a 1969 story rather than a 1968 story because the story's interest in solidarity and obsession with racial figures and the act of representation far outstrip the attention devoted to the anti-ANPO movement itself. In pragmatic terms, 1969 was a year of great celebration for the *buraku* liberation movement. The *Buraku* Liberation League (BLL) led what was arguably the most successful grassroots social movement in postwar Japan. By making its transcript of grievances speak to the public institutions of power, the BLL's actions produced substantial and concrete results in social infrastructure, funding for education, and improved living conditions.[76] The BLL also contested legal tendencies to systematically discriminate against *buraku* residents, both by means of what we might today call geographic profiling and by structural inequities in the legal system such as forced confessions into which often illiterate defendants were coerced, including the Sayama trial.

The first landmark was a 1965 government report, issued by the Delib-
erative Council for *Buraku* Assimilation, that criticized earlier government
attempts to improve living conditions in *buraku* areas.[77] The BLL worked
to affect the concrete result of this report, the 1969 Special Measures Law
(SML), colloquially known as the *dōwa taisaku*, or measures for improving what used to be called *dōwa* areas, an administrative term different
than the more colloquial *buraku*. The year of 1969 was crucial not only
because the SML "set the stage for a new wave of *buraku* activism and
militancy" but because it marked a turning point in court support for the
BLL's use of denunciation as an extralegal means of enforcing its rights
and demanding redress.[78] The stance that discrimination could take place
anywhere, regardless of medium or venue, distinguished the BLL point of
view from an emerging critique of violence that put a greater emphasis on
medium specificity. In particular, the image was felt to represent a great
potential for deceit and duplicity because it could substitute one reality
with another distorted or less realistic one. My next section explores how
Nakagami's critique of the bystander status of Japan implicates the mass
media's misrepresentation of the soldier in the fake account of his deser-
tion. But unlike works of fiction that critique mass media as a vehicle of
illusionism, *On the Japanese Language* indicts the composition of the spectacle by a political group with ulterior motives and bad labor politics, not
the false promise of the medium itself.

Critiques of Spectacle

Criticism by fiction writers and social movement leaders assessed the
end of the 1960s with the gravity usually reserved for fin de siècle affairs
still thirty years in the future. 1968 featured a wealth of indicators that
the postmodern era was just over the horizon. Students took over major
universities to protest technocratic administration and the infusion of
managed society into all spheres of life.[79] The Saison Group, a large chain
of retail stores with ties to a major railway line, opened the first big department store called Seibu in the now flourishing youth capital of Shibuya.
This move would open a retail revolution.[80] The journalistic frenzy over
the 1970 World Exposition in Osaka (Expo '70) promoted a world of consumer electronics and fantastic techno-based visions of the future. It also,
complained writers and activists, packed in far more people than the protests against the reratification of ANPO had attracted. In the disappointed

view of leftists and other critics who advocated national sovereignty, ANPO's failure sealed Japan's dependency on the U.S. military for another ten years in exchange for economic benefits and military protection.[81]

In the atmosphere of Expo '70, late-1960s writers attacked the image and image-based media for their key role in distracting citizens from national politics. Images were denounced as tools of exoticism or escapist entertainment, representations detached from reality, or ways of obscuring a more authentic reality. One common critique decried the way Japan's image as a peaceful nation was sustained by its bystander role to U.S. activities in Vietnam. In other words, although no Japanese troops were sent to the front, members of the public looked on and presumably benefited from more broad economic growth. By 1965, historian Tom Havens writes, the U.S. military had made so many changes to its bases that they could hardly be regarded as merely defending Japan.[82] One hundred and forty-eight installations provided full-fledged launching pads for American strategy in East and Southeast Asia. Bases covered four times as much land as they had during the actual occupation from 1945 to 1952; base staff provided labor for hauling napalm; and contractors cashed in on hundreds of millions of dollars from both direct and indirect procurements, from "lettuce to Sonys."[83]

Because critics sensed that representation stood in the way of accessing reality, and Japan's claim to be a peaceful country was belied by profits made from the war, they were quick to fault images for their capacity to distort as they mediated. The key flaw of the image was to look without acknowledging engagement and to erase the qualities that linked one place, namely Japan, to another, namely the United States. Writings on Vietnam and the Vietnam War in this era were primarily journalistic, but there were a few important exceptions.[84] Kawamura Minato notes that "the crime of 'looking,' or the 'look' as the complicity of warfare" was a frequent feature of later fiction and memoirs by writers such as reporter Kaikō Takeshi.[85] Kaikō's *Vietnam War Diary* (*Betonamu senki*; 1965) reworked columns that he had published in the *Asahi shinbun* a month after returning from an eleven-month stay in Vietnam. These reports later became the 1968 novel *Into a Black Sun* (*Kagayakeru yami*), an I-fiction work about a newspaper reporter's struggles with his assignment in Vietnam in 1964 through 1965. Beginning with his "gravedigger's eyes," the narrator's observations turn existential as he asks himself, in Bruce Suttmeier's words, "how he could look upon the suffering all around him."[86] This doubt culminates in his viewing of a public execution of a twenty-year-old boy. A reporter for a rival newspaper, Hino Keizō of the *Yomiuri shinbun,* published reports that used some of the same incidents. He described the same split of himself as victim and observer, using the style of a "cinematic slow-motion cut" but did not include the graphic spectacles he witnessed until it appeared in a prose fiction work, *Eyes of a Typhoon* (*Taifū no me*), in 1993, a full twenty-five years later.[87] Kawamura argues that this time lag in publishing preserved the fiction that Japan was innocent of any ties to war and placed part of the blame on the routines and distractions encouraged by managed society.

Critics keenly aware of the postmodern and postindustrial manipulation of reality dwelled on the ability of images to displace the everyday person from a sense of real events. Popular writers of genre fiction also explicitly saw spectacle as a replacement for direct democracy or engagement in a public sphere and implicated viewers who looked but did not engage. In this final section, I want to juxtapose Nakagami's novella and its critique of the division of labor in managed society to a well-known story that is more typical of the genre of image critique used in late-1960s antiwar protest. In 1967, Tsutsui Yasutaka's *Vietnam Travel Agency* (*Betonamu kankō kōsha*) was nominated for the Naoki Prize, the most prestigious award given to popular literature.[88] Tsutsui uses irony and satire to lampoon Japanese tourists who are curious about savagery in faraway wild and war-torn places, as long as the strife remains at a safe distance. Most of the spectacles and wild scenes are kept at bay with the luxury of high-tech goods that were becoming increasingly accessible to the everyday consumer in the era of managed society.

Vietnam Travel Agency uses the first-person voice typical of I-fiction to recount the narrator's quest to find the ideal destination for his honeymoon. He wants to travel to a spot that is free of the cares and constraints of his everyday job at a supermarket research center. Set in the near future, the sky is not even the limit in his world of choice: trips to Saturn have become all the rage. People routinely travel by space jet to exotic-seeming destinations that vary wildly, according to the ever-changing buzz generated by travel critics. Though the narrator has prepaid for a voyage to Dakar, when he arrives at the travel agency to finalize arrangements, the boom has already ended. The narrator parks his fiancée in the waiting room and takes a short hop to the Congo with the aim of confronting the branch head in order to make sure the trip happens or he gets a refund.

Though the Congo was the locus classicus of dark continent narratives in the Victorian age, the encounter with wildness in the near future is managed as a scheduled viewing of wild animals from a safe distance as they are trotted out of their cages on a timed schedule and projected onto a "stupidly huge" (*baka dekai*) Jumbotron-like screen.

When the narrator demands a refund for his now obsolete honeymoon plan, the branch manager responds by offering another sales pitch and persuades him to take a trip to Vietnam. The branch manager is desperate to convince customers that they should not abandon their own planet as a source of excitement because Earth still has spectacles to offer. He pitches an alternate plan to the narrator, and they join a space jet package tour for the twenty-eight-minute ride to Vietnam. Here, the viewing is literally spectacular: the war has actually been prolonged due to the remarkable boost it brought to the leisure industry, thanks to visitors like the narrator.

On the trip, passengers are kept safely out of harm's way, as they seek visual stimuli at a distance, surrounded by icons of 1960s travel culture that border on kitsch. The shapely (and ditzy) stewardess explains as they fly over the battlefield that "at this moment, ladies and gentlemen, the huge dirt-covered battle you see below has been going on for hundreds of years, and its old-timey festival atmosphere has given it the status of a local cultural heritage site."[89] An elegantly dressed older man, whose age illustrates how long the war has dragged on, asks why the war broke out. The guide lowers her head and admits, "I don't think that at this point, there is anyone left, who remembers why it broke out."[90] No one even knows what "Vietcong" means, only that the name has attracted tourists.[91] In effect, people only know this spot because of its place in the simulacra of tourist history, not the real events of military history.

The historical amnesia of the war spectators makes them more susceptible to "large-scale spectacle" and to getting fleeced by paying for more and more spectacle.[92] Next to the actual fighting grounds a second industry has emerged, a kind of live-action theme park providing location shoots for a war film. This representation of parallel fake war clearly displaces the real event. According to the guide, among the film income, income from sightseers, and money from use of the battlefield, an actor's salary matches a soldier's. The passengers see an actual skirmish in which a black soldier is killed. A woman runs across the scene carrying a corpse, a white Vietcong soldier, and extras including an American Indian, an Ainu, and a bear appear. The branch manager offers a rational explanation of the useful effects of war, which he says you can understand when you read classical history. War stabilizes economies and helps solve unemployment issues. War even serves as a curb on juvenile delinquency and provides jobs for black fake fighters who side with the South Vietnamese because the North Vietnamese actively hunt black soldiers due to severe discrimination.[93]

Upon hearing how rational this policy is, the space jet driver demands why it is rational to kill black people and walks off the job. Given the pilot's departure, the space jet crashes. The narrator is rescued from the wreckage by a female guerilla. She loans him a petticoat, which he uses to wrap his rifle and flag down a passing helicopter that leads them to safety. The helicopter turns out to be hired by his fiancée who announces she is dumping him and plans to marry the manager of the travel agency instead, followed by a honeymoon on Saturn. Even woman's fickleness is rationalized in a perfect match of supply and demand, as the fiancée's volatile affections find a perfect match in a betrothed whose job is to stoke and satisfy consumer desire. The story ends when the Ainu, American Indian, and bear greet the narrator and offer him a place in their troupe, and he throws down his rifle to join them.

Literary critic Isoda Kōichi remarked that key features of managed society drive the plot of *Vietnam Travel Agency*.[94] All elements of life are rationalized to the extent that structures that are supposed to be playful or spontaneous, such as leisure, follow the same logics as other "mechanisms" of the laboring life, making "a reality whose net has gone so far as to manage the wild beasts in Africa."[95] In Isoda's reading, the only element in the story that manages to break out of management society is war, but it only escapes because it is pure illusion. All "military affairs have become shows for the TV screen, and TV screens have in fact become, conversely, the very preconditions of 'military affairs.'"[96]

Tatsumi Takayuki argues that the story's exploitation of the "pseudo-event" is singular and prescient in Tsutsui's work. The pseudo-event is a notion coined by Daniel Boorstin in his 1961 book *The Image: A Guide to Pseudo-Events in America,* published three years later in Japan.[97] Tatsumi writes that, "in the sixties, Tsutsui tried to figure out the new possibilities put into play by the concept of the pseudo-event (*giji ibento*) and the spectacle, with mimesis as his antagonist."[98] Unlike the critique directed, for example, at Expo '70 where images and entertainment effaced the political realm, for Boorstin, the image was all about giving greater access to knowledge: it is an ambiguous truth. Its key feature was not that it was not a falsehood or that it concealed something. Because someone painstakingly planned it, and it is so intricately managed, its opposite is the spontaneous event, one exempt from planning and standardization, not the real event. Its relation to the underlying reality of the situation is ambiguous, and its chief aim is to make the beholder ask, "What does it mean?" or "Is it planned?" not only "Is it true or real?"[99] The pseudo-event exists for the purposes of being reported, debated, and publicized.

I would like to place *On the Japanese Language* in context of these debates on the bystander, the spectacle and managed society, to show the distinct focus that *On the Japanese Language* fixed on the labor exploitation and the force of ethnography. The focus on language as an interface that can form relations and exert power distinguishes *On the Japanese Language* from other writings on Vietnam. The novella goes beyond a demystifying moment to situate the force of spectacles in interpretive contexts rather than a purely tragic mode or an ironic mode that exaggerates features of complicit looking with kitsch and absurdism. A brief reminder of the spiraling climax of Nakagami's novel is first in order. Suddenly, without warning Boku, the leftist group publishes a story in a student newspaper. The article announces the results of the front's mission by claiming that the group has convinced the soldier to desert the army and has awakened the soldier's solidarity with anti-imperial causes. The story does not mention the soldier's race, but the article is published alongside a photo where the soldier stands alongside the narrator.

In the photo, Boku's arm is draped around the soldier's shoulder to dramatize the two youths' cross-cultural, cross-racial, and cross-national solidarity. The photo is juxtaposed with a fabulated caption, and the image of supposed solidarity is referred to in the story by a gloating leftist as a *monogatari* (story, tale). At no point is the soldier himself interviewed or quoted. Boku narrates:

I was written up in the newspaper as well.
"This heroic Black soldier Ludolph L. Witt (age 20) has responded to the anti-imperialist measures persuasion of our anti-war student front, in this imperial policy and reactionary system known as Japan, and announced his refusal to return to the fighting front.
This action is based on international proletarianism, in the face of U.S.–Japan anti-revolutionary league. And is a clear indicator of strong support for the fight of Vietnam's people. S-kun (age 19),

who helped with the persuasion, as well as we, the anti-imperial
Anti-War United Student Front at large, now hope for your widespread participation in the movement to corrode the morale of
these soldiers, and persuade them to desert."[100]

When the soldier sees the story, however, he panics and spirals into a suicidal mania. He realizes that he has been a tool in the students' *monogatari*,
or plot, instrumentalized like a product to be a metonymic example for
the crisis of conscience felt by minoritarian soldiers in the U.S. armed
forces who realize their double consciousness and ally with the global
subaltern. The crowning blow to the soldier is dealt by the photograph of
himself with the narrator's arm draped about his neck in apparent solidarity. Nakagami's contextualization of the photo in a concrete media form
with a caption shows the work's preoccupation with the process of interpreting images, even in propagandistic settings. It is not the image itself
that is degraded but its mode of interpretation. The term of *monogatari*,
while used here in a fairly quotidian way to mean "story," is in 1968 already
being primed for the revisionism it will undergo in the 1970s and 1980s as
a literary critical centerpiece.

In this climactic scene, the students not only conscript Ludolph into
their laboratory but also outsource the dirty work onto Boku who, without their work, is unemployed. The scene differs from the Brotherhood
sequence in *Invisible Man* because it imagines a potential ally. *On the
Japanese Language* depicts the exploitation of the soldier through Boku's
conscription into a series of routines, forced mobility, uses of technology to give reports, and a vertical hierarchy in relation to his employers.
Where he had thought himself a subject of his own historical actions,
he is revealed to be an object. His situation reprises the logic of the Suiheisha Manifesto but relocates it to the context of managed society. The
students' anticipation of the economies of scale more typically found in
large industrial concerns shows the structural similarity of their scheme
to the larger national military-industrial complex. The contribution of
this story to a discussion of Japanese and global postmodernism is to
show how critiques of popular manipulation can no longer be based
solely on the illusionist nature of photographs or screen media and their
abilities to deceive.

While many accounts of the student movement stress its dimension
of class struggle, Nakagami's story stresses the effects of race and ethnic

difference, aspects of the struggle sidelined by the activists who only see liberation in national terms or terms of teleology in which authenticity is displaced by spectacle. In *On the Japanese Language*, the manifesto provides a place to imagine a lateral, transnational alliance modeled on a proletariat but based on an experience of racialized exile from the nation. Ultimately in the novella, race and ethnic difference stay in the realm of the prepolitical. Neither revolution nor liberation comes to fruition, and Boku does not assert the right to denunciation that the BLL fought for in the courts.

This chapter has explored how a set of lower frequencies operates in the 1968 novella *On the Japanese Language* as subtexts to the main story. These allusions locate the novella's themes and tropes, I argued, in a literary historical perspective that insisted that I-fiction must be socialized and must be socialized in particular ways in the late 1960s to question the consequences of Japan's alignment between the West and the rest. Neither narrative nor characters present anything like an overall critique of U.S. military presence or a desire to get rid of ANPO. In fact, Nakagami's caustic treatment of the 1968 student movement in this story is substantially different than the aura of nostalgia or failed revolution that prevails in many later accounts.[101] By using allusion to speak what the inaudible man could not say directly, Nakagami Kenji's work departed from the strongly voiced mandate of *buraku* literature and literary criticism that insisted that *buraku* characters should be described in the lived texture of realistic, everyday life. Instead, Nakagami turned to the tools of Japanese postmodernism, the intersections of exchange with word and image culture, as venues for exploring a politics of solidarity through the heightened attention they brought to relationships between characters in the United States and Japan during the Vietnam War era. I argued that typographical modernism and the embedded diary structure that organize the novella socialized the genre of I-fiction by using the hidden transcripts of African American literature and the political organizing device of the manifesto.

The novella operates on the one hand as a critique of Boku's tenuous status as a part-time worker who is outsourced the disagreeable parts of a job, a characteristic feature of managed society, where dirty work is often consigned to *buraku* characters and residents. On the other hand, the novella depicts how a political community might emerge out of imagining a shared experience between characters of different races, ethnicities, and nations. Where both early twentieth-century critics and failed 1960s revolutionaries saw nothing but gloom and defeat in the aftermath of 1968, the focus on the soldier and the hidden transcripts pertinent to 1969 prompts us to ask what sort of political commitments might be imagined to follow out of their imagined solidarity. My next chapter turns to examine concretely how one of these imagined solidarities with Korea worked when interpreted in terms of South–South relations.

CHAPTER 5

The 38th Parallax

Nakagami in/and Korea

A Second Life for Asian Modernity

The ideas of exchange and exile punctuated Nakagami's works. During a period of intense travel beginning in the late 1970s, he transposed these questions from the immediate domestic context of Kumano and *kokubungaku* (national literature) to the regional context of East Asia. He paid special attention to the national context of Korea, itself fraught with ideas of Southernness—divided by a border from the North, a former "South" of Japan's imperial reach and emerging from its position in the global South to become a modern industrialized nation. Between 1978 and 1985, Nakagami visited Korea seven times and traveled extensively from his base in Seoul. Korea would become one of the largest subjects in his oeuvre. Nakagami initially imagined Korea as an alternative to Japanese modernity but became disillusioned with the revival of nativist culture by leftist intellectuals because they abandoned its roots in outcast culture when they mobilized its cultural forms for antiauthoritarian protest. Although his initial expectations do not pan out, his interest is vindicated by the vitality of street life in Seoul and the new styles of writing and photography that he engages to capture Korea as a whole.

Nakagami idealizes Seoul and Korea as a whole because there literature is closely tied to life; war and modern nationalism give that life a clarity it lacks in Japan: "Korea has an animated kind of energy. If you are in Seoul for even ten days, in this energetic Korea, it becomes obvious this is a place where literature is constantly bubbling under. That is something I am envious of as a novelist. First of all, there was a civil war (*nanboku sensō*) within the same people, and national boundaries were laid down as if to draw a line on a map. Neither of these two things exists in Japan."[1] Through these travels, Nakagami observes the heightened "sense of entropy" resulting from the tensions between North and South.[2] Nakagami benefits from this entropy by being one of the few Japanese intellectuals to interact with Korean writers, editors, and intellectuals in the years following the 1980 Kwangju Massacre. Seoul may have been under curfew, as he writes in the essay *Dancing, Seoul* (*Rinbu suru, Seoul*), but it was also the stage for the democratization movement of the 1980s and after-hour editorial summits. He uses his forays into the literary worlds and the performing arts venues of Seoul and Chŏngju to describe the "exceptional" yet exemplary kind of modernity that may be experienced in Korea.[3] These works both redefine the critical term of *monogatari* and use media forms that draw their rhetorical and documentary power from immediacy.

This chapter considers Nakagami's immersion in journalistic essays and roundtables about Korea. It then turns to look at places that show his search for direct contact with the vital elements of folk forms, political resistance, and a sense of time that was anti- or nonlinear and multiple and therefore unstructured: markets and photography. I follow his attempts to determine whether populist culture is still attached to outcast culture, a question he poses to dissident poet Kim Chi-ha and other writers as well as scholars and performers engaged in conserving folk forms. I conclude that he ultimately decides that, despite his initial high hopes for accomplishing a salvage ethnography, Korean intellectuals, too, have channeled *hisabetsu-min* (outcast) folk forms into the greater cause of modernization. Partisans of the democratization movement have subordinated the specific historical character of *hisabetsu-min* culture to a more generalized populist (*shomin*) resistance against aristocratic (*yangban*) culture. The resistance, too, has repeated Japan's embrace of modernization and made itself too modern to be salvaged. An outside to this structure, however, can still be found in the live action of the marketplace and in the populist kinds of exchange that sustain it. Finally, to show this marketplace vitality, I look at works of fiction published during and after his stays in Korea.

The Mirror Curtain

Nakagami's publications on Korea begin with the series of reportage essays published in 1978 in the *Tokyo shinbun* newspaper, compiled as *On the Other Side of Landscape* (*Fūkei no mukō e*). The term "landscape" clearly refers to Karatani Kōjin's description of modern subjectivity in Japan as formed by a subject-object relation that severs the human observer from the world she or he lives in, which she or he must represent in mediated form as objects to which the observer is external in both time and space. The other side of landscape is on the one hand unknown, across what Nakagami calls the "mirror curtain" that sometimes distorts and reverses things across the Sea of Japan. But it is also perhaps some greater immersion in reality, a different ontological state that is directly experienced, as the curtain transforms conventions of representation.[4] The essays highlight an extensive network of public intellectuals that Nakagami consults and travels with. Interviews, site visits, notes, tape recording, and scholarly reading give an explicitly ethnographic cast to the interpretations of folk forms. "I'm going not as a novelist who tries to capture 'things as they are' (*ari no mama*), but like a formal scholar," Nakagami writes (55). If a novelist would use the tried-and-true naturalist technique of routing representation solely through his own personal sense of the phenomenon, the scholar collects information and provides interpretive contexts.

Nakagami's most intense period of writing about Korea, primarily on literature and performing arts, occurs between 1983 and 1988. By 1985, his writings on Korea are published in Japanese venues ranging from men's magazines to leftist weeklies, while in Korea he is thoroughly in conversation with both scholars and editorial staff in journalism and publishing. He finishes one long work of prose fiction, *The Ends of the Earth, Supreme Time* (1983), while living in Seoul and publishes a book-length roundtable with the Korean writer Yun Hŭng-gil, *Located in the "East"* (*Tōyō ni itchi suru*; 1981). Although he never learned to speak Korean well or read Hangŭl script, Nakagami began to broker Korean writing into Japanese by working closely with writers and editors in Korea. When a major Tokyo bookstore asks him to fabulate an imaginary library in 1984, the shelves feature more translated Korean fiction than any other single group of writings.[5] His roundtable partner Yun is one of his selections and one of the thirteen writers Nakagami includes in a volume he edits, *Contemporary Korean Short-Story Fiction* (*Kankoku gendai tanpen shōsetsu*; 1985). The selections of "the most cutting-edge writing" introduce a range of styles and ideologies of Korean writing.[6] Nakagami includes So Nu-fi (1922–86), the conservative editorial writer of the *Chōsen nippō* newspaper, as well as Yun's stylistic experiments using a modern perspectival form of first-person narration. The story of Yun's that he includes has a monophonic narration, which Nakagami reads as a "calm within the storm" where events, one after the other, seem volatile from the outside, but an inner stasis is observed.[7]

In addition to showcasing Korean writers, the collection serves as a reprimand to the postwar literary production of Japanese writers in light of the gravitas and vitality found in Korea's postliberation fiction. Historical circumstance has produced an atmosphere where "themes" and "literary materials are roiling around" like objects waiting to be put into contexts.[8] Where Korean writers take up the "split of the ancestral country" and the "tragedy of fighting kin against kin and recounting the travails of soldiers sent off to Vietnam," Japanese writers are busy lamenting the end of history, not making or even looking for it.[9] And where a "galaxy" of Korean writers has emerged, no fictional forms appear that might make up a "post-ANPO generation."[10] (ANPO, the 1960 U.S.–Japan Security Treaty, stipulates terms for U.S. military presence in Japan, given Japan's constitutional prohibition against war according to Article 9 of the Constitution. It was greeted with mass protests and forced the resignation of Prime Minister Kishi in 1960 but has been reratified every ten years since.) In Nakagami's eyes, Japanese writers have succumbed to political melancholy after the movement against renewing ANPO failed in 1970. "Speaking at a gut level," Nakagami writes, this generation that paralleled the first postliberation generation in Korea has "lost its sensibility for fiction and ability to confront life with the resources of language" in the era of high-speed economic growth.[11]

The traditional barometers of literary vitality and the slimmed-down numbers of Akutagawa and Naoki Prize winners indeed confirm Nakagami's frustration that fiction writing stalled. Between Nakagami's 1975 Akutagawa Prize and 1985, the Akutagawa (given to pure literature) went unfilled eight of twenty-one rounds, and the Naoki (given to popular literature) was similarly blank in six of twenty-one rounds. About the same time in 1984, a debate between New Left stalwart Yoshimoto Takaaki and Haniya Yutaka broke out over the relation between fashion and politics and provoked wider discussion on New Aka's abandonment of populist struggles in the context of an affluent economy. Yoshimoto appeared in a photo shoot in *An•An* magazine, the Japanese edition of *Elle*, wearing an outfit by the avant-garde designer Kawakubo Rei's couture label Comme des Garçons.[12] Yoshimoto essentially established consumer society leftism from its inside, a position that Nakagami cites as evidence that Japanese writers seem to be embracing an "impoverished notion of 'the end.'"[13] His object of critique, "the end," refers to the discourse on the end of history that suffused the 1980s climate of Japanese postmodernism and literature and set the stage for later millennial discussions of subculture.

This preface signals a parting of the waters between Nakagami and adherents of postmodernism who see history periodized in a fundamentally modern way, claiming an "end" to history in a historicist scheme. Nakagami's own writings of this period implicitly contradict the idea that history has ended. He establishes in three ways that a relation to history as narrative is still very much in effect by looking at how characters encounter eruptions of the "law and system" of discrimination in his pure fiction works like *Kumano Stories;* by turning to subcultural forms like manga and genre fiction that engage with imperial history; and by immersing himself in a place (Korea) where, in his view, the tie of daily life not only to the social but to world-historical events is evident.[14]

Nakagami publishes a series of mass-market writings in which his role as cultural interpreter against the backdrop of comparative modernities is established apart from his fictional writing. Many roundtable conversations with writers and intellectuals follow and feature Nakagami in dialogue with scholars and public intellectuals like Han U-san, cultural editor of the *Kankoku nippō* newspaper in "A New Era for Japan-Korea Exchange," with the pop anthropologist Kim Yang-ki in "A Fundament of Culture—Korean Shamanism," and with pianist and electronic musician Sakamoto Ryūichi on Korean music in a long roundtable on what the new diplomatic relations mean at a popular (*minshū*) level.[15] Nakagami publishes a book review of a scholarly work on Korean shamanism and comments in *Penthouse* magazine on the opening of the ferry between the southern port cities of Shimonoseki, Japan, and Pusan, Korea. That article defends film director Ōshima Nagisa's outburst in a TV shoot on board the ferry. Shortly after President Chun's 1984 trip to Japan, the first by a Korean head of state, a group of intellectuals from the two countries met on the ferry as it traversed the Korea Strait. The in-between location was meant to free up discussion and demonstrate goodwill by taking place in open territory on the twentieth anniversary of the 1965 Treaty of Basic Relations (*Nikkan kihan jōyaku*) between Japan and the Republic of Korea. The treaty stipulated that Japan would pay eight hundred million dollars in reparations and loans to South Korea and deemed it the exclusive representative of Korea in exchange for dropping further claims on Japan related to its colonial rule, essentially reconciling both economic and psychological war debts. But Ōshima became so needled by continual questions raised about Japan's wartime aggressions that he exploded and screamed, "*Baka yarō!*" (Fuck you!) at his questioners. Nakagami charges the Korean news media with "caricaturing" Ōshima and Japan as barbarians and promoting itself (10). He says that the news media raised issues from the colonial era to the extent he has "calluses on his ears" (12).

His impatience with what he acknowledges as the "thirty-six years of the imperial nightmare" Japan exercised over Korea sometimes compels Nakagami to opt out of the conversation and agree with the "new era" interpretation that celebrated the present alliance without any narrative of past relations.[16] Writing in *New Japan Literature* (*Shin Nihon bungaku*), Oba Kazuyuki charges that this celebration of twenty years of exchanges (*kōryū*) following the 1965 treaty does not take place at the popular level as it pretends to. Instead, culture is employed to further the dominance of the developmental dictatorship that drives President Chun's policies (13), a celebration that attracts the collaboration of even purportedly left-ist Japanese intellectuals.

Magazines such as *Playboy,* the *Economist,* and the *Asahi Journal* all commissioned Nakagami to write essays on his impressions of Korea and other Asian, Southern places. His writings began to be published along-side visual materials and even apart from the three photo-prose works set in Korea I examine later; Nakagami's magazine work was increasingly twined with photos. *Looking for a Spanish Caravan* (*Supanisshu kyaraban o sagashite*; 1986) and *Buffalo Soldier* (1988) feature meditations on current events and tours through Asian and North African cities, beginning with Seoul. *City* (*Machi yo*), published in *Playboy* and *Subaru* from 1977 to 1989, is a collection of short stories about men who drift into worlds of under-ground political intrigue or transient sexual relations with locals following political upheavals in Singapore, Spain, Tangiers, Seoul, and Manila. The Seoul story of *City* in *Subaru* was accompanied by a photo shoot of young couples by Morita Kōzō; the Manila story in *Shōsetsu Subaru* features layouts of dancers by Seto Masato and was referred to as a "color novel"; and Nakahira Takuma's photos accompanied the Hong Kong, Spain, and Tangiers stories.[17] The photos were all atmospheric rather than illustrative; none are more so than the panoramas, ethnographic crowd shots, and the anonymous prostitutes depicted in the works set in Seoul.

Throughout Nakagami's writings, Seoul is depicted as a city full of vital-ity, where literature is imagined as part of a larger substrate of political resis-tance "bubbling under." Having witnessed this vitality erode once in Japan and Japanese fiction, Nakagami is poised to capture it in Korea before it disappears. Nakagami's perception of vitality is no doubt underwritten by new kinds of exchange, diplomacy, and trade between the two nations that increased after 1965.

In the fifteen years before Nakagami arrived, Korea's gross domestic product had advanced, Michael Robinson notes, at a remarkable average rate of 8.2 percent a year.[18] The developmental dictatorship of Presidents Park Chung-hee and Chun Doo-hwan following the Korean War had achieved certain criteria of modernization, as seen in a rise in education levels, industrial development, and tax reforms. In Kim Hyung-A's words, Korea changed "from a predominantly peasant agricultural society into a dynamic industrial nation in less than thirty years."[19] Less sanguine critics of modernization, particularly those engaged with the *minjung* (people's) movement, remarked on how economic growth resulted in kinds of capitalism that disempowered workers and caused widespread proletarianization.

Nakagami frames his account of Korea's vitality in *Dancing, Seoul* by establishing the context of the economic boom, always with reference to Japan and what he perceives as the toll modernization took on Japanese culture, particularly outcast folk culture. His writings on Korea hinge on documenting elements of folk culture in Korea that echo those that were effaced in Japan's modernization. This work is ethnographic and comparative in that it begins by establishing what anthropologist James Clifford calls "domains of equivalence."[20] These categories—like kinship, religion, gender, and modernization—are optics that Nakagami seeks to transfer to his understanding of Korea based on his knowledge of Japan: "The differences between Korean and Japanese structures of politics and society are vast."[21] With its plenitude of cultural data that seemed to flourish even in the context of rapid economic development, Korea seems to offer a kind of second life, an example for what Japanese modernity might have been but failed to be under high-speed economic growth of the 1950s through 1970s.

In *Dancing, Seoul*, Nakagami attributes the real estate boom of what was called "the miracle on the Han" to government-regulated economics that incorporated all forms of economic activity into its system and "blocked any exit and caused a huge whirlpool" of activity.[22] He reprises the critical position of writers and scholars he met that emphasizes the gap between those in possession of land and the means of production and "the property-less" (*musansha*, or proletariat). The result was to make

Korea's manufacturing sectors such as shipping, steel, and clothing sur-
pass the fabled "worker bees" of Japan.[23] Nakagami departs this hive of
productivity just as Korea is moving into the orbit of world—especially
Japanese—markets.

Korea's national economic productivity shifted upward just as changes
in diplomatic and economic relations made it easier for visitors to travel
between the two countries, as signaled by President Chun's 1984 visit
to Japan and the 1988 Seoul Olympics. Both celebrants and skeptics of
modernization judged the new exchanges with respect to the twenty-
year anniversary of the 1965 treaty. The Korean government rejected a
Japanese government request to sponsor an official "joint cultural council."[24] Instead, Chun's visit was held against a backdrop of televised performances of Korean folk arts, including the narrative song form of *pansori*
and *namsadang* male dance troupes. These genres would interest Nakagami when he visited and would become the materials he translates to a
Japanese public.[25]

Works Nakagami published in and about Korea beginning in 1978
emphasize kinds of aesthetics and experience that revitalize the idea
of *monogatari*. *Monogatari* shifts from working as the "law and system"
and the daily life-cum-structure that links political and cultural discrimination through units, principles, and overall grammar as it does
in Japan. Nakagami finds *monogatari* active at a populist (*shomin*) level
in Korea, as a proliferating, dynamic deconstructing structure, more
akin to a Bakhtinian vision of polyphony.[26] *Monogatari* puts into modern social and material settings the formal elements itemized by scholars of classical Japanese but does so in the present moment. These
premodern elements found in contemporary Korea include lack of
centralizing perspective, a layered narrative expressed through polyphonic forms, complex and subtle perceptual demands on the reader,
and an open-ended process of composition. *Monogatari* "dance" (*rinbu
suru*) in the dynamic, polyphonic, ethnographic space that is Korea.
The drastically different characteristic from classical *monogatari* is that
Korean *monogatari* have a decidedly modern origin, "the civil war and
the completely senseless artificial border."[27] Korea's dynamism allows
Nakagami to imagine that active resistance against state and popular
discrimination might be possible in a modern, Southern Asian setting
as it is presently not in Japan.

When Nakagami first arrives in Korea, however, he discovers that traces of the old "are being uprooted by those buildings going up one after another."[28] As early as his trip into Seoul from the airport, he laments he has arrived to find what he seeks: "The editor from *Korean Arts* (*Kankoku bungei*) told me that the landscape of Seoul reminded her of the construction boom around the Tokyo Olympics. When I heard her say that, to tell you the truth, it gave me an ominous feeling. My hometown of the Kii peninsula, Kishū Shingū was like that. Actually, all of Japan was like that. When you build new things, inevitably you tear down the old" (20). Poised on what he sees as a threshold, Nakagami investigates folk forms to see how Korean modernization could follow a centrally planned mandate of economic and social reform but also accommodate folk cultures that originated in nomadic outcast life. When he looks at the folk form of Korean mask drama and contemplates the coexistence of *hisabetsu-min* folk forms with modernity, he wonders "what has Japan been doing for the last hundred years?" (35).

Routes of Song

Nakagami's first visit to Korea was prompted by the element of exchange (*kōtsū*) that preoccupies him beginning in the 1970s. His brother-in-law was a *zainichi* Korean resident of Osaka who built and operated a large supermarket chain with branches in Korea. Nakagami first went to Korea to attend a party for a branch opening in the booming industrial city of Ulsan that was the home of Hyundai and boasted Korea's highest per capita income.[29] As he reminds his *zainichi* Korean interlocutors in roundtables, his early first-person stories like "The Very First Happening" feature Korean characters.[30] The story revolves around three boys, including a *zainichi* Korean boy, who build a playhouse called "secret."[31] The boy claims not to be Korean, despite the social world's insistence to the contrary. The status of the narrator's identity remains cryptic. But his acute sympathy with the *zainichi* boy's doubleness suggests an open-ended but structurally similar alienation.

Physical displacement to Korea and a disconnect from the parallax life commuting between center and periphery in Japan seem to have been necessary preconditions for investing in Korea in terms of traveling, writing, and thinking concretely about the specificity of how exchange might affect discrimination for others than *buraku-min*. Encounters with Korean children appear intermittently both in Nakagami's fictions and in descriptions of his own childhood. But they never seem to catalyze his reading and writing like the on-site encounter with people, markets, and performing arts in Korea. It is not until 1985 that he centers a work on a minoritarian character not from the *roji*, a bionovel of the *zainichi enka* singer Miyako Harumi, *Song from the Heavens* (*Ten no uta*).[32] After returning to Japan from his first trip to Korea, Nakagami meets with family members, including a nephew who has moved from Osaka to Ulsan, because "there were only lousy jobs" in Japan.[33] Nakagami remarks that he would "never have had the wherewithal" to listen to the young man at home, and he had not imagined he would "run into" and make connections with "the 'issues' of resident Koreans" (77). Moreover, he writes that he did not start reading Korean fiction until his visit in 1978.

Nakagami's story of what spurred his interest in Korean cultural forms has several variations. All of them revolve around the search to understand popular song. In a roundtable discussion with the *zainichi* Korean actor Ri Saburō, he notes that he was "bowled over" by Yi Saeng-ae, the first singer of Korean popular songs (*minyō*) to become popular in Japan.[34] When she peaked in 1978, the same year of Nakagami's first visit to Korea, Nakagami's karaoke friends urged him to go look for "the roots of popular song," the title of a Yi album.[35] But he did not want to "let it end there" and pursued the materials of song in "something more cultural, more literary" than "the industry" (436). The song that finally propels him to Korea narrates a sibling suicide (*kyōdai shinjū*). The sibling suicide song was local to Shingū and served as the skeleton of his most celebrated work, *The Sea of Withered Trees*. The song was rumored to have been brought there by young women who went to work in the Japanese industrial version of the Silk Road, the Cotton Road, the textile mills of the Nishijin neighborhood in Kyoto. These movements of work song, or exchange, purportedly came back with the young workers to Shingū from the capital where they performed it at O-bon, the annual commemoration of the dead.

The song tells a story of a young man who falls in love with his sister and begs for her to sleep with him for "just a single night." The sister feigns consent and meticulously dresses and puts on makeup. The brother glimpses a figure he thinks is the sister's husband, his archrival. He shoots the figure only to discover it is his sister in disguise. The song rushes to an end as the brother vows to die. Nakagami reads this song as a symbolic inversion of the story of the *Kojiki*, which tells the birth and unfolding of the Japanese imperial family from the incestuous coupling of two sibling gods. In his interpretation, the young girls sent out to work use their improvised songs to link South and capital with their story. The murder of one half of the incestuous couple at the end of the story effectively terminates the imperial line. The sibling suicide song makes impossible the ultimate flourishing of the imperial industry that necessitates the hard commute between Kumano and capital along the Cotton Road.

The 1978 essay "On the Other Side of Landscape" suggests a kind of bridge from Kumano to Korean folkic materials. "On the Other Side of Landscape" opens with a transcription of the song's lyrics followed by a series of questions. Why is the song from Kyoto sung in Kumano? Why does the brother speak so baldly about incest? What is the nature of the bridge where the confrontation occurs, and why does the brother die underneath it? No question is ultimately ever answered. Nor is the origin of the song found. But Shimao Toshio suggests a way to connect popular song in Kumano and Korea through a "hint" in a roundtable in 1978, one that connects Nakagami's prior interest in a Japanese South with a more regional South in Asia. Shimao had published a series of essays on Okinawa between the mid-1950s and 1970, just before Okinawa's reversion to Japan from U.S. possession in 1972. Shimao's essays attempted to redraw the cartography of Japan's cultural identity by emphasizing the dependence of metropole and mainland on peripheral regions such as the Ryūkyū Islands.

His key concept was Yaponesia, a neologism that described an identity he found in the Ryūkyū Islands linking it to Japan geographically, phonically, and culturally. Shimao suggested that southern territories were at the crux of modern Japan's prosperity and had been even since the days of the Satsuma domain's control over the Ryūkyū Islands in the Tokugawa era.[36] He suggests to Nakagami that the same song is sung in Okinawa, "if you change the names of the brother and sister," based on cultural flows within Asia, exchanges that seem apart from mainstream or nationalist Japanese culture.[37] Later, Nakagami was told that the same song exists in Kanagawa and Tokyo (78), two other points in the open-source network of destination cities for workers from the provinces. Nonetheless, Shimao's suggestion leads Nakagami to "look for the roots of song in Korea" through travel, live performances, talking to journalists and performers, and other "improvisational meetings" at competitions and gatherings of musicians.[38] "Drawing that line," he concludes at the end of his trip, "allows us to draw almost an entirely different map of Japan" (79). Nakagami's map, however, goes beyond Japan to connect to a regional imaginary of the South.[39]

To some Korean intellectuals, Nakagami's interest in the folk forms that flourished in the 1980s "Korean boom" recalls Japanese expatriates' attachment to Korean folk forms in the 1920s and 1930s, following on policies of cultural rule (*bunka seiji*) initiated in 1919 in unsettling ways. Nakagami sees his work as different because he is interested in celebrating Korea's vitality, resistance, and capacity to be modern and multiple, not the sorrow and stagnation that earlier commentators found.[40] Writers such as Oba are wary that a "new version of the Japan-Korea treaty system" is being put in place with President Chun's visit. Despite the influx of funds after 1965 and the new cultural flows expected after 1985, Oba fears that, "consciously or unconsciously," new forms of exchange and investment would result in economic vitality that would support the military government and its policies of national defense and state suppression of worker and citizen welfare.[41] Oba suspects that the influx of foreign investment will prioritize industry and transport infrastructure over the needs and welfare of citizens.[42] In effect, he is concerned that soft power will work in the service of hard power. Oba worries further that even though Nakagami celebrates the new diplomatic arrangement that distances itself from colonial domination, his knowledge of Korean folk arts continues to be informed by materials produced by colonial-era Japanese scholars whose fieldwork was conducted under police supervision. Where Nakagami emphasizes their "direct contact" (*sesshoku*), Oba stresses that their job had been to "destroy folk belief systems that were part of the soul that drove the many independence movements after 1919."[43]

Nakagami initially seems unaware of some of the contradictions of embracing Korean folk forms as a salvage ethnography. Namely, he seems unaware of contemporary historical context: the fact that folk forms, like shamanism that he seeks out, were repopularized by students in the context of protesting against normalized diplomatic relations between Korea and Japan that might lead to Japanese neocolonialism by bringing in Japanese capital to finance the military government.[44] Nakagami seems to believe that folk forms and art are enabled by new structures of exchange but that they can exist at a civilian level apart from the government alliances that make them possible. Oba, to the contrary, claims that cultural artifacts cannot be understood apart from their diplomatic conditions of exchange. He backs his own opinion up with dissident poet Kim Chi-ha's writings in the

Japanese magazine *World* (*Sekai*): "The political and economic dependence is already there" pushed by the Nakasone administration such that "all that remains is the cultural dominance in tune with military rule."[45]

But among devotees of Korea, Nakagami was not unique in putting folk forms at the center of his interest in Korea. In the late 1970s, a string of Korean *enka* singers had become popular in Japan. Nakagami was like many newly fascinated with Korea in that his interest was fired by contact with mediums like film and music that promoted liveness as both performance and kinds of media circulation that facilitated contact with real-time events in Korea. In a 1984 interview, Yon Ta-ku, cultural consul at the Korean embassy, had lamented that it was hard to interest people in "contemporary Korean art," and schools and culture centers had difficulty filling the new Hangul reading classes they opened to ride the wave of interest in the mid-1970s.[46] But in contrast, contact with media seen to promote direct contact with Korea thrived. Tourism to Korea doubled in the late 1980s as the Seoul Olympics neared (1). The Mitsukoshi Department Store featured an exhibition on Korea that was so popular that, in 1988, three of eight video stands showing a promo film about Seoul had broken down from overuse. The consul Yon remarked wryly that there were more "splashy" sushi restaurants in Seoul than in Tokyo but that most Koreans still traced Korean-Japanese relations back to Hideyoshi's 1592 invasion of Korea on the heels of his unification of Japan.[47]

Like Yon, for Korean intellectuals who observe Nakagami as *he* observes, Nakagami seems uncomfortably close to reprising a different second life: the life of a Japanese empire whose emissaries had collected Korean folk forms in the 1920s and 1930s. These objects of folk art were "a source for demonstrating that Korea and Japan were one body" but that Japan occupied the role of intellectual head.[48] His first assessments of performing arts admittedly spring from a process of trial and error involved in looking for the cognate of Japanese popular song (*kayōkyoku*).[49] The source of the sibling suicide song never appears, and the personal aesthetic connection between Korea and Japan never pans out. In fact, Nakagami discovers his Japan-based perceptions are so off that their blind spots threaten to make the materials he does see "go to waste."[50] Over time he starts to apprehend structures in Korean cultural forms that both resemble Japanese forms and at times supersede them because they are successful in resisting the state. He begins to look for stories that, like the sibling suicide song, would parody or invert symbolic hierarchies. The new kinds of contact with a Korean South displace his understanding of the highly structural nature of the South as seen in Japanese cultural production like *kokubungaku*. This shift draws on an established rhetoric of the therapeutic South to promise innovation, healing, and escape from the rigors of Tokyo and its literature's focuses on "landscape, confession, interiority and expression."[51]

The sought-after vitality is seen in new kinds of writing and a new emphasis on direct experiences of intensity, immediacy, depth, color, and contrast that follow upon this new phase of travel. Ironically, given Nakagami's chronically agonistic distance from "landscape, confession, and interiority," the emphasis on the idiosyncrasy of personal experience ties him firmly to the twentieth-century idiom of I-fiction. His particular emphasis on experience acquired through encounters with the South derive less from naturalism and more from the writing pioneered in the early twentieth century that sees narrating life (*seimei*) as the primary goal of fiction writing. Known as Taishō vitalism, these philosophical and literary writings were published by people such as Tanabe Hajime, who coined the term, as well as a side array of thinkers that include socialist Osugi Sakae, fiction writers Shimamura Hōgetsu and Arishima Takeo, and poet Hagiwara Sakutarō. All of these people placed the human desire to unite with universal "life" at the center of meaning and sought to see the working of this life beneath the dynamism of a civilization based on machinery and the laws of the physical world.[52] Though they drew on thinkers like Henri Bergson, these Taishō-era writers often sought ways that departed from, or transcended, forms of modernity that were painted as Western. When they looked for ways to overcome modernity, some writers looked at pan-Asian sources that seemed to signal a common cultural context with Japan but suggest that Japan was more advanced in apprehending the universal forms it could use to guide other Asian countries, some of which became colonies. One key difference is that Nakagami's focus on vitality and overcoming modernity by seeing its second life in Korea occurs in external moments of contact, especially in performances and markets. It is not found within the internal psychic space of recollection, memory, and interiority.

Liveness

In contrast to textually oriented archivists or object collectors, Nakagami turns to kinds of performance that can exploit the element of "liveness" in a direct relation with an audience. Philip Auslander defines liveness as "the functions and values attributed to live performance" in a mediatized age when media threaten to usurp the live form's position in a cultural economy.[53] Part of the appeal of liveness is populism, and part is dynamism: "In Japan, there are things like Noh and *kyōgen*, but they are really highbrow. They have gotten high-class, and the most important thing has been lost. But in Korea, there are many [traditional arts] left."[54] After all, Nakagami complains, Japan is so inert that people use recorded karaoke to entertain themselves when they go out drinking. In contrast to this accommodation to mass recorded culture, energetic Koreans "bang on the tables and really sing."[55] Such a successful salvage is impossible to accomplish in Japan. He expresses despair and anger at Japan's discrimination against folk forms, especially those derived from outcast culture in favor of "artificial music programmed into a computer and tidied up to satisfy consumer demand, like Pink Lady."[56] For Nakagami, the collective production of folk forms preserved an attachment to "nature" that was mocked in mediated mass cultural forms. Pink Lady was a stylized and TV-friendly duet of girlish singers. When they became popular, they traded in the rustic overalls of their debut and performed by ripping off kimonos to unveil slinky beaded dresses to the tune of disco cover songs. Needless to say, in Nakagami's interpretation they diverged fatally from the folk tradition and darkness (*yami*) of *enka* song, with its open-source interchangeable elements filled by local contexts of negativity and suffering produced by modernity.[57]

Korea contrasts favorably to Japanese vestiges of folk forms. Nakagami derides Osore-zan, the site of Japan's biggest annual festival of shamans. People throng to Osore-zan to consult mediums who converse with the world of the dead, a practice called *kuchiyose* (literally, putting your mouth close to both god and client to mediate between the spirit world and human world). The mountain is located in the rugged far north of the main island of Honshū, a long difficult journey whose distance in space is often felt to correspond to a distance in time. Despite this seeming separation from daily life, Nakagami complains that "the kind of shamanism you get at Osore-zan is different than the real shamanism we've been talking about . . . It's gotten to be a real spectacle . . . I used to be delighted because they gave voice to spirit thoughts by *kuchiyose*, but these days it feels like you're buying a hamburger at McDonald's."[58] His irritation at the almost franchised nature of *kuchiyose* shamans derives from the sense that prophecies and channelings are not distinct from one to the next. Also, Nakagami dislikes that in the Osore-zan tours visitors choose one over another because they are able to place a spiritual order that is duly delivered in a standardized and cost-effective way, just as they would do at a fast food restaurant. The shamans then respond to competition and marketing as part of a tourist constellation, not to the actual relation (or performance of one) between visitor and spirit world. This disenchanted vision of *kuchiyose* provides a far less satisfying spiritual and communal reality than Nakagami's interpretation of Korean shamanism does: "You notice that shamanism has a hold at the bottom of Koreans' daily lives. It only remains in a tiny bit of Japan, but in Korea, it lives on visibly in daily life."[59]

Nakagami is first obsessed with Korean shamanism because its instruments, song forms, and performers' origins in outcast classes seem to correspond to a successfully salvaged version of outcast (*senmin*) arts lost in Japan.[60] His admiration for Korean shamanism is explicitly tied to its ability to maintain an original connection with life. In Japan, Nakagami writes, the former "killer of cows"—or outcast who was once charged with transporting life (*seimei*) from one realm to another in Noh theater, kabuki, ikebana, and other artistic practices (*gei*)—has become a mere worker and lost touch with both art and religion (30). Korea has salvaged that connection and preserves (*hoji*) shamanism as the first "interpretation" (*kaidoku*) of nature. The dichotomy formed between Japan and Korea breaks down along lines of original and copy but also around commodity forms that seem to demand no dialogue between cultural form and reader and no act of reading in the performer.

Nakagami takes a series of trips around Seoul and around the southwest Chŏlla province with an eye to viewing shamanism, *pansori,* and mask drama as exemplary folk forms in which performers and producers make direct contact with an audience. Nakagami's knowledge of *pansori* and mask drama comes from scholarly books, conversations with scholars, and site visits to both the National Art School in Seoul and more vernacular mask drama performances in Chŏngju. He weaves an elaborate ethnography of the role performers play in social resistance. Most importantly, these performers might maintain a relation to outcast folk forms because, even into the twentieth century, the narrators of *pansori* and *kwangdae,* typically come from hereditary shaman households.[61]

Pansori is a solo oral technique that is dramatic, musical, told in verse, and accompanied only by a drum. Performances are often held outdoors, include audiences of aristocrats as well as commoners, contain a great variety of rhythms, and are products of serial composition. Like the *sekkyō-bushi* songs Nakagami admires from Kumano, *pansori* comprises a huge archive of plots, effects, allusions, and local details. Like *sekkyō-bushi,* it was not put into written notation until several hundred years after it began, in the late nineteenth century; and despite being anthologized in a standard form, it has many improvised elements. *Pansori* is also most likely conceptually agreeable to him because it probably comes from the geographic South of Korea, Chŏlla province.[62]

The *pansori* about which Nakagami writes most extensively is a song about a love affair between a prostitute and a member of the *yangban* aristocratic class. Unable to tell what is standard and what is improvised when he listens, Nakagami later seeks out a standard version of the libretto in an anthology. He emphasizes the elements he sees that are mobile and structure openness into their form. It is as if he transposes the mobile narrator, multiple enunciative position, and use of figural language straight from classical scholars' undoing of *monogatari* in Tokyo and finds its living qualities in Korea. Most importantly, the open-source flexibility of parts signals to him the unfixed nature of its narrator's social status. Like his opaque nature of the *roji,* he is excited by a refusal to represent a speaking position that could be mobilized for populist political resistance and recuperated by the democracy movement. This unfixed nature of the form marks a historical condition, not a historical identity: "not wandering performers, but discriminated-against people who were shooed away from fixed living situations" (35) and not even mobilized to legitimate or decorate formal religious ceremonies.

Nakagami perceives that the situation of *hisabetsu-min* in Korea was similar to that in Japan but even more extreme. They were not granted protection by temples or shrines and thus did not have connections to the emperor, which resulted in a status as both exalted and abjected. This distinction marks Korean outcast performers as different from Japanese performers who are beginning to be the object of writings in the late 1970s. Amino Yoshihiko's pioneering writings about medieval itinerant culture articulated how the commercial economy of medieval Japan was intimately related to mobile populations who earned their livings through primarily nonagricultural means.[63] One of the implications of his writings was that Japanese multiculturalism was not suppressed by imperial power but intimately dependent on it, precisely the point Nakagami made about exchange (*kōtsū*). Amino stresses that in Japan some drifters and travelers were forced into itinerancy, but other artisans and entertainers maintained patron-itinerant relationships and were allowed freedoms denied to people with fixed residence. Nakagami does not quote Amino, but this framework is evident when he compares Japanese itinerants to Korea. Here in Korea, he says, folk performers were forced to keep moving and could only stop moving in marketplaces. The elements of market interaction and market survival are key to Nakagami's appreciation of *pansori* and mask drama as an itinerant art.

> Mask drama and kabuki and Noh, all have to be acknowledged as starting from itinerant arts.
> After some time, Noh was taken under the wing of temples and shrines, and was patronized by the warrior class ascending in power, and in a similar way, kabuki, though it was started by *kawaramono,* started to be supported by the rising merchant class, and took off. In the end, both Noh and kabuki found their place, their "topos." The topos for Noh was in the singing, for kabuki it happened in collusion with the accompaniment and the stagehands, and they came into their own by cumulatively adding elements.
> How does it work with mask drama, I wonder? Fixed forms and improvisation mingle in the performance, and in the case of *pongsan* mask drama, you can see the remnants of five hundred years of discrimination and exclusion held against its artisans during the Yi dynasty. If there's no temple or shrine to provide nomadic artists with a space there's no patronage. This is speculation on my part, but the fact that there was not a money economy or that the money economy hadn't taken off, must have made the performer's lives one step bleaker. Which is to say, what is striking about Korean performing arts, especially the practitioners of mask drama, is the mark of the topos-less topos, the *mudan*.
> I find this fascinating. The luster of rawness, or what you might call the abject (*sen*) quality, one of the great pulls of performing arts, still persists, where it has been lost given that Noh and kabuki

have found their place. This is where the appeal of the *namsadang*
troupes—which have as good as vanished—and the musical *samu-*
runori groups comes through.[64]

Nakagami is also able to see performance of *pongsan* mask drama, the genre
he favors. In 1967 *pongsan* drama had been named a National Treasure.
Some librettos were anthologized in Japanese, including the production
Nakagami reads. The seven episodes of the play tell a standard story filled in
around with separate episodes. Four young monks abandon their strict rev-
erential ways upon meeting eight more dissolute monks. One of the elder
monks falls in love with a shamaness and is punished. Nakagami singles
out three elements that elevate *pansori* and mask drama above Noh or any
Japanese folk form. First, the protagonist is collective: "There is nothing personal about it."[65] Second, the stage is on the same plane as the spectators.
This reprises the open-air locations where the players were chased to put on
drama and dance shows. Existing on the same plane also allows for the audience to be part of the drama, use "lots of ad-libs," and look right back at the
spectators.[66] And, third, playing to farmers meant that a social critique could
take place. This social critique, however, is limited by contemporary Korean
interpreters to satire against bureaucrats, officials, and corrupt elites.

    Nakagami is confident of his own viewing of this "luster," which has sur-
vived two expulsions: one from the *kan* (bureaucrats) and another from
the *min* (people).[67] But gradually he becomes frustrated by the fact that
some of the forms that he embraced, like mask drama, have been singled
out for reward and recognition by the state's National Treasure System and
have become severed from their nomadic outcast roots—a disappointing reprisal of Japan's mass culture transformation with similar effects in
the high culture realm. The fact that resistance writers and scholars have
praised these folk forms as satire of elites by populists also disappoints him.
"Isn't taking it as satire" of the aristocratic classes "too much like pure ideology?" (46). Alternately, "seeing it as just *yangban* versus populist (*shomin*)
satire leeches out the fullness of *pansori* and mask drama."[68] The element
that is cut out is the intense sexuality of the male players' eroticism that
makes it a "magnetic field of sex."[69] It is not clear whether it is the male-
male sexuality itself or the open possibilities of sexual transgression writ
large that overturn the order, but the play contains, like Bakhtin's carnival,
a "force of gravity that overturns" conventional relations between men and
women, aggressor and aggressed.[70] This relation is neither sanctioned by

formal religions like Buddhism nor patronized through the imperial system like *Noh*.[71] Nakagami's ideal as seen in Korean folk forms seems to combine elements of a premodern oral past with value on form that is open enough to incorporate contemporary references, an openness that itself refers back to the existential situation of its performers in a way that exalts rather than laments their on-the-run aesthetic of the marketplace. To Nakagami, this mingling of past and open form is most accessible in the marketplace as a whole, even outside of the performance space.

Marketplace and Museum

Tearing down the old in favor of the new, conceding to linear time, is what Japan has done too well, in Nakagami's opinion. In Korea he pursues a different relation to time, one that furnishes kinds of experience that used to exist in Japan but are no longer available. Not only does time not move in a linear fashion, but it is multiple and dynamic and best witnessed in outdoor markets, the latter-day equivalents of the outcast performers' "topos":

> As is well known, there is no place that is as misunderstood as Korea. Sometimes you suspect the misunderstanding is welcome, and this makes a *monogatari*-writer like me shout for joy, and if I can explain to Japanese readers the multi-polar, multi-layered dancing *monogatari* so they can see it, they will understand this country's populist folk customs, the landscape of the elderly men and women who sell things in the crowded marketplace and street-corners, and readers will be able to get a glimpse of how what's going on in 1981 can co-exist at the same time as court-era customs. This is the populist folk landscape of the Silla and Yi dynasties, but at the same time, to a *monogatari*-writer, the situation suggests the Japanese medieval court period (*ōchō-ki*), and just when I realize that suggestion is unsustainable the perspective breaks, and the *monogatari* starts to dance.[72]

His comparison to the market of the "Japanese medieval court period" suggests a social ideal that is popular and apart from imperial life—fluid, decentered, and dynamic. His ideal combines elements of the museum and the market and is presented in media that incorporate visual elements and have the effect of intensifying the direct contact with Korea. Realizing that his vision of the populist landscape of hundreds of years ago is actually "unsustainable" breaks Nakagami's reverie. But the conceit that Seoul's residents, especially elderly ones, can traverse these multiple temporalities unconsciously as part of their daily life sustains his writings and transfers on to writings that are set in Japan. The Korean marketplace is at once the showcase of "a new young country, and also an old country that possesses four thousand years of history."[73] He urges other tourists to go for a viewing of elderly people: "You should take time and venture away from your tour group and peek around this corner, if you have time to see the market, the elderly people who 'sell things in order to live.'"[74] The elderly transcend a possible contradiction between capitalism and tradition and make public space into an open-air sort of museum, unbounded by walls and institutions.

The market is Nakagami's most privileged site of insight and vitality, offering the kind of epiphany he is unable to secure even in performing arts because they have been sacralized and suffocated, either in the National Treasure System or by dissidents who want to claim them for antiauthoritarian purposes. I take the term "market epiphany" from Alfred López and Ashok Mohapatra. They coined this term to describe the encounter that writers profess when they visit India and find informants who support their predisposed views. Neoliberal journalist Thomas Friedman quotes an Indian engineer to ratify his delight that the "world is flat."[75] The Indian engineer-pundit he interviews declares to him that globalization is "a good thing . . . a new milestone in human progress and a great opportunity for India and the world."[76] For ethnographer Paulo Favero, the bustling street market is a "sensory experience . . . representative of public space in contemporary urban India."[77] López and Mohapatra disagree with the conclusion held by each, writing that, "in each case, India is the catalyst for a desired epiphany . . . in both examples, the writer/researcher deploys a particular image of India that in turn informs their staged epiphany in a calculated and predictable way."[78] For Friedman, this is the human intellectual capital, and for Favero it is the street-level market with tour guides. For each writer, the moment of contact with the market that allows the epiphany fosters both a kind of personal transcendence and an epistemological revelation at the same time. One could add to this list Lafcadio Hearn's classical ethnographic account of a night market at a temple that features insects for sale, whose exchange and commerce enables human consumers to connect not only to the natural world but to a past in which nature, technology, and poetics mingle on the same plane.[79] To call Nakagami's epiphany "staged" plays up the preparation rather than the after-the-fact crafting of the incident. But it does offer a simi-lar sense of transport and fusion of episteme and affect.

In *Dancing, Seoul*, published seven years later, he places the same ideas of market and museum at the center of his description. Korea exhibits a histor-ical continuity that is both unbroken and appears like a museum of artifacts that are extinct in Japan: "Korea has lots of old, nostalgic things that make you think of the things that people in Japan knew before the war but are no longer here in the 1980s."[80] And every time he goes out, he writes,

> Especially in Seoul, I saw the place become more and more brim-ming with mysteriousness and overflowing with interest . . . Anyway, one of the special features of Korean culture is that it is full of mul-tiple *monogatari*, and, moreover, these things still give off a luster of the primitive . . . You can get a glimpse of these multiple *monogatari* first and foremost in the daily life around the market and the streets. To put it simply, until 70 years ago Korea was dynastic. Life around the market and the streets—to put it in the perspective of Japan— was the vibrant life described in the world of *Konjaku monogatari* and *Uji shūi monogatari*, the world outside the court in medieval tales (*ōchō monogatari*). After it was liberated from the seed of modernity of the era of colonial governance that Japan had brought in, Koreans fostered the seed that America brought as modernity.[81]

The idea of Korea as a museum has been a persistent and a contested model in Korea-Japanese relations since the colonial era. Envisioning Korea as a museum of forms that recall Japan but are no longer there updates ideas about aesthetic nationalism that were published a cen-tury earlier but locates them in Korea. In 1906, art educator and scholar Okakura Tenshin wrote that Japan's isolation made it the "real repository of the trust of Asiatic thought and culture . . . thus Japan is a museum of Asiatic civilization."[82] His essays on Japan's leading role in pan-Asian spirituality and aesthetics were later taken to be intellectual justifications of Japan prevailing over other less developed Asian followers through imperial rule. In the 1920s and 1930s, the split between Japan as theorist and other Asian regions as producers was illustrated in the practices of Japanese collectors and connoisseurs of folk art. Japanese residents and tourists in Korea collected crafts that were mass produced by hand and included pottery, textiles, and calligraphy. Koreans themselves were, in the collectors' dominion, oblivious to the beauty of these objects because they produced their works as "unknown craftsmen" without the effort of consciousness and without subjecting them to the standards of a dualistic world such as "beauty" and "ugliness."[83]

The new category of *mingei,* or folk craft, was invented by Yanagi Sōetsu (1889–1961) and colleagues like the potters Hamada Shōji (1894–1978) and Kawai Kanjirō (1890–1966). *Mingei* referred to what Yanagi characterized as "unself-consciously handmade and unsigned for the people by the people, cheaply and in quantity" found in objects of unstressed and ordinary everyday life (*getemono*).[84] Nakagami likens his own observations to those *mingei* collectors in a roundtable with comparative anthropologist Han U-san: "The thing that really struck me the most was that visible things (*miru mono*) and audible things (*kiku mono*) were the soul of culture. Even though modernization has taken place, these things are still very much present. You hear this often, but Yanagi Sōetsu made a big fuss over a bowl (*owan*) that a cat uses. To him it was a magnificent thing. As a metaphor, I think that still holds."[85]

The museological elements of *monogatari* that Nakagami singles out are different than the *mingei* objects because he finds these "visible things" and "audible things" primarily in the social and cultural forms of the people who trade them rather than in the material objects themselves. The bowl functions as a metaphor for *monogatari* because Nakagami transfers it from the register of objects to one of social forms, the experience of vitality one has when seeing and hearing, encounters with reality that stimulate the senses. Both approaches clearly elevate the Japanese traveler over the Korean objects. Nakagami's appreciation differs because his is a traveling connoisseurship. He pursues direct contact with reality that requires immersion on location where cultural forms are produced, rather than collecting and carrying away the artifact. The arts that most offer this direct contact with reality are performing arts of *pansori* narrative singing and mask drama. But when Nakagami writes elements of Korean folk forms into his own fiction, it is the marketplace venue that most acutely captures direct contact with *senmin* vitality.

Photorealism

The sense of a heightened animated contact with reality in Korea is most vividly conveyed in a series of photo-prose works Nakagami does with photographers. All three books are lushly designed mixed-media ethnographic books published outside of pure literature publishing houses. *Korea*, part of a series of 1982 coffee-table books featuring Shinoyama Kishin's panoramas of the Silk Road, was published by Shūeisha, a magazine and manga publisher that also produced *Weekly Playboy*, where Nakagami often published essays, and *Shonen Jump*. *Dancing, Seoul*, another photo-prose work with Shinoyama, was published in 1985 by Kadokawa shoten. Kadokawa was run by the charismatic Kadokawa Haruki, pioneer of the "media mix" strategy that changed Japanese film production by delinking it from pure literature and tying blockbusters to genre fiction and huge advertising campaigns.[86] Parco, the publisher of *Monogatari Seoul*, revolutionized department stores by installing small couture boutiques that featured primarily Japanese designers in its Shibuya store. Parco also exhibited subculture art and was connected to many subcultures of the New Aka era, including Libro Bookstore and several performance halls. Nakagami's turn away from pure literature and Japanese sources material to Korea and more visually oriented media had the ironic effect of showcasing authentic moments of cultural contact that were themselves enabled by the relativization of media forms.

The first collaboration with Shinoyama was titled simply *Korea* and is essentially a road trip through Korean villages and major cities following Shinoyama's prolific "just take it" (*gutto yotte toru*) style of candid photography. He had pioneered this style on popular journalistic subjects such as nudes, "idol" singers, and food in Japan, as well as old-world locales like Venice, Rome, and Egypt, done in frequent collaboration with the architect Isozaki Arata. *Korea* begins with a night ferry from Cheju and tours through a number of rural villages, featuring candid shots of houses, massive varieties of food, and groups of single-sex workers in fields. The color photos present Korean land and people literally closer to life. Images are framed either in close up to capture facial expressions or in wide shot to capture a panoramic landscape. Shots of domestic life are interleaved with many festivals and pageants, like performances of the song "Arirang," folk dance competitions, and uncaptioned photos that capture people— farmers, children, and masked people—going to or from festive occasions in uncomposed scenes of movement.

Nakagami's commentary hinges on the power of photos to circulate rather than specific responses to Shinoyama's images. As in other works, he singles out the market as a place of open access where "anyone" can enter and enjoy, thronging (*afureru*) with people and things abounding in a disordered state, spanning "5,000 years of history from the classical past to now."[87] He is fascinated by the market because unlike in Japan, except for Osaka, the goods are not all brand new; they, too, have been passed from place to place and life to life. The market features many amateur entrepreneurs who sell second-hand goods, improvising their touts and their goods depending on the needs of the day, without an official plan.

Nakagami's second work with Shinoyama, *Dancing, Seoul,* was a result of their travels together, composed in a style called "Shinorama." This showy neologism riffed on the supersized and colorful atmosphere of Cinemascope and the curved screen of Cinerama projection in movie theatres. Cinerama was designed to provide a sense of depth and realism by using a wide, curved screen whose field of view tugged at the viewer's peripheral vision, challenging the eye's ability to take in the scene as a whole. Shinoyama's photo composition follows Cinerama's way of composing images, which had originated in photography of travelogues and surveys of spectacles. Each image is formed from three separate thirty-five millimeter films, or three cameras.[88] The effect in both media formats is to project a landscape that is just out of visual reach, larger than life and probably more colorful, to immerse the viewer in a reality in which he finds himself a "participant": "a man walking down a city street, for example, hears not only the sounds directly in front of him, but also those on the side, and behind him as well. The Cinerama film process attains these effects of real life by surrounding the viewer completely with action and sound in an environment."[89] *Dancing, Seoul's* panoramas are printed on two-dimensional glossy paper that folds out from the book, and the curve must be supplied by the reader who unfolds the image. But their panoramic dimensions and vibrant colors underscore the sense of outsized scale and plenitude of the markets that Nakagami describes.[90]

These kinds of direct contact with reality and the mode of ethnographic capture enabled by media that privilege "liveness" and plenitude begin to transform Nakagami's fiction writing. The photos emphasize the vitalist register of South-ness. This animation and dynamism is apparent in Nakagami's colloquial narrative style, in the parallel glosses (*okurigana*) in Hangŭl of particular words like "market" and elderly "granny," and in his choice of descriptions clustering around the ideas of vitality (*katsuki*), dynamism, and things that overflow (*afureru*). This emphasis on vitality occurs in ways that recall his earlier literary uses of recorded music, especially free jazz, as models outside Japan that have achieved relationships with received tradition that exceed structures of domination and subordination. *Monogatari Seoul* is composed of a novel intercut with photo plates. The prose tells the story of migrants who move between center and periphery seeking work and bringing the energy of action and conversation to the metropole. This vitality is the basis for Nakagami's reassessment of fictional style. *Monogatari Seoul* concerns a woman who comes to Seoul a few years after the Korean War, against a market as its backdrop. It interweaves two stories. One, the focus of the narrative, is the story of this female immigrant from the countryside we know only in her collective function as "the woman" for two-thirds of the novel. The drama occurs as her life intersects with a male folk hero named Changil, a "grand thief" on the order of Robin Hood whose experience in Vietnam soured him on the corruption of elites. Araki's photos of interior spaces in hotels and houses punctuate the story about the woman whose life is completely overturned by the Korean War.[91] She drifts from the country to Seoul and ends up selling scavenged goods in a marketplace. The photos seem to map out possible lives for the woman or sights she might see in the market or streets or in her bundles of second-hand goods. Her alternate lives as a prostitute in a functional but tattered hotel room are also envisioned. *Monogatari Seoul*'s protagonist is defined entirely by terms that give her value from within the market and its collective inhabitants. The idea of "exchange" that Nakagami first theorized in his discussions with Karatani now drives the fictional world:

> It all started because of the civil unrest, when everyone in the market came from somewhere else, and put down a tiny bit of money to lay in a stock of things to sell. When the world calmed down, somehow people figured out who came from where. But when the woman showed up, not in the immediate aftermath, but now, carrying her small children, asking everybody around the market if they had seen her husband who had just randomly walked off one day, everyone thought she cut a strange figure. The women who worked at the market said, "Well, if he just walked off like that, he'll probably come wandering back just like that one of these days."

Men are like that they said, and laughed. Most of the male laborers who worked for the stores in the market said, "It's no longer a crisis time when we run out of food in the early spring." But carriers, one or two levels of sub-contractor below those who worked in the stores, or wanderers who would deliver any kind of a thing if you would ask them, nodded, "You've got that right." The laborers who worked as movers knew well the reasons that would lead anyone to walk out of the house "just like that," just as they knew exactly why a man would come sashaying back to his wife and kids.

Should she still keep looking for that guy, or should she just give it up and consider him a bird that flew from its cage? But even though she had just started and had barely started to make any money, she'd gotten a real attitude and got into fights with customers over petty little amounts of money. At the chaotic cross-roads she lined up some hideously colored cheap panties or plastic shower caps on a sheet of plywood sitting on top of a hand-drawn trolley-turned-to-a-stand. Pulling on the elastic of some flamingly red kids' panties, she said, "No matter how much you'd get discount on these, they'd never fit you well," and tried to holler them. The female customers would just retort right back, "you're really trying the hard sell, aren't you."[92]

The story is, on the one hand, a rags-to-riches ethnographic narrative. It follows a displaced entrepreneur who starts from scratch with no resources after the Korean War, bands with other war refugees, and looks and listens in participant-observation tradition to clear a space for herself in a scavenger's economy. Her story contains elaborate descriptions of material culture that are packed with an amount of realist detail not found in other Nakagami works. These objects and practices include the space she makes to live, her choice of street-worn goods for sale, her daily routines, her ongoing and increasingly tight-knit relations with the other people in the *roji*, and even her travails of PMS.

At the same time, the story is underwritten by the highly generic plot conventions of melodrama that typically structure Nakagami's works with female protagonists. Secondary characters, too, retain the integrity of their peasant station while protesting the corruption of civil servants and businessmen, bandits in disguise who exploit them in narratives by writers such as Kim Chi-ha. The backstory of elite corruption that spurred the character Changil to turn to the underground economy also inspired Kim's spleenful comic masterwork *Five Bandits,* one of the star texts of the *minjung* (people's) movement.[93] *Monogatari Seoul* is a melodramatic pica-resque tale about the woman's accidental encounter that takes the side of the bandits. Her story begins—in the market, naturally—with Changil, a larger-than-life personage she first meets when he does her a good deed. He helps her carry some heavy sweets to her lodgings. It is only after gos-sip whirls that she discovers he is a legendary thief whose name falls from "elderly ladies' lips like that of a lover, and he is treated like the young-est brother of the old men."[94] They run into each other at night in the street, and, just as the light goes out, he confesses under the moonlight that he is a "formidable thief who runs around the city and stirs things up."[95] While he is whispered about and adored by the people (*shomin*), his efforts are directed to a Robin Hood–like sabotage of corporate entities and infrastructures.

One night the woman passes a truck being loaded with appliances from a department store, loot supplied by Changil. His machinations grow in scale from household goods to stock market manipulations, and the story ends by turning into a piece of speculative fiction. The woman becomes friendly with a group of Vietnam vets and is a secret member of their activities as aides to Changil. Changil vanishes, leav-ing many rumors in his wake, as if "an action movie lead had died in the middle," trailing only an echo of cicadas in the *roji* and in the mar-ket.[96] The reference to action movies most likely refers to the narrative of "turning the world upside down" (*gekokujō*) or inverting the hierar-chy between vassal and lord that structures many postwar action films, ninja movies, and *yakuza* films, as well as many episodes of rebellion in the medieval historiography of Japan. Seven days after Changil's disap-pearance, as if the world turning upside down were a memorial to him, the "only *zaibatsu* in Korea dissolves, and people setting out for the market saw a wealth of stocks, private wealth, state capital, savings, dia-monds and rubies floating down the middle of Seoul in the Han River," followed by bottles of Suntory whisky, blankets, alligator wallets, and a bounty of luxury goods.[97] The market people recover all these items, and Changil is remembered "like an action-movie hero."[98] In his stead the woman rises, "like another Changil."[99] The triumphalist ending of this work is entirely unlike that of previous Nakagami works. Many of his celebrated middle works, such as *A Thousand Years of Pleasure,* are striking for the early, violent deaths of young men. Each chapter of *A Thousand Years* tells the story of the sad end of a young man unable to use bad-boy gang lives as an exit or even an economically viable alternative to mainstream life. While Changil vanishes mysteriously, perhaps killed by a Vietnam war buddy or a rival, in no other Nakagami work does a story end with a woman poised to succeed, much less in the male field of gangsterism.

In keeping with the ethnographic elements of the South that Nakagami had highlighted in his essays, the populist version of the market is the site of all crossings and the place where experience acquires its greatest value. The two fictions that Nakagami imagined with respect to Korea, the perpetrator, and the action hero, are fused together in the next phase of his work. This choice of heroic genre is absolutely appropriate, given that Nakagami's idealism of Korea centers on its ability to manifest medieval dynamics without anachronism in modern times. And, moreover, it fulfills a narrative pattern that, in his eyes, was unavailable or invisible to Japanese history. The outsider hero is useful for things he does rather than useful as Ushimatsu was in *The Broken Commandment*, useful because he left. This, too, inverts the hierarchy of the tragic outsider as an example of tragic enlightenment that Nakagami had tried to write against for decades in Japan.

Panorama and Perpetration

The new process of encounter with the direct reality of Southern spaces, beginning with Korea, furnishes a frame for reimagining Japan in terms of a regional Asian identity, one that comes to terms with its perpetrator past in the Pacific War. Nakagami's works following his Southern turn consist of narratives that feature Japanese national characters who identify with the Southern regions of their own country and try to establish postcolonial relationships with the Souths of Japan's historical past. In his extended tour to look for the roots of folk songs in Korea, Nakagami stands on an overlook in Chŏngju. The point of view that narrates produces the same formal sweep as the coffee-table book images. Using this synoptic point of view, he narrates a historical account of Japanese writers' engagement with Japan's history in Korea. He uses this panoramic view to assert an overview of Japanese literary history in which he "discovers"

the postwar writers and the Third Generation are the same. They
have consistently described the war from the side to whom damage
was done (*higai-sha*), and there has not once been a time when
they tried to describe it from the perpetrator's (*kagai-sha*) side.
Looking at the landscape over the river of Chŏngju, I was overcome by the urge to do so, like an urge to scratch my foot through
my shoe, and as someone born after the war, a glimpse of such a
novel describing the war and the invasion floated through my head.
The novel that I would write, knowing nothing actual about the
war and the invasion, would be about a student who comes to this
city, Chŏngju, to study the traditional arts of *pansori* and *kamen-
geki*, and while exploring the past, and the history, and the customs
of the Koreans he meets, starts to take notice of the debates on
invading Korea (*seikan-ron*) and becomes gradually aware of the
beginning of war and invasion.

   He will investigate. To investigate is to disclose (*abaku*). Not
exactly to Korea as a nation state, but to this quiet town Chŏngju
in Northern Chŏlla province. To gestate a *monogatari*, it might be
a good idea to draw on the *Kojiki* and the *Nihon shoki*. Looking at
Chŏngju, instantly reading the novel that would take Chŏngju as
its focal point, knowing that this is to disclose the things that our
fathers and mothers did, and also disclose myself, my thoughts
grew heavy.[100]

Four things are worth noting in the above reverie. First, is the wholesale
claim that no writer since 1945 has written about wartime complicity,
violence, or collaboration. This seems overstated considering the scenes
of anti-Korean violence in Ōta Yoko's 1948 atom-bomb memoir *City of
Corpses* (*Shikabane no machi*) or village violence against foreigners held
captive examined in Oe's *The Catch* (*Shiiku*) or *The Silent Cry*, not to
mention the memoirs and first-person stories of Yasuoka Shōtarō, Endo
Shūsaku, and Kojima Nobuo, for example, published in the 1970s. What
I take from this rather broad claim is that postwar and Third Generation writers tended to emphasize a quality of loss. In Van Gessel's words,
the Third Generation writers dwelled on a "loss of a sense of place, of a
spiritual home from which they could derive solace or inspiration," and
investigated this "self-dismantlement" largely in works about family and
domestic life.[102] For Nakagami, as I mentioned earlier, the postwar period

was a time of gains, not losses, because it began to legislate education for *buraku* children. This point is related to the second, the significance of the time period when Nakagami would set his novel. *Seikan-ron* refers to the 1873 debate over a Japanese attack on Korea because it did not recognize the authority of Meiji Japan. The effect was to contest the unequal treaties that would knit Korea, through the terms of international law, into a modern economy of nation-states. In effect, this plot would be a historical novel examining the motivations of elites beginning the initial stages of annexing Korea into the empire.

Third is Nakagami's claim that he is not writing about "Korea as a nation" but about the specific locale of Chŏngju. Because of its intensity of relation to folk arts, it qualifies as a regional South, connected to the larger idea of the global South. Behind this specificity, I think, is the doubled sense of subordination experienced by folk artists he seeks out in Chŏngju who are both Korean and outcasts. And fourth is the choice of verb for "disclose," *abaku*. Instead of a more neutral verb like express, disclose, or even represent, Nakagami uses a word that contains a character for violence (*bō*, 暴), connecting words and discourse. The student's dawning awareness of his position vis-à-vis the two nations is framed in terms of violence and complicity of Nakagami's parents' generation. While the novel is never written, fictionalized portraits and essays demonstrate Nakagami's attempt to sketch the perpetrator actions of the earlier generation without "falling into a weird masochism."[103]

This chapter traced the meanings of South that Nakagami employed in order to understand and convey the South as a structural position vis-à-vis an industrial North, with a focus on Korea as a developing country that still maintained its South-ness though it was in danger of disappearing. I looked at how three registers of South appear in Nakagami's writings on Korea: the biographical, the vitalist experiential, and the colonial-historical. Korea, as a country with an enviably anterior relation to time, offered materials for experiencing a second chance of modernity where multiple senses of time could coexist without becoming obsolete, and a kind of vitality to daily life prevailed in small-time entrepreneurs. Nakagami's emphasis on person-to-person exchange in a marketplace—the "live" form of a market—sidesteps debates about the different ontological statuses of live and mediated forms. Rather, it both reprises the observing stance of collectors of the colonial era and anticipates the dynamics of collecting and exchanging put into place by historically contingent *otaku* and fan communities characteristic of subculture, thoroughly saturated in capitalism and economic relationships.

My final chapter takes up the popular media of comics and a gangster serial novel that continue to represent the perpetrator in terms of conflicted colonial desire. Well before Murakami Takashi's Superflat movement and popular character novels, Nakagami's work anticipated millennial shifts in characterization and media forms that discarded psychological realism as the benchmark of a good story while retaining strong links to major themes and conflicts of canonical literature now told in the mode and medium of genre fiction. Ironically, as I discuss in the next chapter, at the very time that his long-term mission to bring together writing and ethnography seemed to be appearing in popular genres and venues, it was also the most scorned. Critics did not admit that popular forms like manga and anime could be in informed dialogue with historical issues, and they have ignored the thematics of anticolonial and antiracist solidarity that this collection of characters strongly promotes. Characters in the works I now turn to are all young men who revisit sites that the Japanese military invaded or occupied in the last years of the Pacific War.

· CHAPTER 6 ·

Subculture and the South

Literature versus Subculture

Distribution of fan-based subcultures like character goods and anime has flourished outside Japan since the mid-1990s. At the same time, most new research and venues that explore these new subculture exchanges and their social forms have almost entirely dropped prose fiction from their analysis.[1] The Superflat aesthetic comes from the field of visual fine arts.[2] "Cool" comes from discussions of soft power in international relations circles and in both Asian and Asian American contexts draws on cultural forms "from pop music to consumer electronics, architecture to fashion, and animation to cuisine."[3] Discussions of fan culture focus on the world-ing qualities of shared objects and information. In Anne Allison's words, toys are the source of understanding "the constructed world premised on the very notion of difference itself—of endless bodies, vistas and powers that perpetually break down into constituent components that reattach and combine in various ways."[4]

Subculture treatments that include the written word tend to limit themselves to manga, with exceptions for new kinds of girls' culture like cell-phone novels and light novels.[5] The *New Yorker* as well as prestigious Japanese literary journals like *Kokubungaku* and *Nihon bungaku* all devoted substantial page time to cell-phone novels in 2008.[6] While acknowledging the aesthetic inventiveness and economic heft of visually oriented subcultural forms, this chapter is an effort to clear a place for understanding the role of writing in the subcultural world, to show how subculture has roots in postwar literature and debates on postwar Japanese cultural nationalism, and to ask how Nakagami's arguments about ethnography within Japan fit in the field of subculture. Most pointedly, I ask how subculture still registers within it and how some of these differences are more different than others. How would Nakagami's work to bring the parallax identities of *kokubungaku* national literature and ethnography together sit in the field of subculture? The best route to this question is through the works themselves.

I begin with a brief introduction of reasons writers and critics of fine fiction have spurned subculture. I show how the equal and opposite retort on the part of subculture critics claims its new territory by drawing on unacknowledged properties of prose fiction: namely, the idea of *monogatari* (narrative) and a conception of fiction strongly tied to but restricted to the literary naturalism of the early twentieth century. I argue that Nakagami's subculture works sit in the space between these two partisans of media specificity and serve as one way of opening subculture to narratives beyond the common traumatic narrative of U.S.–Japan relations by shifting to Asian, Southern locales. I focus on two works revived by the same new media critics who have put literary fiction on the back burner, Ōtsuka Eiji and Azuma Hiroki. These works are a long picaresque work of genre fiction, *Different Tribes* (*Izoku*; 1984–92) and a manga that depicts the journey of a young sports star as he retraces his family history within the history of the Japanese empire, *Eternal Return of a Southbound Ship* (*Minami kaiki-sen*; 1989–90).

Different Tribes and *Eternal Return* use the coming-of-age story to dramatize choices for Japanese characters in a world that is not only multicultural but composed of minoritarian cultures that work to build worlds using the narrative modes and kinds of characterization typically found in subculture works. Ten years after Ōe Kenzaburo's lament of the death of engaged literature in his 1994 Nobel Prize speech, Ōtsuka and Azuma have republished or written about *Eternal Return* and *Different Tribes,* works that in fact engage just the sort of topic Ōe advocates, by placing them in the context of subcultural narrative forms that have emerged since the 1980s. Nakagami's late works all take place in regions outside of Japan broadly conceived as its historical South. They explore the motivations for exile and the ambivalent possibilities of colonial desire on the part of minoritarian Japanese citizens through a rueful awareness of the infusions of prewar history in the present. Their contact with former colonial worlds is cut with a yearning for anticolonial alliances and the desire for self-determination. *Eternal Return* and *Different Tribes* mark a kind of utopian desire that a Japanese character's relation to Asia can extend past revivalist trajectories of hybrid empire and use the new nomadism to show a social world composed of collaborative members of different scales of the South, local to Japan but also present in other structural Souths and the geographic South.

Critiques of Subculture

The Japanese use of the term subculture is less interested in deviance than studies have historically been in the United States. There, subculture appeared as a field of study in sociology and anthropology, especially in studies of deviance and immigrant assimilation (or its perceived failure) in urban America.[7] Interpretations coming from Japan tend to be more sympathetic with two other lines of inquiry. One was pursued by Albert Cohen who saw the specific rules of subcultures as "solutions" with autonomous ideas about how to respond to mainstream cultural pressures.[8] We see this line clearly in fan culture studies, especially in Azuma's emphasis on communication as the goal of *otaku* culture, made of people who "fanatically consume, produce, and collect comic books (manga), animated films (anime) and other products related to these forms of popular visual culture and who participate in the production and sales of derivative fan merchandise."[9] The second line is pursued beginning in the 1970s by British writers whose focus on outsiders drew on fieldwork but also on the scenes and media forms of subculture, in addition to participant-observation on how class forms were socially reproduced through ideology and institutions. Rather than seeing them as problems demanding solutions, Dick Hebdige is interested in how subcultures change the "ideological character of cultural signs" so that they might be doubly read. [10] Stuart Hall and Tony Jefferson emphasize "resistance through rituals," ways that style in music or clothing worked to realign "shifts in class and power relations, consciousness ideology and hegemony" that existed between "delinquents and control agents."[11] These approaches did not represent practical kinds of problem solving but analyze the way that hegemony funnels subordination into different, expressive, creative directions, new idioms like punk and reggae that ultimately result in a transformation of mainstream culture. This line is more important in works like Nakagami's that demand or benefit from the switch of double reading, where new referent can replace old but keep it indeterminate. Subculture in Japan is more likely to be autonomous and tends to be more obsessed with norms and less concerned with deviance. This is true of both promoters and detractors of subculture. Two key norms are the display of postwar nationalism and a focus on social mobility—both of which are anchored in a strong history in literary subculture.

Since the mid-1970s, fiction writers such as Ōe Kenzaburō and critics such as Etō Jun have been wary of what they perceive as a decline in pure literature at the hands of subculture.[12] When Ōe delivered his Nobel Prize acceptance speech in 1994, he criticized two contemporary writers who were becoming popular worldwide, Murakami Haruki and Yoshimoto Banana, by labeling them "subculture writers." [13] Ōe read subculture less as a style or method of exchange—as later critics will—and more as a genre and related set of themes that revealed that writers were disengaged from the postwar era. This distance, in his view, was political and ideological as well as generational but was significant because it departed from his ongoing effort to locate Japan in a twentieth-century history of imperialism. Subculture characters were too involved with self and consumer culture when issues of empire still lingered traumatically, and their lack of resolution haunted Japan's relation with other Asian nations.

In 1976, Japan's most famous literary critic, Etō Jun, had set the tone for discussing the "sub" of subculture as inferior (*kai*), failing to support the cause of cultural nationalism by deferring to American culture. He protested when a novel set next to a U.S. military base won the Akutagawa Prize.[14] The youthful protagonists of Murakami Ryū's debut novel, *Almost Transparent Blue* (*Kagiri-naku, tōmei ni chikai burū*), and the setting outside a U.S. military base incensed Etō. Murakami's characters were most vividly described when they flaunted their habits of dependency acquired from U.S. soldiers. Etō charged that Murakami did not "express" anything new but merely reflected the "realities" of base culture.[15] The economic and political dependency acted out through the stylistic dependency was fortified by Murakami's own camera-like, mannered realism.

The novel opens with a medley of perceptions focalized through a first-person consciousness:

> It wasn't the sound of an airplane. The buzz was somewhere behind my ear. Smaller than a fly, it circled for a moment before my eyes, then disappeared into a dark corner of the room.
>
> On the round white tabletop reflecting the ceiling light was an ashtray made of glass. A long, thin, lipstick-smeared cigarette smoldered in it. Near the edge of the table stood a pear-shaped wine-bottle, with a picture on its label of a blonde woman, her mouth full of grapes from the bunch she held in her hand. Red light from the ceiling trembled on the surface of the wine in a glass. The ends of the table legs disappeared into the thick pile of the rug.

Opposite me was a large dressing table. The back of the woman sitting at it was moist with sweat. She stretched out her leg and rolled off a black stocking.[16]

This style captures a series of objects through a central perspective but does not comment on the assemblage of reality it describes. In Karatani Kōjin's words, *Almost Transparent Blue* was a "base novel based basically on the base."[17] For example, the succulent marbling of the "blonde woman's" mouthful of grapes springs from the realm of the neopinup, certainly an occupation leftover. Karatani's piled-up description also parodies the way that material and style in Murakami's work are redundant, dependent, and stuck on the single absurdly repeated phoneme "base." Each subsequent syllable imitates but does not interpret what came before, performing the very flaw that Etō condemns.

The book has been most "controversial"—which is to say, mentioned but not analyzed—because of the way that orgy scenes reproduce the observer dynamic on the part of its Japanese characters. Japanese women defer to American men; the scenes show African American men as uncontrolled appetites who seduce Japanese women into sexual submission. Etō sidesteps the issues of representing interracial sex to see these scenes in national terms: they reveal the reality of an incursion into national sovereignty. The narrator, who looks on, registers the events in the detached style evident above registering impressions like a rapidly clicking camera shutter. Etō's impression of mimetic dependency is heightened because he observes but doesn't intervene. Two years later, Etō threw down his pen altogether and stopped reviewing books in his *Mainichi shinbun* column. He justified his decision as a response to the decreasing quality of fiction that followed its encounter with subculture.

Looking over my shoulder at the nine years of this column, I have to acknowledge the regrettable fact that prose fiction has been ejected from the seat of culture, and has been wandering in the dregs of subculture. Nine years ago, Kawabata Yasunari, Funahashi Seiichi, Mishima Yukio, Takeda Taijun and Hirano Ken were all in good health. Each of these people is now dead, and those that live are likely going to be fading away one by one. After they have passed on, that equitable critic we call time will leave the things that should be left, and bring back to life those that should be back to life, and will bid farewell to everything in a gulf of forgetfulness. *All is gone, old familiar faces* [italics in English].[18]

The first critical wave of literary studies' interest in subculture judged works according to how they displayed Japanese cultural nationalism and saw aesthetics as domain that fell under Japanese national sovereignty.

Both Ōe and Etō, however, overlook the fact that the subculture they chalk up to crises of globalization actually had literary roots. Popular journalism immediately after the war pulled an example from the fiction of Dazai Osamu to showcase what Mabuchi Kōsuke names as the first term for subculture, *zoku*. Mabuchi writes that *zoku* became popular when it was employed to describe the social rupture felt by the nobility in the immediate postwar era. Where most people assume that *zoku* (族) had an anthropological referent like the term *minzoku* (民族, folk), it actually referred to *kizoku*, the nobility.[19] When the occupation army abolished Japan's prewar system of aristocratic ranks and took away its stipends after the war, most of these families were forced to sell their property and belongings to generate income. While this *zoku* may refer to a social class rather than the lone teenage trader of collectibles, the two versions of subculture have common elements at their core: they are based on trading as the source of social mobility, and they have an acute sense of how objects traded have value attributed to them by their possessors beyond their use value.

The *zoku* that popular journalism used as its signature example came from Dazai Osamu's 1947 *The Setting Sun* (*Shayō*).[20] When Dazai and his mistress committed suicide in 1948, journalists applied the elegy for refinement found in *The Setting Sun* to the contemporary social world and coined the term "setting-sun tribe" (*shayō-zoku*). *The Setting Sun*'s characters had a keen awareness of the way cultural capital found in mannered attention to banal objects bound its characters together socially while subjecting its economic fate to the market.

The Setting Sun is the first-person story of a young woman, Kazuko, who nurses her sick mother after relocating to a modest house in the countryside. Her brother suddenly comes back from the fighting front addicted to booze and morphine, and his expensive habits threaten to completely ruin the family. While he flees to Tokyo to become further dissipated, Kazuko stays at home caring for her delicate mother who she calls the "last aristocrat."[21] This character's littlest motions are endowed with an elegance that sets her apart from the common woman: "Her head still averted, fluttered another spoonful of soup between her lips. Mother eats in a way so unlike the manner prescribed in women's magazines that it is no mere figure of speech in her case to use the world 'flutter.'"[22] Kazuko declares that her mother's aristocratic bearing, her mode of consumption, can compensate for the object's shoddy material quality: "It is amazing how much better soup tastes when you eat it as mother does."[23] The value of taste added to the soup by aristocratic manners is a clear case of cultural capital providing a richness that the object itself can't provide. From the occupation period forward, *zoku* was used in journalism to describe booms or fads often involving style, leisure, or youth culture. It also set the tone for critics to judge subculture according to its position on postwar Japanese nationalism.

Subculture and Worlds

In the mid-1980s Ōtsuka Eiji began to advance a much broader formulation of how subculture worked by using the term *monogatari*. He spun the term in a different way than either Nakagami or New Aka critics had used it and sidestepped its literary meaning. On the surface, his frame of *monogatari* might seem quite distinct from Nakagami's interpretation of subculture as a kind of double reading that engages the history of a more specific, perhaps indeterminate, semantics of history. Ōtsuka uses subcultural forms to explore how metanarratives of history's shaping by leaders channel desires for collective self-determination. His works revisit the themes of alliance and self-determination that underwrote Nakagami's most critically celebrated pure fiction and also preoccupy postmillennial fiction, given its focus on the new proletariat class of the information economy.

In 1989, Otsuka published a book called *On Monogatari Consumption* (*Monogatari shōhi-ron*).[24] Manifestly a book about how marketing creates "worlds" (*sekai*), Ōtsuka chronicled how objects for children were increasingly packaged in story forms that encouraged collecting. Ōtsuka's key example was Bikkuriman (amazing man) chocolates, a kiddie snack that packaged a set of stickers along with its peanut-waffle candy product. The stickers had a character on the A-side. There was no original backstory gluing the characters together as in *Star Wars* or like Pokémon provides in the mythic Count Tajiri, the beasts' original collector. Instead, there was information on the stickers' B-side. As children collected the stickers, he writes, they invented stories, "small *monogatari*" that were ministories formed through exchange.[25] The more stickers collected, the more complex the interlocked relations of the story world became and the more variable according to the miniworld held by each collector. As more points of view were added to described key dramatic events and backstories, the story world was made deeper and more complex. Their do-it-yourself small *monogatari* placed young consumers within a larger story world that existed beyond the information they were given, creating a composite "large story" (*ōki monogatari*) but one that post-dated their encounter with the information.[26]

Ōtsuka's definition of subculture is instructive because it refers to a set of ideals, not a "concrete set of cultural expressions," and has "no interest in literature," only in understanding how the dilemma of the simulacral legacy of the U.S. occupation and postwar era appear in subcultural forms and expressions.[27] We should note that many of the concerns with sociality and alienation that infused Anglo-American subculture studies are absent, as are Etō's doubts about Japanese culture's autonomy. Ōtsuka has been responsible for bringing attention to Nakagami's more mass-oriented work in the magazine he edits, *New Reality* (*Shin genjitsu*), as well as in mainstream publishing houses. Ōtsuka's vision of subculture is more based on his understanding of the formal quality of media and styles and how they might be reconnected to prewar, perhaps, imperial contexts. He uses histories of style to write his politics into a historical account of subculture. For literary analysis, the problem is that the only traits he recognizes are those that already have a resonance with the styles of manga or anime.

When Azuma and Ōtsuka began to emphasize *monogatari* as story worlds, it was not new to claim that Nakagami's literary works dealing with Kumano and the *roji* constituted a coherent world. In fact, it was Faulkner critic Ōhashi Kenzaburō who first broached Nakagami's works as a conceptual "world."[28] It was not new to claim that a geographic story world was a new postmodern kind of literature. Kawamura Minato concludes his history of postwar literature with a section on contemporary fiction that uses the device of an imaginary map. He cites Nakagami's Kishū saga, *Different Tribes* and *Miracles* (*Kiseki*; 1989), and works by Ii Naoyuki, Yoshimeki Hirohiko, Satō Yasushi, Maruyama Kenji, and Murakami Haruki.[29]

But it *was* new to argue that this saga-like structure with multiple points of entry was consistent with the way that popular subculture narratives were organized and that there is an investment in contemporary issues (*gendai-sei*) in subcultural forms as a whole and in Nakagami's works in specific. Nakagami is a rare point of convergence between two registers of discourse: those that saw *monogatari* as story world and those who saw *monogatari* as a fabricated system of narrative operations. Moreover, he was the only one to persist with the fieldwork in race and ethnicity that the earlier structuralist texts had been built from, adding a third register of meaning to *monogatari*. His use of *monogatari* had three dimensions—narrative, classical, and ethnic—only two of which were used by other writers at any given time.

Azuma also brings Nakagami into conversation with contemporary fiction and worlds by connecting *Different Tribes* to new styles of flatness and characterization that are common in light novels and other low cultural forms.[30] Azuma's interest in bridging literature and subculture springs from a break with the journal *Critical Space* (*Hihyō kūkan*). This journal was one of the main publications where postmodernism and critical theory (*shisō*) were translated and situated. In the New Aka era, the journal was ideally situated to showcase the political potentials of subculture, a direction it did not follow. Azuma maintains that although Nakagami was the only fiction writer taken seriously in the journal's pages, its editors only treated Nakagami's "early works."[31] He argues that the journal's high culture agenda had "no relation to reality" (*genjitsusei*) and neglected contemporary writers like Murakami Haruki and Tsutsui Yasutaka. Three editors of *Critical Space*, Asada Akira, Karatani Kōjin, and Watanabe Naomi, along with Yomota Inuhiko, also edited Nakagami's complete works, which included only a small selection of genre and subculture work. Because Nakagami's growing interest in the South and his subculture works happen at the same time and are both excluded from the collected works, both these elements drop out of critical discourse. "Sub," in the context of selection criteria, consigns mixed-media and subcultural material to an inferior or unaesthetic status.

In contrast to Ōtsuka's market orientation, Azuma is interested in the philosophical question of "what words to use to describe contemporary reality?"[32] For Azuma, reality *itself* took a turn that subculture has responded to better than theory has. Namely, in 1995, after the Kobe earthquake and the subway gassings committed by followers of the AUM religious cult, people started looking for simpler realities. This search was reflected in the way pure literature and high culture theory stopped being a place for experimentation, as sociology and psychology took over the task of putting forth a discourse that represents the real. Azuma writes that "reality is something that has overcome the communal illusion" that literature is still invested in.[33] This phrase refers to Yoshimoto Takaaki's 1968 essay collection, *On Communal Illusions (Kyōdō gensō-ron)*, that argued that ideology was poised between different layers of personal, coupled, and national ideology. Following Azuma's hint, literature might learn from subculture in reckoning with its own posthistorical status and focus on the kinds of communication that work or falter between microsocieties of people.

Ōtsuka also makes his mark in Nakagami criticism by departing from the domain of high culture. Ōtsuka considers it "mysterious" (*fushigi*) that the manga script for *Eternal Return* has not been published, while film scripts and unfinished novels are included in Nakagami's complete works.[34] Because of similar disputes about the cultural status of mass culture works, he has been perhaps the most controversial guest at Kumano Daigaku (Kumano University). This annual summer symposium held in Shingū, founded with "no grades, no exams, and no graduation" and staffed by town volunteers, is typically programmed based on an anticipated split between high and popular cultures.[35] Each year features new scholarship on Nakagami's work as well as performances and readings by musicians and writers. The list of performers is usually headlined by a writer or performer who knew Nakagami in his lifetime and who contributed to changing the relation between mainstream and minor cultural forms. Participants include spoken-word writer Itō Seikō, who used rhythms of rap and hip hop in Japanese to invent a kinetic, oral writing and performance style in the mid-1980s, and the widely popular *zainichi* Korean *enka* singer Miyako Harumi. Opening the afternoon session of the 2006 symposium, regular Asada Akira remarked that it would be markedly different from Ōtsuka's morning session. The disrespect was lost on Ōtsuka: he had already turned his own cold shoulder and left to catch the train back to Tokyo.

This missed connection seems all the more ironic because Asada himself was no stranger to popularization of difficult texts. Asada published a best-selling pop explication of poststructuralist theory, his 1983 collection *Structure and Power*. But although Asada had been hyped in mass journalism, his works aimed to make intellectual history more accessible, not to popularize their application or insights in the mass- or pop-culture worlds of manga, anime, genre writing, or entertainment-oriented media, commodity cultures that trivialized thought. His own rejection of popular culture as an object of analysis underscores even more the limited field of the initial highbrow reception of poststructuralism and shows how distinct Nakagami's path was. The title of *Eternal Return* is indeed indisputably high culture in one sense, despite the *yakuza* backdrop and the plot's garnish of boxing superstars and prostitutes with hearts of gold. The Japanese title, *Minami kaiki-sen*, even owes a nod to Asada because an alternate reading of the characters 南回帰船, "Minami kaiki-sen," is a near homonym of the Japanese translation of *Tristes tropiques, Kanashiki nankai kisen*, whose author Asada had helped to popularize in *Structure and Power*. In its context, Asada's withering dismissal of Ōtsuka's introduction to Nakagami's work carried an extra punch because Asada had been an editor of Nakagami's complete works. Asada's writings, however, were framed in the genre of New Aka and featured outlines of complex poststructuralist theory.

The slight of Ōtsuka is only one episode in a decade-plus running dispute between the two writers hinging on the value of mass and pop culture. Their initial difference of opinion had come to a head after the massive and traumatic AUM subway gassings of Tokyo in 1995. If the planes flying into the World Trade Center took their spectacular imagery from cinema, AUM drew its sense of apocalypse from manga, and the cult even published its own apocalyptic manga series. Asada had argued that popular culture gave undue attention to AUM and its new-age-ish ideologies. Asada made essentially a false-consciousness argument against AUM's significance. He wrote that the religious group was a "stunted" (*waishōna*) phenomenon that should not be taken seriously as "either religion/spirituality or thought."[36] For Asada, seriousness meant significant in a genealogy of philosophical inquiry, not contemporary reality. In contrast, writers and critics with ties to subculture saw the AUM gassings as significant on the same scale that U.S. scholars saw 9/11. Murakami Haruki published, for example, two volumes of interviews with both survivors and perpetrators of the 1995 attacks in the style of New Journalism. While rightists like Kobayashi Yoshinori tapped into desire for community in his revisionist comic books, the world of high theory consigned Nakagami's fantastic Southern works to the realm of subculture.

The manga *Eternal Return* is in some ways a subculture reprise of *Monogatari Seoul*. It, too, emphasizes collaboration between diasporic, disillusioned but tenacious characters from the margins of history who are thrown by destiny into more central roles. Where the photos in *Monogatari Seoul* stood out as separate tableaux from the story, the text and image both work in the service of the narrative of the story's hero, Takashi. Nakagami wrote the prose outline (*gensaku*) for the manga, which was then illustrated by Tanaka Akio. The specific panel divisions and page sequences I treat below show some interpretation by Tanaka, especially his treatment of time in action scenes. But the narrative idioms of South Seas paradise and dream sequences were scripted by Nakagami and locate him in a textual tradition of South Seas reveries pioneered in the 1880s.

The journeys in Nakagami's works to Southern settings direct readers' attention to genres and events that stretch from the Meiji era to the Pacific War beginning with utopian narratives from the 1880s where political rebels take flight to the South Seas (*nan'yō*). The Southern engagements of these works give subculture a different genealogy than we find in the prevailing account by artists like Murakami Takashi or critics like Azuma Hiroki and Etō Jun that traces it back to the post–World War II context of U.S.–Japan rivalry or dependence.[37] *Different Tribes* and *Eternal Return* present Japan's relation to Asia but do so through a different lens than the transnational cultural flows that have emerged since the 1990s to connect Japan with Asia through digital culture and postmodern forms.

Modern Japanese stories of self-determined utopias stretch from the 1890s to Ōe's *Seventeen* to Abe Kazushige's 1996 *Individual Projection*, a noirish novel about a charismatic leader's attempts to use a crew of discontented lumpen workers to corral nuclear weapons into a plot of world domination.[38] Nakagami's literary fiction was about developing neologisms like *roji* that prevent exteriority from being incorporated into a totalizing system within Japan. His subculture works explore how this story of self-determination might be told within the scale of Asia and the global South and might incorporate desires for self-determination in both diasporic and fantastic contexts. Both *Different Tribes* and *Eternal Return* work because of elements of small *monogatari* and exchange—along with new ideas about the flat nature of information-heavy characterization—and are conspicuously different from the thick textures of psychological interiority, intertextuality, and figural language that the prose fiction of pure literature (*jun bungaku*) has conventionally privileged. *Different Tribes* is a serial novel stocked with genre elements of the spy, adventure, and gangster genres.

Dubbed "flat" (*heiban*) and lacking a sense of dramatic pitch by Yomota Inuhiko, it focuses on three characters: Tatsuya the low-level gangster, the *zainichi* Korean Simu, and the Ainu Utari.[39] It tracks the three and several friends as they band together and travel from the fictional *roji* city of Fujinami in Japan, to Okinawa, to the Philippines to find a series of hidden treasures. The novel is punctuated, as Murakami Rori reminds us, by two actual incidents committed by people Nakagami researched, both of which bear on the idea of sovereignty.[40] One was the 1987 incident of a flag burning in Yomitan village in Okinawa by Chibana Shōichi. Nakagami had interviewed Chibana on the subject of the mass suicides in Okinawa that the Japanese army provoked when they fanned the hysteria of an invasion. The second incident was Nakagami's "improvised" interview with a man he identifies as "the anti-government leader of the New People's Army" but who "feels more like a cousin" than someone in charge of a group, two of whose members are killed in terrorist incidents each day.[41] Both incidents stress anticolonial self-determination through a lens of romanticized kinship. This is precisely the kind of utopian fraternity that *On the Japanese Language* had imagined in 1968.

Like *Eternal Return*, the characters in *Different Tribes* are led by a charismatic boss who aims to recreate the Qing dynasty's alliance with Japanese rulers of Manchukuo and form a new empire, this time in Davao, an old Japanese merchant colony even before Japan's 1941 through 1945 occupation of the Philippines. *Different Tribes* employs the same idea of a found family comprising young men of different parentage on a quest but sets it in postcolonial terms. The youths travel through Asia; and, as in *Eternal Return*, the story ends suspended in Davao while the armed conflict of the Filipino New People's Army roars in the background.

Popular Cultures of the South

The regional name of *nan'yō* is attributed to Shiga Shigetaka, who in 1887 published the first travelogue of the South Seas in Japanese, a record of a ten-month trip. Shiga's title, *Nan'yō jiji* (*Matters of the South Seas*), was patterned on other maritime regions like the "western seas" (*seiyō*) and the "eastern seas" (*tōyō*), and his concerns were patterned after Charles Darwin's accounts of voyages on the Beagle. In the 1880s and 1890s, a flurry of political novels (*seiji shōsetsu*) dramatized adventures by political refugees and adventurers in the South Seas. As Thomas Schnellbacher reminds us, the sci-fi tendency to locate utopian stories in outer space is relatively recent.[42] The most popular of the nineteenth-century stories is Yano Ryūkei's *Story of a Floating Castle* (*Ukishiro monogatari*; 1883). *Floating Castle* recounted the story of three young men who capture a pirate ship and use it to launch their exploration of the Indian Ocean.[43] Its vision of Polynesian splendor and receptivity was the backdrop for many voyages of colonial anticipation and later nostalgia. Kawamura Minato argues that the "motifs" of the popular Orientalist "yearning for the South Seas" found in Meiji-era political novels and pleasure reading did not fit into the category of literature.[44] While these works are certainly exiled from the mid-Meiji-era ideal of realism and manners, Robert Tierney and Yano Tōru note that slightly later writers including Natsume Sōseki, Shiga Naoya, Akutagawa Ryūnosuke, Nitobe Inazō (the popularizer of the warrior ethos of Bushidō), Tanizaki Jun'ichirō, and Nakajima Atsushi all included representations of South Seas expeditions and expositions as set-pieces in well-known works.[45]

The presence of the South was featured in 1930s mass culture works. From 1933 to 1939, a popular manga series, *The Adventures of Dankichi* (*Bōken Dankichi*), reprised the journey of discovery in the South Seas, but in the cute form that Kawamura calls mass-culture Orientalism. This cluster of materials included comics, travelogues, fiction, and tourist literature, all of which depicted "natives" or "primitives."[46] Many of these, including *Dankichi*, dramatized relations between civilizing Japanese voyager and local inhabitants. *Dankichi* depicts a boy hero who falls asleep in a fishing boat with his pet-friend mouse and washes up on the shores of a remote island. After, he conquers both the wild animals and the "race of dark head-hunters."[47] This story emphasizes pacification through affection and governance rather than swash-buckling force and sets a narrative precedent for the multicultural alliances of Nakagami's works. Nakagami's Southern works return not only to these settings. They also revisit tropes and stylistic markers from wartime fiction set in the South Seas.

The four volumes of Nakagami's comic were illustrated by Tanaka Akio without direct consultation with Nakagami. As we see in Figure 1, the places where the visual account of the South Seas has to supply details unexplained in the original script suggest how popular work about the South Seas is embedded in multiple sets of conventions that exceed Nakagami's own hints. The story begins as Takashi, a beat-up but happy-go-lucky boxer, is walking through a low-rent part of Nakano ward. It is shown as a grungy neighborhood strewn with old newspapers and homeless men, street touts, and dubious looking clubs. A game center arcade catches Takashi's eye, and he comes upon a young chubby Taiwanese man on the motorbike ride. Chigu, whose name is written with characters that mean "succeeding revolution" (継革), will later display his chops as a kung fu champion. But at the moment, he abandons his ride in deference to Takashi who rides it almost into the ground to the amazement of a

Figure 1. Chigu pushes back against threatening yakuza. Image courtesy of Futabasha. From the manga Minami kaiki-sen (Eternal return of a southern ship), *by Tanaka Akio, based on a script by Nakagami Kenji.*

crowd of *yakuza* thugs and a nubile young off-duty hostess, Gina. Takashi's destiny as leader-hero of a collaborative of nomads is established from this first encounter with the Taiwanese youth. Meanwhile, another hostess collapses after a drug overdose, showing the desperate measures she clutches at in order to desert her job and get out from under the exploitation of her *yakuza* bosses. When Gina's manager attempts to roughhouse with Chigu to get rid of this chubby nuisance, Chigu unleashes an unexpected and wicked barrage of kung fu moves. In a series of zig-fractured panels from multiple points of view, the kung fu flattens the manager.

The upper panel depicts Chigu standing obliviously as two thugs approach him. The splintering of the three midright panels into new and distinct shapes indicates the power of each blow he delivers as it chops and injures the manager and the other *yakuza*. The difference in sizes and geometry of the panels emphasizes the multiple, serial, and varied nature of his blows, all of which do grave damage. Manga critic Ōzawa Nobuaki thinks that Nakagami's highly literary script was adapted into the wrong comic genre for its story. In his opinion, the script uses a "-like" (-*no yō ni*) style of metaphoric writing whose emphasis on states and emotions expressed through objects might have worked better with an expressive style more typically found in *shōjo* manga. He does praise the dilated action scenes such as this one where "like" is exhibited in fragmentation and speed rather than naturalist detail and interior affect.[48]

As the fight dies down, Chigu walks with Takashi and Gina into the neon sunset, into a coffee shop where they each confess their desire to quit the racket that grinds each of them down. Gina confides that she has perfected a highly effective *shinjū* (double love suicide) hustle and convinces another friend to join in so that he can acquire money to finance a motorbike purchase. They take strong medication as if to kill themselves. Then, a friend of Gina's calls one of her most reliably milquetoast customers and extorts him for a million yen. The suicide scam succeeds; but when the friend, Marianne, persuades Takashi to commit *shinjū* joint suicide, they extort the wrong man: a *yakuza* boss. Not only does Marianne die, but Takashi, Chigu, and Gina are pursued by the right-wing boss's patriot biker flunky. They ditch him, only to run into his associates just as they are making their mark in the motocross circuit. Takashi is riding high with success until he starts having flashbacks in which he sees Marianne, the dead hostess of the failed suicide attempt (Figure 2), superimposed in memory over the softly backlit image of his mother (Figure 3). The image of his

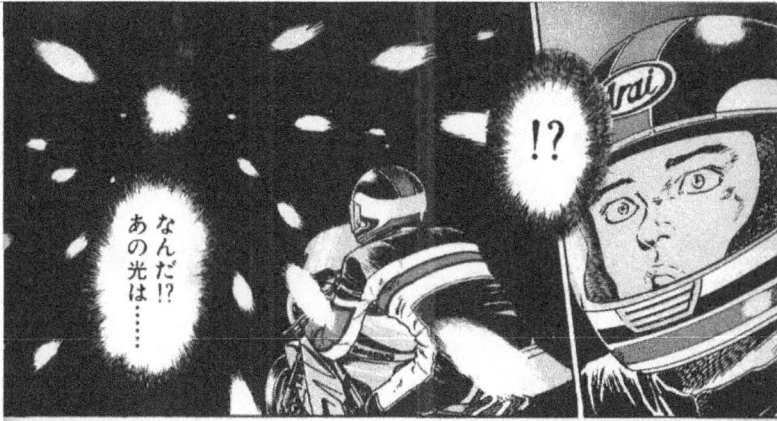

Figure 2. Takashi is addressed by Marianne from the great beyond. Image courtesy of Futabasha. From the manga Minami kaiki-sen (Eternal return of a southern ship), *by Tanaka Akio, based on a script by Nakagami Kenji.*

Figure 3. Takashi remembers his mother even more transcendentally, and rides into the past to find her. Image courtesy of Futabasha. From the manga Minami kaiki-sen (Eternal return of a southern ship), *by Tanaka Akio, based on a script by Nakagami Kenji.*

mother is drawn in the same style in which Marianne had smiled wanly at him from a heavenly otherworld in the center of the otherwise dark page. Underscoring the superimposition of lost friend and lost mother is the likeness of the name Marianne to Nakajima Atsushi's most famous story about the South Seas published in 1942.[49]

A complicated sense of perpetrator guilt is imagined through this juxtaposition. As a newborn baby, Takashi could not possibly have committed the sort of ethical lapse that he did with Marianne. Nonetheless, a structure of loss and guilt and an overlapping visual language associates the two figures and links the journey to find and reconcile with his mother to a sense of perpetrator guilt and unfulfilled responsibility. Although this is an action comic for boys and need not display a *shōjo* manga's infatuation with subjective depth and interiority, the story dwells on Takashi's unconscious life as a way to connect his life as a Japanese citizen in the present to a colonial past, especially the Southern emigrant past on both sides of the family he did not know he had. As the story continues to unfold, the narrative is paced in a series of episodes that present strangers and antagonists who, after a confrontation and test of mettle, turn out to be allies, devoting themselves to Takashi's cause to finance his trip to the South Seas, all the while the net of *yakuza* thugs threatens to close in on them. Marianne's sister Mitsuko (written with the character for "light" 光) arrives on the scene, and she and Takashi fall in love. He reveals to her one of his deepest secrets, that his father is (was) a legendary racer-turned-boxer who has disappeared after bequeathing Takashi what a right-wing *yakuza* calls his legendary "thoroughbred"-like genes.

The plot develops into a conflict between the *yakuza* desire to quash Takashi and the desire to support him as a pure-blooded "thoroughbred" corresponding to their belief in national spirit. Takashi becomes an overnight sports media sensation. A nosy reporter shows him a photo of the mother he thought he had lost (Figure 4) and probably killed when he was born, now living in Saipan, a princess in exile.

Takashi is lured to Yokohama's Chinatown where he is seduced deeper into the right-wing plot by a high-ranking boss who has a history with Takashi's parents, a history Takashi is eager to unravel. The landscape and detailed scene drawings in the manga cite many signifiers of Chinese-ness, including food fetishes and kung fu, all of which are very Japanese-ified versions of Chinese codes and suggest the leaders' vision of a cosmopolitan compatibility between Chinese materiality and Japanese spirit, in willing

Figure 4. Takashi's mother is revealed to be alive in an English-language newspaper. Image courtesy of Futabasha. From the manga Minami kaiki-sen (Eternal return of a southern ship), *by Tanaka Akio, based on a script by Nakagami Kenji.*

deference to Japanese fascist ideology. The plot hinges on a change in leadership, or spiritual guidance, from elderly Manchus to the yet-to-be-tested Takashi. The *yakuza* pull Takashi into a back room, crowded with a large mass of gaudily dressed and stern-looking elderly men. The men, who turn out to be ninety-year-old eunuchs, force him to fight an exhibition match. His daunting opponent is Mike Tyson (at the top of his game in 1989), who appears to be in the ring for the massive prize stakes. Takashi scores a last-minute knockout win, and Tyson congratulates Takashi, perhaps the most revealing in the series of deferential moves by opponents. All of them demonstrate Takashi's natural leadership, but Tyson's global status in the sport of boxing places his obedience at the highest level of competition. Like the faithful and clever mouse sidekick of *Dankichi* or the highly coordinated pheasants and rabbits of *Momotarō*, or even the Benkei to his Yoshitsune,[50] Tyson follows the pattern of faithful retainer. Even though Tyson makes a vast sum of money, the enthusiasm with which he jumps to Takashi's rescue after his gracious defeat also implies a certain evident and natural aristocracy falling into place with Japan at the helm.

The *yakuza* reveals to Takashi that the real history of China, theirs, has been betrayed by products like the reviled film *The Last Emperor*, made by Bernard Bertolucci. The film tells the story of the last Qing emperor by showing how he was elevated into being the "puppet emperor" of Manchuria, "built by the evil power of Japan."[51] After having waited for decades for their long-desired and prayed-for child (*mōshi-ko*), their plan is to depose China and restore the Qing Empire to its rightful place, for which they require Takashi's help. Only after he complies will he know all about his parents and their history. The elders banish Takashi's girlfriend Mitsuko in order to broker a marriage between the new champion and a beautiful girl that he understands even without words to be a Qing princess.

Takashi integrates the new fragments of story into his personal memories. He realizes that there were world-historical reasons for his personal history of exile and alienation. His father had taken him away from the South Seas in order to protect him from his destiny as an imperial breeder. The new information explains why his father claimed his mother died and he himself disappeared. The right-wing leader explains that he is trying to make up for the lost time, when Japanese citizens emigrated to the South because they couldn't feed themselves in Japan. Outside the helicopter, a bomb is being tested, but Takashi has a stronger will and more loyal friends who instinctively run to his aid, as if guided by the destiny proper to a quest narrative. He absconds with the princess and Tyson to a guerilla camp near the Filipino city of Davao, where the story remains unfinished. The friends stand alert at the edge of a tiger-filled forest as the New People's Army approaches, and Douglas MacArthur is rumored to live nearby.

Eternal Return seems to suggest that Japan was mistaken in both allowing its population to leave and in constructing the puppet country of Manchuria. But at the same time, the comic also suggests that Japan can contribute to a second chance at Chinese modernity and in fact may be necessary to help restore China's former glory. Takashi's refusal to collaborate is the road not taken by Kobayashi Yoshinori's manga, though it, too, centers on the young man's drive for independence and self-determination. *Eternal Return* is set in the large frame of the South Seas, but its precise choice of Tonga as the main character's destination—the group of about 170 islands northwest of New Zealand—is significant in terms of Nakagami's interest in independence and self-determination movements. Tonga was the only Pacific Island nation to retain native governance through the Pacific War. Unlike much of Micronesia, annexed by Japan in 1919, mandated as a trustee for the League of Nations after 1922, and held even after Japan quit the League of Nations in 1933, Tonga was a British protectorate. Although Tonga's residents suffered disease and had settlers after contact with explorers and traders, from a point of view that seeks to show a potential solidarity with self-determination, Tonga stands out.[52] It had not been compromised in the role of agricultural cash cow that much of the South Seas served for Japan. Nor had it been placed like Micronesia in protectorate status. It did not thus experience the Japanese colonial regimes of village governance, health care, second-class wages, education, and land reform that followed when Micronesia was named a Japanese protectorate in 1922.[53]

In *Eternal Return*, Nakagami's representation of Tonga as lush, fecund, and sentimentalized is consistent with earlier representations of the South Seas that emphasize its dimensions of friendliness and untouched purity and counter to the chronicles of drudgery and oppression that Japanese fiction writers like Nakajima Atsushi penned about Japanese-occupied areas. Takashi is visually introduced in drawing styles that project his point of view about his imagined past as if he were a mixed-race child. His father is drawn with darker skin, waving farewell to a Polynesian looking woman who is his mother. In his imagination (Figure 5), she looks very much like signifiers of Polynesia that infused

Figure 5. Takashi's father's mother and siblings as he imagines them, waving good-bye from Tonga. Image courtesy of Futabasha. From the manga Minami kaiki-sen (Eternal return of a southern ship), *by Tanaka Akio, based on a script by Nakagami Kenji.*

ethnographic writings and political novels since the 1880s: plump, dark skinned, with flowers in her hair, surrounded by palm trees and children.[54] The image of Tonga uncontaminated by colonial structures—seen in the representation of Takashi's affectionate grandmother—follows the same logic as representations of anticolonial rebels in *Different Tribes*. Though one is docile and the other fierce, both are firmly committed to independence and self-determination, even as they ally politically and romantically with nomads of other ethnicities.

The six-hundred-page *yakuza* colonial novel *Different Tribes*, written at roughly the same time, is based on similar themes of multiethnic alliance, destiny, a wandering prince, and a resurgence of empire in former Manchu territory. *Different Tribes* is a rewrite of the late Edo-period classic *The Eight-Dog Chronicles* (*Nansō satomi hakken-den*; 1814–42) by Takizawa Bakin. *Different Tribes* is set against the backdrop of a contemporary recolonization of Manchuria by a league of minoritarian youths. Each young man is marked with a "blue mark" that resembles, as Nakagami writes, both the failed colony of Manchukuo and the "city map of Davao, thought of as the prewar paradise of the South Seas."[55] In the history of realism in Japan, Bakin holds the place of enemy number one. In Meiji-era programs of literary criticism, such as Tsubouchi Shōyō's *The Essence of Prose Fiction* (*Shōsetsu no shinzui*), his works were criticized because they brimmed with all the vices of pre-Meiji writings that critics wanted to consign to the historical past, such as moral judgment, fantasy, religion, minimal coverage of social class, and lack of psychological realism.[56] Bakin's works also showed a debt to the array of Chinese textual traditions that Meiji-era scholars who were then building the canon of Japanese literature excised from their curricula and anthologies of literature.[57] Nakagami's reclamation of the supernatural themes, moral righteousness, and signifiers of Chinese-ness is consistent with his overall commitment to renarrating modern literature by including elements that the Meiji institution builders of *kokubungaku* had purged.

Eight-Dog Chronicles is a massive samurai serial work, a supernatural romance set in the fifteenth century. It features eight characters, each of whom is the spiritual son of a dog-human relationship, a marriage that ends in tragedy. A princess is impregnated by a dog-hero who took her father's challenge and brought back the head of her family's archrival. The princess is wounded and kills herself before being murdered by the rivals, taking her unborn children with her. As she dies, eight glow stick–like beads fly off; later eight sons are born to different human parents. Each child's name contains the word for "dog" and represents a Confucian virtue. The eight youths work together to lift the curse from the princess's family and end up restoring the family's fortunes by setting up their own domains to rule over.[58]

The original *Eight-Dog Chronicles* closes as the eight warriors journey to Kyoto, where they are given land in the province of Awa to build their own kingdom. The late twentieth-century incarnation of this story, *Different Tribes*, moves through a series of locations and events in locales all over Asia as the band of youths is under the sway of a right-wing leader, Makinohara. *Different Tribes* features a scriptwriter as a metanarrator who frames and interprets the main story. Unlike *Eternal Return*, *Different Tribes* is complete. The scriptwriter's filter of the story through perpetrator guilt and structures of fantasy expands on the reconciliation of myth, national literature, and comic forms that makes up the quest narrative of *Eternal Return*. This in turn links to examples of Nakagami's fine fiction, especially the story world of *A Thousand Years of Pleasure* (*Sen'nen no yuraku*; 1982). Azuma reads *Different Tribes* as a "flat" narrative for several reasons.[59] It is dialogue heavy and does not hover in the depth of characters' psychological space. The characters' identities are informationalized, or filled with content, in a way he likens to database narratives because the signifiers are stereotyped as shorthand for identities. The Ainu character, for instance, is named Utaru. His name resonates closely with the name of the largest Ainu association in Japan, the Utari kyōkai, or association of comrades/fellows, which changed its name from Ainu in 1963.[60] And the story of the generic *yakuza* plot is given a context inside the novel itself at a metalevel through the "scenario writer."

The scenario writer plays a trickster role and comments on events, occupying a metaconstructive role like that of a database-friendly reader speaking from within the text to a more conventional novelistic reader outside the text. The story ends as its youthful protagonists wait for the writer to arrive and tie up the loose ends, while dipping in and out of a resort swimming pool in Davao. The scene is almost camp in its attention to clingy swimsuits and a casualness that contrasts with the graveness of the story that unfolds. The young men are trying to piece together information and rumors to explain what motivated their leader Makinohara to organize their elaborate transplant to the war-torn Philippines. He is rumored by some to be a cousin of the Qing emperor, whose supporters

buried treasure during the war in the mountains near Davao, now occupied by the New People's Army. Others think he is a Japanese imposter,
posing as Chinese to avoid the anti-Japanese sentiment that lingers from
the wartime occupation of the Philippines. With these rumors on the
table and unresolved, in "a Southern country whose light blinds them," a
man with a rifle appears and orders the main character, Tatsuya, to get out
of the pool.[61] The story ends as he rises from the pool like a neowestern
film where the limits of the frontier are finally reached, and the settler has
nowhere left to run.

In the story world of the subcultural South, the plotlines never quite
live up to the high hopes of postcolonial fantasy. None of the rumors is
supported or excluded; but, through the poolside showdown, the heroic
status of Tatsuya as the predestined agent of triumphant return to the
metropole is drastically qualified. Tatsuya falls into the *yakuza* drifter, and
the quest plots through a fairly distinguished literary route and brings new
contexts and challenges to it. The wandering prince is a common trope
in the loftier textual realms of *kokubungaku*, with examples dating back to
the classical Heian period.[62] The theme of the prince in exile reconciles
kokubungaku with the realm of subculture genre fiction via the quest narrative in *Eternal Return*. It also adds a narrative of political history that is
not common in quest narratives of the 1980s by reengaging Japan's imperial past and its settlement of the Pacific Islands.

In the version of the wandering prince motif systematized in the twentieth century, folklorist Orikuchi Shinobu notes that the ur-instance of
the trope is in *The Tale of the Bamboo-Cutter* (*Taketori monogatari*), written under the status system of the eighth century, which referred to the
bamboo cutter's family as *senmin* (outcast, outside the system). A typical
example of the trope that features a male hero is found in *The Tale of Genji*.
At a key moment, the hero, Hikaru Genji, is stripped of his rank and post.
He departs the capital to journey to the far periphery of a beach at Suma.
This self-exile seems to crush his chances to approach the throne. At the
end of the Suma chapter, however, he is aided by the gods and comes
back not only in triumph but in terms that challenge the way that power
is exerted at court. In 1984, about the time he started writing *Different
Tribes*, Nakagami established this quality of exile as one of his criteria for
writing prose fiction. Takashi's journey to the South Seas island of Tonga
suggests that an outlier colonial subject may pose a threat at court and
may have a chance at reshaping the rules that establish who takes charge

at court, how succession is determined, and how politics works at court. In essence, although the comic is suspended after four volumes, setting this story world as a round-trip journey from Japan to the Pacific Islands suggests Nakagami's interest in challenging the idea of imperial rule to include overseas development and cross-ethnic relations and integrating these ideas into the conventions of a popular story world whose conventions crossed an increasing number of media following on the 1980s boom of interest in myth.[63]

Reconciling with *Kokubungaku*

The unimpeachable market orientation that Ōtsuka uses to introduce *monogatari* is certainly at odds with the process of canonizing Nakagami's works as part of high culture *kokubungaku*. *Kokubungaku*'s standards are more likely to be fixed in light of scholarly or aesthetic value rather than market value. Given the way we have seen that subculture directly confronts buried elements of popular culture history to mine the temptations and costs of sovereignty, it becomes clear that even Nakagami's earlier and most lyrical and literary works experiment with the structures of subculture narrative. One example of this kind of amplification and deepening of a story world through additive narratives is the world of the *roji* first inhabited by *The Cape's* protagonist, Akiyuki. *A Thousand Years of Pleasure* expands the single-protagonist story set in the *roji* into a world inhabited by six main characters with the same geography and some overlapping characters. *A Thousand Years of Pleasure* is a serial *monogatari* narrated by an elderly woman, Oryū no oba, based on conversations Nakagami had with Tabata Ryū, a Shingū resident.[64] Oryū has been midwife to all six members of a beautiful yet doomed extended family, the Nakamoto clan. She narrates the stories of each beautiful youth from birth to death in the all-seeing manner of a mythic chronicler who tracks the world from creation to extinction. Etō Jun calls this space "another world," while Yoshimoto Takaaki calls it "Asian" or a "classical" world.[65] Moriyasu Toshiji, who as director of the Suiheisha Museum is devoted to chronicling the *buraku* liberation movement, calls it a "mythic" world, too far removed from reality to compel him.[66] These are all, ironically, typical complaints both *buraku* activists and high theory partisans put to Nakagami's subculture works. But Yoshimoto insists that the work is a "forcible retaking" of *monogatari*. The narrator tells us, in long sentences broken as if by breaths, that the title's "thousand" refers on one hand to Oryū's powers of endurance. This chapter concerns the life and tragic death of the first of six characters, Fumihiko. It contains, I think, two kinds of discursive realism that contradict critical opinions that the story flees from reality but still maintains the deepening and additive tendencies of the narrative that Ōtsuka describes: "Oryū vowed that she would live on another thousand years, just as she had lived a thousand years along with the *roji*, and tamped down her own irritation at the unreliable young men of the *roji* by thinking of the other young men related to the clear but settled blood of the long-suffering Nakamoto clan—Hisashi's face, or the incredibly strong and muscular Fumihiko."[67] Oryū's longevity is superhuman even in this passage. This effect is amplified because she outlives each young man. She is a mythic type of narrator we are more likely to see in a role-playing game or quest narrative than in modern pure fiction.

Critics such as Etō, Yoshimoto, and Moriyasu see the transcendental viewing position of Oryū's narration as dislocated from history because it resembles a fantastic or mythic story. *Monogatari* may be powerful, but it is still literary. I see it in dialogue with intertexts of *buraku* rhetorical activism and *kokubungaku*. Oryū's endurance and antirealistic lifetime of over one hundred years are made even more significant because of two extraliterary references to texts from *buraku* rhetorical history that work in the way that subculture typically mobilizes signifiers of history, a pattern common in global postmodernism. One, the "thousand" refers to Takahashi Sadaki's 1924 *A Thousand Years of Hisabetsu Buraku Discrimination*. As we saw in chapter 1, Takahashi's thousand stood for the long-standing relations between exploiter and exploited classes. Oryū's characterization in terms of that history suggests that she, too, is aware of this, or has even collected the six serial episodes to illustrate that narrative by creating a story world that collects representative cases of thousand-ness. Her description of her own relation to the historical past through descriptions of the 1871 Emancipation Edict establish that the *roji*'s history is intimately related to the failure of the Meiji restoration to create a level socioeconomic playing field, even in the idealized moment of the proclamation abolishing the Tokugawa status system. What Nakagami brings to the media mix is an understanding of *monogatari* in terms of relations of exchange and coexistence within the thematic elements of the works themselves and a revisit of themes of quest and adventure that still inform Japan's present in the South.

Nakagami's frame of South in both high culture literature and mass culture manga and fiction shows terms of exchange operating in a concrete geopolitical framework. In turn, the way that relations of exchange featuring the South play out across the two separate registers of high- and pop-culture bridges between an interest in deconstructing "thought" (*shisō*) and a populist stake in constructing narrative. While the terms of the South vary in Nakagami's works, from the *roji* to Korea to the South Seas, what his works foreground is that differential identity that places a value on Southern-ness is always in play. Depicting the South as a virtual, speculative place, but one with a history, is markedly different than the version of South popularized after World War II in which Japan itself was imagined as a defeated South. It reprises some of the early twentieth-century dreams of *buraku* emigration or expatriation as well as a revisiting of wartime empire building in the South Seas, seen through the lens of defeat. Nakagami's interpretation of the South also differs from the generation that came before him. These writers and thinkers saw the South as a place of postwar defeat and ruin in terms of a bilateral relation with the United States. He sees the South—the Japanese South—in terms of a structural relation to a developed and imperial North, a relation he then sees extended between Japan and other Southern parts of Asia and the Pacific Islands. Through specific comparisons between Japan's modernity and a postbellum America or contemporary Korea, his South is comparative, imperial, and global.

Conclusion

Both/And

I began *Nakagami, Japan* by showing how the notion of parallax was integral to Nakagami's writing and how his doubled point of view attempted to run counter to the myth of Japan's postwar world as a monocultural, homogenous society that prevailed in the 1970s and 1980s. Parallax provided a way to talk about the two viewing positions of *buraku* and mainstream that helped shape the contours of Nakagami's biography as well as the two audiences who clustered around his work, readers of fine fiction and discursive readers familiar with an archive of *buraku* rhetorical activism. It also provided a way to account for stark differences in opinion between Nakagami and *buraku* activists regarding the role of culture and whether it called for a response at a semantic or structural level. Parallax was also useful to show a view of literature that is different than what we see through the monocular lens of *kokubungaku* nationalism in either its Meiji-era version or its postwar configuration.

These *kokubungaku* examples I just listed are cases where two positions cannot accommodate the same view on the same object. But the metaphorical use of parallax in Nakagami's work also proposes something else: the capacity to experience places—and texts—simultaneously and through scales of both, instead of inside/outside and either/or in the positions provided by a society outside of society or an imperial syntax. To read for *buraku and roji*, for South *and* modern provides a way to talk about how writing and power are exercised in similar ways in very different realms. This includes the important connection bridged by imperial syntax or literature and the legal system as we saw in the trope of confession that traverses the Sayama trial and literature from wildly different venues, from coterie magazines to mass leftist periodicals. If Nakagami's novels, especially his late ones, never quite live up to the high hopes of solidarity that they seem to long for, they nonetheless push us to look beyond the postwar idea of a monoculture to explore some earlier eclipsed and plural histories of how parallax was experienced, critiqued, or made livable.

My primary aim in this book has been to introduce a new lexicon for talking about differential identity as it is manifested in multiple scales of space-based identity that situate Japan in the context of global post-modernism and information society. The second goal has been to clarify how Nakagami's periodization of modern literature along lines that privilege the Great Treason Incident, alongside its precedents and fallouts throughout the 1970s, would show an expanded notion of writing that includes extraliterary texts that share repertoires of rhetoric for depicting ethnicity, defining representation in both textual and political forms. I wanted to show how indebted modern literature was to ethnography and how certain patterns of writing persisted in writing the *buraku* over time. I also pursued how Nakagami's socialized self, defined through exchange rather than self-consciousness, might produce a different idea of the literary producer. To do so I introduced the unconventional nature of his apprenticeship as an autodidact, a worker-writer, a traveler, and a volatile and compelling conversationalist. In roundtable conversations, mugging for the tape recorder showed exactly how Nakagami parlayed the assumption that "I is an 'Other'" into communicative situations that he sometimes spurned, sometimes took charge of, sometimes got lost in, and sometimes treated as a space of self-mythology. I showed how the distribution of I-ness in his works happened less through controlled unilateral self-representation and more through writing himself into ongoing conversations and debates on the status of ethnicity, the relation of language in books to language outside of books, and the relation of Japanese fiction to ethnography, many of which highlighted the situation of living in parallax.

I showed other examples of activism that clashed with Nakagami's own agendas in chapters 1 and 2 in key figures like Noma Hiroshi and Hijikata Tetsu as well as in foundational historiographers. This divergence suggested not only that there was a sense of canonicity in *buraku* writing but that this canon was understood to privilege history, realism, and social engagement, and that although Nakagami's works evaded the transformational self-consciousness that liberation literature writers advocated, he drew on a shared archive of *buraku* rhetorical activism, such as confession and the somatic pain caused by words, and applied its repertoire with historical particularity to contemporary events (the Sayama trial and the Vietnam War). We saw in chapter 3 how he used the rhetoric of the *buraku* as a dark continent to excavate folk stories and oral narration that uses tropes common in the national histories while using local names and toponyms to write an open-source history, one that is both localizable and encourages us to think at the circulation of (even folkic) cultural forms in terms of multiple scales: local, regional, national, and global.

By looking at manifestos and histories, I underscored that the literary history to which Nakagami gestures is based on retrieving the elements of writing that are not literature per se. While poststructuralist critics were documenting, asserting, or lamenting the end of literature, he was constructing a new archive of writing that traversed venues known both as pure literature and the legal system and those known as subcultural forms. I argued that Nakagami's approach to using the pop structuralist term *monogatari* added an ethnographic twist to the linguistic turn that underwrote the booming field of theory (*shisō*) in the 1970s and 1980s. This, I argued, connected Nakagami's work in fiction, reportage, and public speaking to the project of making a claim on mainstream identity in postwar Japan, often through hidden transcripts that are available to a discursive reader who has informed him or herself about *buraku* history and can read for parallax. This hidden transcript also allowed for cross-cultural comparison by depicting geopolitical alignments in the human and economic terms of suffering and solidarity. I argued that issues of differential identity—namely race and ethnicity, not the resurgence of class discussion that has emerged with discussions of the "gap" society (*kakusa shakai*)—were left unaddressed by youth-oriented leftist politics and critics of the postmodern image. I maintained that these differentials, social neologisms like the *roji*, need to be relinked to the material transformations of labor taking place in the postmodern managed society of Japan.

By situating Nakagami's work in concrete discussions about historical context and cultural modernization in the early twentieth century, I worked to show how including new media and subcultural forms of narrative and mixed-media work adds to our understanding of the role that writing can be seen to play in the postwar landscape. Much writing about subculture is disappointing because it succumbs to the same kind of modernization theory assumptions that literary scholars have been trying to undo for thirty years. In this dirge, literature is claimed to be obsolete purely because of its age and doomed to dodder wanly into obsolescence when newer, more technologically savvy or gadget-friendly media appear on the scene. When literary studies responds to new media defensively, rather than looking at the parallax relations that different storytelling forms adopt and have adopted, it becomes claustrophobic. The suffocating effect of canonization on Nakagami's works and their sheltering from conversation in terms of subculture and mixed-media works is apparent. When these works drop from the conversation, entire constellations of important themes go with them. I hoped to show in chapters 5 and 6 that this dropped material includes the global South and the relation to the multiple Souths that Japan is connected to. This forced separation prohibits Nakagami's literary works from taking part in ongoing conversations about story worlds and serial narratives and genre fictions that traverse media and incorporate both visual and literary semiotics in their expressions.

What might be learned from looking at Japanese literature or any global postmodern literature in light of these findings? Five specific programs come to mind. First and most broadly, if we followed Nakagami's lead here we would never be able to look at a library, a university, or an edition of complete works without asking about how literary institutions are intimately related to other kinds of writing race and ethnicity in the modern age, especially the formation of a national canon based on separating text from image, oral from written, and native from foreign. Second, we could follow Nakagami's lead in transforming literature and literary history by treating oral literature and folk art as something besides lyricism and something besides document, taking it beyond debates of authenticity. In his work, oral culture is neither for the pure purpose of connecting to an originary holistic past nor for documenting sociohistorical fact. Rather, it works as a kind of criticism to interpret local events in a broader context by improvising key narrative elements in shifting scales of context. The third page we might take from Nakagami's playbook is a more acute understanding of how a national literature is constructed around discourses that produce an enemy within as a way of heightening and verifying national identity. The terrorist of "Map of a Nineteen-Year-Old" and the serial killer in the 1969 essay "Letter from Nagayama Norio" feature angry young men who respond to a structure of dispossession with "a pistol, not a pen."[1] The story is fiction and the imagined letter speaks from the point of view of a historically real person. Suggestive comparisons are easily found in Japanese literature, beginning with *The Broken Commandment*. Abe Kazushige's 1996 *Individual Projection* depicts the film noir–like story told in flashback of a world-weary twenty-something freeter—a free-lance contract worker who cobbles together jobs to survive in a recession economy—who becomes embroiled in a plot to build a nuclear bomb while making a school film project. Outside Japan, Michael Muhammad Knight's *The Taqwacores*, about a Muslim punk rock house in Buffalo, New York, explores issues of orthodoxy and rebellion through the musical and philosophical landscape of the two self-reflexive belief systems of its twenty-something protagonists in a disenchanted Rust Belt town. Allegories of managed life in works such as Margaret Atwood's *Handmaid's Tale* or China Miéville's *Perdido Street Station* all hinge on systems that represent multiple worlds full of social neologisms, ones that dramatize worlds based on differential identity and feature subcultural protagonists that collaborate to invent new forms of social life under conditions of neoliberal and fascist life that attempt to name and regulate the enemy within.

Fourth, the implications for literature seen in a frame of global post-modernism include how writers write for multiple audiences and for different scales of readership. Nakagami's works, along with other sub-culture works in the 1980s, show a developing consciousness of a set of regional connectivities across national boundaries linked by writers who read in translation and are themselves translated. One such body, as I have argued, is the global South. There is no reason that East Asian area studies need restrict itself to the Cold War constellation of the C-J-K character set. Going beyond the Chinese, Japanese, and Korean presets can produce fruitful regional analyses that respond to new scales and political or aes-thetic alignments. In the context of global postmodernism, these might include postmodern treatments of received tradition in an era of high-speed economic growth or rapidly, unevenly modernizing examples such as the northern and southern landscapes of Michelangelo Antonioni's cinematic Italy, the Lebanon of Rashid Al-Daif's *Dear Mr. Kawabata*, the frontier morality of Octavia Butler's *Fledgling*, or Junot Díaz's Dominican Republic via New Jersey in *The Brief and Wondrous Life of Oscar Wao*.

And finally, as we consider future directions for engaging contempo-rary literature from Japan, Nakagami's stress on differential identity can remind us that in translation we are all too apt to flatten the difference that we see as the obstacle of translation so that we may accommodate and naturalize our own understandings of identity. His *roji* can prompt us to use the new, the unfamiliar, or the neologism to refer to specific kinds of alterity and allow them to establish genuinely other narratives. In the politics of translation that broker Japanese fiction into English, difference seems fixed in a vocabulary that derives from a sociological abstraction of the Civil Rights imaginary of the mid-1960s. It is not able to accommodate either shifts in black history or any other minority presence, including an Americanized Asian presence. The structure of this time lag is most vividly illustrated in the respective ways of taking in Nakagami and Murakami Haruki: the most literary and black of postwar writers and the most popular and white of postwar writers, respectively. The unspoken assumption that difference should be articulated in racial terms is brought out when we consider the British English translation of Nakagami's works. Andrew Rankin's translation of *Snakelust* interprets Nakagami's Kishū characters through the lens of class. The cockney flourish seems jarring to a reader of American English; the reverse is probably true of the British or other English reader who reads the U.S. translation of *The Cape* and looks for evidence of the subtitle that the book has acquired in translation, "stories from the Japanese ghetto."

Nakagami's work prompts to ask questions about the relations between literary representation and political representation. It introduces compelling questions about the relations, moreover, between social movements and aesthetics and about the personal responsibility of being one of a kind in a cultural marketplace, refusing to follow an activist mandate but also refusing to give up a materialist approach to textual historicity in the context where most of this writer's intellectual colleagues were claiming the end of history. To say the least, postwar Japan has not typically been a place one looks for model understandings of culture beyond monoculture. I think this assumption is, to conclude by invoking my visual metaphor one final time, shortsighted. Nakagami's *roji* teaches us that we may have to unlearn our habitual vocabularies of difference and identity and understand the neologisms of experience—literally, its new words. Perhaps the temporal orientation of my interpretation of difference, rooted in the new, should prompt me to rethink why alterity is productively described as future oriented. I mean it also to ask what the politics of exchange are in the relations of *kōtsū* that increasingly structure our daily lives and the ways that media and differential identity constantly ask us to think, act, depend, and translate given the very real fiction that we live, the ways in which "I is an 'Other.'"

Notes

Introduction

1. All English translations are by author unless otherwise noted. Nakagami Kenji, "Watashi wa 'Nihon'jin na no ka?" in *Nakagami Kenji hatsugen shūsei*, ed. Karatani Kōjin and Suga Hidemi (Tokyo: Dai-san bunmeisha, 1999), 338–58.

2. Nakagami, "Watashi wa 'Nihon'jin na no ka?" 340.

3. See Yanase Keisuke, *Shakai-gai no shakai: eta hinin* (Tokyo: Daigaku-kan, 1901).

4. W. E. B. Du Bois, *The Souls of Black Folk* (Chicago: A. C. McClurg, 1909), 3.

5. Ibid., 3; Nakagami Kenji and Karatani Kōjin, *Kobayashi Hideo o koete: taidan hyōron* (Tokyo: Kawade shobō, 1979), 143.

6. For the use of the camera obscura by Nietzsche, Marx, and Freud, see Sarah Kofman, *Camera Obscura: Of Ideology*, trans. Will Straw (Ithaca, N.Y.: Cornell University Press, 1999).

7. Carl Cassegard, "Exteriority and Transcritique: Karatani Kōjin and the Impact of the 1990s," *Japanese Studies* 27, no.1 (2007): 5. Parallax is also the basis of Karatani's reading of Kant, which he takes up in *Transcritique on Kant and Marx* (Cambridge, Mass.: MIT Press, 2003).

8. Étienne Balibar and Immanuel Wallerstein, *Race, Nation, Class: Ambiguous Identities* (London: Verso, 1991), 8.

9. Kurokawa Midori, "Jinshu-shugi to buraku sabetsu," in *Jinshu gainen no fuhensei o tō*, ed. Takezawa Yasuko (Kyoto: Jinbun shoin, 2005), 276–97.

10. See Michael Brownstein, "From *Kokugaku* to *Kokubungaku*: Canon-Formation in the Meiji Period," *Harvard Journal of Asiatic Studies* 47, no. 2 (1987): 435–60; and Tomiko Yoda, *Gender and National Literature: Heian Texts in the Constructions of Japanese Modernity* (Durham, N.C.: Duke University Press, 2004).

11. Theodore C. Bestor, Patricia G. Steinhoff, and Victoria Lyon-Bestor, *Doing Fieldwork in Japan* (Honolulu: University of Hawai'i Press, 2003), 3.

12. James Clifford and George Marcus, *Writing Culture: The Poetics and Politics of Ethnography* (Berkeley: University of California Press, 2010).

13. Bestor, Steinhoff and Lyon-Bestor, *Doing Fieldwork in Japan*, 3.

14. Nakagami Kenji, *Kishū: ki no kuni, ne no kuni monogatari* (Tokyo: Asahi shinbunsha, 1978), 251.

15. Umezawa Toshihiko, Yamagishi Takashi, and Hirano Hidehisa, *Bungaku no naka no hisabetsu buraku-zō: sengo-hen* (Tokyo: Akashi shoten, 1982), 271.

16. Moriyasu Toshiji, *Nakagami Kenji-ron: Kumano, roji, gensō* (Osaka: Kaihō shuppansha, 2003), 1.

17. Watanabe Naomi, *Nihon kindai bungaku to "sabetsu"* (Tokyo: Ōta shuppan, 1994), 32–40.

18. Hamamura is constantly seen as a man of cryptic origins.

19. The Cotton Road should be read as an analog of the Silk Road and modern industrialization, but also with reference to Erskine Caldwell's novel *Tobacco Road*. Poet Yaguchi Yasufumi tells me that Nakagami was a good friend of the Ainu novelist Uenishi Haruji and that *Tobacco Road* was a major inspiration for Uenishi, a countertext to Faulkner's works.

20. David Harvey, "Neoliberalism as Creative Destruction," *The ANNALS of the American Academy of Political and Social Science* 610 (2007): 21.

21. While generative works such as Michael Hardt and Antonio Negri's *Empire* and Naomi Klein's *The Shock Doctrine* treat Japan, Japan remains outside the scope of the main analysis. None of the key Japanese texts is yet translated. See Sakai Takashi, *Jiyū-ron* (Tokyo: Seidosha, 2001); and Shibuya Nozomu, *Tamashii no rōdō: neo-riberarizumu-ron* (Tokyo: Seidosha, 2003).

22. For early discussions, see Murahashi Tadasu, *Dowa kyōiku no jissen* (Kyoto: Buraku mondai kenkyūjo shuppanbu, 1963).

23. Matsune Hisao, Kurimoto Hideichi, and Mukai Takashi, *Hirakareta yutakana bungaku*, ed. Takazawa Shūji (Yokohama: Kyū bunkakai, 1994), 8.

24. Nakagami Kenji, "Hisabetsu buraku no kōkai kōza hakkai de uchikiri no hansei," in *Nakagami Kenji zenshū 15*, ed. Karatani et al. (Tokyo: Shūeisha, 1996), 257–60.

25. Nakagami, "Ki no mama no kora," *Kaihō kyōiku* 8 (1983): 14–17.

26. Umezawa, Yamagishi, and Hirano, *Bungaku no naka no hisabetsu buraku-zō: sengo-hen*, 303.

27. Moriyasu, *Nakagami Kenji-ron*, 5.

28. Nakagami and Karatani, *Kobayashi Hideo o koete*, 51.

29. Nakagami, "Watashi wa 'Nihon'jin na no ka?" 345.

30. See Yoshikuni Igarashi, *Bodies of Memory: Narratives of War in Postwar Japanese Culture, 1945–1970* (Princeton, N.J.: Princeton University Press, 2000), esp. chapter 3.

31. For an anthropological history of the concept, see Harumi Befu, *Hegemony of Homogeneity: An Anthropological Analysis of "Nihonjinron"* (Melbourne: Trans Pacific Press, 2001). Recent works include David L. Howell, *Geographies of Identity in Nineteenth-Century Japan* (Berkeley: University of California Press, 2005); Richard Siddle, *Race, Resistance and the Ainu of Japan* (London: Routledge, 1996); Sonia Ryang and John Lie, *Diaspora without Homeland: Being Korean in Japan* (Berkeley: University of California Press, 2009); and Ken Kawashima, *The Proletarian Gamble:*

Korean Workers in Interwar Japan (Durham, N.C.: Duke University Press, 2009). English-language *buraku* socioanthropology that contested the myth of a monoculture began with George Devos and Hiroshi Wagatsuma's *Japan's Invisible Race: Caste in Culture and Personality* (Berkeley: University of California Press, 1966).

32. See Kim Jung-mi, *Suihei undō kenkyū: minzoku sabetsu hihan* (Tokyo: Gendai kikakushitsu, 1994).

33. See Edward Fowler, "The *Buraku* in Modern Japanese Literature: Texts and Contexts," *Journal of Japanese Studies* 26, no. 1 (1998): 21–25; and Kim, *Suihei undō kenkyū*, 543–80.

34. Tomotsune Tsutomu, "Nakagami Kenji and the *Buraku* Issue in Postwar Japan," *Inter-Asia Cultural Studies* 4, no. 2 (2003): 228.

35. Nakagami, *Kishū: ki no kuni, ne no kuni monogatari*, 216.

36. Christopher Kelty, *Two Bits: The Cultural Significance of Free Software* (Durham, N.C.: Duke University Press, 2008), 18.

37. Kanai Mieko, Karatani Kōjin, Kōno Taeko, and Yasuoka Shōtarō et al, "Tsuitō Nakagami Kenji," *Bungakkai* 46, no. 10 (1992): 135. The speaker is Shimada Masahiko.

38. Kobayashi Yoshinori, *Sensō-ron* (Tokyo: Gentōsha, 1998). In English, see Mark Driscoll, "Kobayashi Yoshinori Is Dead: Imperial War/Sick Liberal Peace/Neoliberal Class War," *Mechademia* 4 (2009): 290–303.

39. Nakagami, "Ki no mama no kora," 16.

40. On *buraku* activism in terms of human rights, see John H. Davis, "Blurring the Boundaries of the *Buraku(min)*," in *Globalization and Social Change in Contemporary Japan*, ed. J. S. Eades, Tom Gill, and Harumi Befu (Melbourne: Trans Pacific Press, 2000), 110–22.

41. Nakagami, "Watashi wa 'Nihon'jin na no ka?"339.

42. Ibid., 340.

43. Takayama Fumihiko, *Erekutora: Nakagami Kenji no shōgai* (Tokyo: Bungei shunjū, 2007), 63. Thanks to Robin Colomb for introducing me to this book.

44. Ibid., 69–72.

45. Nakagami Kenji and Ōe Kenzaburō, "Tayō-ka suru gendai bungaku—sen-kyū-hyaku hachi-jū nendai e mukete," *Gendai shi techō* 77, no. 1 (1980): 198.

46. Yomota Inuhiko, "Sanshu ni tsuite," *Gengo bunka* 14 (1997): 164. Rimbaud is foundational in the Japanese reception of French poetics because of Kobayashi Hideo's early works on realism and symbolism. See Kobayashi Hideo, *Ranbō, X e no tegami* (Tokyo: Shinchōsha, 1978).

47. Nakagami published a roundtable on haiku with Kadokawa Haruki, arguably the most important impresario in postwar independent film production. See Nakagami Kenji and Kadokawa Haruki, *Haiku no jidai: Tōno, Kumano, Yoshino seichi junrei* (Tokyo: Kadokawa shoten, 1985).

48. Certainly he is among the most mythologized. His death at the age of twenty-five, after living for eleven years in Africa, is often seen by critics to be

prefigured in his poetry's ambivalent claims on French racial history and the Africanist discourse in his poem "Mauvais sang" (Bad blood), in *A Season in Hell* (Boston: Little, Brown, 1997), 8–23.

49. Arthur Rimbaud, *A Season in Hell*. For the effect of the autobiographical fallacy on interpretation of Rimbaud, see Christopher L. Miller, *Blank Darkness: Africanist Discourse in French* (Chicago: University of Chicago Press, 1985).

50. Rimbaud, *A Season in Hell*, 9.

51. Nakagami and Murakami Ryū, *Jazu to bakudan* (Tokyo: Kawade shobō, 1983), 92.

52. Nakagami Kenji, "Jūhassai no koro," *Bungaku-kai* 31, no. 10 (1977): 166.

53. Nakagami, "Jūhassai no koro," 166.

54. Van Gessel, *The Sting of Life: Four Contemporary Japanese Novelists* (New York: Columbia University Press, 1989), 40; Nakagami, "Jūhassai no koro," 166.

55. Nakagami Kenji, "Tenjō no nagame e—tsuitō Mori Atsushi," in *Nakagami Kenji zenshū 15*, ed. Karatani et al. (Tokyo: Shūeisha, 1996), 599.

56. Nakagami Kenji, "Ichiban hajime no dekigoto," in *Nakagami Kenji zenshū* 1 (Tokyo: Shūeisha, 1995), 209–63.

57. Takayama, *Erekutora*, 15.

58. Watanabe Naomi, *Nakagami Kenji-ron: itōshisa ni tsuite* (Tokyo: Kawade shobō shinsha, 1996), 6.

59. Ibid.

60. Eve Zimmerman, *Out of the Alleyway: Nakagami Kenji and the Poetics of Outcaste Fiction* (Cambridge, Mass.: Harvard University Asia Center, 2007), 32–34.

61. Moriyasu, *Nakagami Kenji-ron*, 5.

62. Tessa Morris-Suzuki, *Beyond Computopia: Information, Automation and Democracy in Japan* (London: Kegan Paul International, 1988). Tsurumi Shunsuke's writing on pragmatism and Peircean semiotics in the journal *Science of Thought* (Shisō no kagaku) began in 1946.

63. David Harvey, *The Condition of Postmodernity: An Enquiry into the Origins of Cultural Change* (Oxford: Blackwell, 1989), 66 and 75.

64. Ikegami Yoshihiko, "Gendai-Shiso: Making Use of Postmodernism," *Inter-Asia Cultural Studies* 2, no. 3 (2001): 370.

65. Marilyn Ivy, "Critical Texts, Mass Artifacts: The Consumption of Knowledge in Postmodern Japan," in *Postmodernism and Japan*, ed. Masao Miyoshi and H. D. Harootunian (Durham, N.C.: Duke University Press, 1989), 26.

66. Playboy Nihonban henshūbu, *Playboy Interview Selected* (Tokyo: Shūeisha, 1990), 97–114.

67. Fujii Sadakazu, *Monogatari riron kōza* (Tokyo: Tokyo daigaku shuppankai, 2003).

68. Hasumi Shigehiko, *Fūkō, Durūzu, Derida* (Tokyo: Asahi shuppansha, 1978).

69. Karatani Kōjin, *The Origins of Modern Japanese Literature* (Durham, N.C.: Duke University Press, 1993), 193.

70. Karatani, *The Origins of Modern Japanese Literature*, 193.

71. Kobayashi Hideo, "Discourse on Fiction of the Self," in *Literature of the Lost Home: Kobayashi Hideo—Literary Criticism, 1924–1939*, trans. Paul Anderer (Stanford, Calif.: Stanford University Press).

72. Nakagami, "Karatani Kōjin e no tegami," in *Fūkei no mukō e/Monogatari no keifu* (Tokyo: Kōdansha bungei bunko, 2004), 88–114.

73. Jacques Derrida, *Dissemination*, trans. Barbara Johnson (Chicago: University of Chicago Press, 1981), 98–118.

74. Fujii Sadakazu, "Barikēdo no naka no *Genji monogatari*," *Tenbō* 127 (1969): 123–34.

75. Tomiko Yoda, *Gender and National Literature: Heian Texts in the Constructions of Japanese Modernity* (Durham, N.C.: Duke University Press, 2004), 83.

76. Hyōdo Hiromi, *"Koe" no kokumin kokka Nihon* (Tokyo: Nippon hōsō shuppan kyōkai, 2000); and Hyōdo Hiromi, *Monogatari, oraritī, kyōdōtai: shin katarimono josetsu* (Tokyo: Hitsuji shobō, 2002).

77. Kobayashi Hideo, "Discourse on Fiction of the Self," in *Literature of the Lost Home: Kobayashi Hideo—Literary Criticism, 1924-1939*, ed. Paul Anderer (Stanford, Calif.: Stanford University Press, 1995), 67–93; and Kobayashi Hideo, "Watakushi shōsetsu-ron," in *Shintei Kobayashi Hideo zenshū* (Tokyo: Shinchōsha, 1978), 118–45.

78. Gessel, *The Sting of Life*, 68.

79. Kobayashi, "Discourse on Fiction of the Self," 75; Kobayashi, "Watakushi shōsetsu-ron," 127.

80. Kobayashi, "Discourse on Fiction of the Self," 80; Kobayashi, "Watakushi shōsetsu-ron," 132.

81. Kobayashi, "Discourse on Fiction of the Self," 82; Kobayashi, "Watakushi shōsetsu-ron," 134.

82. André Gide, *The Counterfeiters, with the Journal of "The Counterfeiters,"* trans. Dorothy Bussy and Justin O'Brien (New York: Vintage, 1973), 189.

83. Kobayashi, "Discourse on Fiction of the Self," 84; Kobayashi, "Watakushi shōsetsu-ron," 136.

84. See Hibi Yoshitaka, *"Jiko hyōshō" no bungaku-shi: jibun o kaku shōsetsu no tōjō* (Tokyo: Kanrin shobō, 2002).

85. *Hisabetsu buraku* is the phrase most commonly used in official or public contexts to refer to *buraku* neighborhoods. *Hisabetsu* (被差別) means "suffering or experiencing discrimination"; *hisabetsu buraku* refers to a neighborhood where people who have historically experienced such discrimination live.

86. Nakagami, *The Cape and Other Stories from the Japanese Ghetto*, trans. Eve Zimmerman (Berkeley: Stone Bridge Press, 1999), 180.

87. Kawamura Jirō, "Nakagami Kenji," in *Shinchō nihon bungaku jiten* (Tokyo: Shinchōsha, 1988), 901.

88. "Sengo umare hajime no Akutagawa-shō sakka Nakagami Kenji-san shi-kyo," *Sankei shinbun* (August 13, 1992), 27; Etō Jun, "Waga tomo yo, yasashii kyojin yo," *Mainichi shinbun,* August 15, 1992, 36.

89. Tatematsu Wahei, "Tsuitō Nakagami Kenji—Kajōna nikutai no sakka," *Shūkan dokusho-jin,* September 7, 1992, 1.

90. Etō, "Waga tomo yo," 36.

91. Nakagami, "Watashi wa 'Nihon'jin na no ka?" 338.

92. Nakagami Kenji "Monogatari no keifu—hachi-nin no sakka—1—Satō Haruo," *Kokubungaku kaishaku to kyōzai no kenkyū* 24, no. 2 (1979): 141. For photos and coverage of the earthquake and subsequent tsunami and fire damage, see, for example, "Shingū-shi wa zenmetsu ka?—kinan no shosho ni kasai," *Asahi shinbun,* Osaka ed., December 22, 1946, 2.

93. Nakagami, *Kishū: ki no kuni, ne no kuni monogatari,* 141.

1. An Archive of Activism

1. For a more elaborate description of Tokugawa status distinctions, see David L. Howell, *Geographies of Identity in Nineteenth-Century Japan* (Berkeley: University of California Press, 2005).

2. Harada Tomohiko, *Hisabetsu buraku no rekishi,* Asahi sensho 34 (Tokyo: Asahi shinbunsha, 1975), 182.

3. Yanase Keisuke, *Shakai-gai no shakai: eta hinin* (Tokyo: Daigakukan, 1901).

4. Yanagita Kunio, "Iwayuru tokushu buraku no shurui," in *Suihei=hito no yo ni hikari are,* ed. Okiura Kazuteru (Tokyo: Shakai hyōronsha, 1981), 105.

5. Takahashi Sadaki, *Hisabetsu buraku issennen-shi,* ed. Okiura Kazuteru (Tokyo: Iwanami shoten, 1992), 20.

6. Kimura Ki, *Bungei tōzai nanboku* (Tokyo: Shinchōsha, 1926), 50–93.

7. My point of reference is Gayatri Spivak's essay, "Can the Subaltern Speak?" in *Marxism and the Interpretation of Culture,* ed. Cary Nelson and Lawrence Grossberg (Urbana: University of Illinois Press, 1988), 271–316. Spivak reads the word "representation" in the two registers of political and literary representation.

8. Christopher Kelty, *Two Bits: The Cultural Significance of Free Software* (Durham, N.C.: Duke University Press, 2008), 3–11.

9. A number of local protests, petitions, and initiatives had preceded the edict. Mere months before the Meiji Restoration in 1868, *eta* leader Danzaemon petitioned to have the status of sixteen of his men raised after he was raised to *heimin* status after pledging to help the *bakufu* military government in battle. In Watanabe village, an *eta* village petitioned to the *bakufu* in 1867 that discriminating against them because they ate meat was untenable since foreigners whose interests they courted also ate meat. It was finally Ōe Taku, a bureaucrat in the Ministry of Popular Affairs, who put through

the decree, although his version contained economic provisions for artisan training and resettlement to the frontier of Hokkaidō among other measures. The Emancipation Edict is actually a name applied later to this edict. Variations on its name reveal a great deal about the power the interpreter wants it to have. Some critics object to the term "emancipation" (*kaihō*) because while the colloquial name of the Emancipation Edict echoes Abraham Lincoln's Emancipation Proclamation of 1865, the edict didn't actually "free" anyone. Nor were the pre-1871 lower echelons of the status system actually slaves. One paraphrase has called it the "*senmin* liberation edict" (liberation of the outcasts, exploited, abjected), which is more direct about who is imagined to be liberated when the *eta* and *hinin* nomenclature is abolished. Other scholars reject the term "liberation" and emphasize the specific concrete effects of the decree, attributing to it names such as "edict that abolishes abject names."

10. See Ogushi Natsumi, *Kindai hisabetsu buraku-shi kenkyū* (Tokyo: Akashi shoten, 1980).

11. Hirota Masaki, *Sabetsu no shosō* (Tokyo: Iwanami shoten, 1990), 76–77.

12. For extended analysis, see Harada, *Hisabetsu buraku no rekishi*, and Harada Tomohiko and Uesugi Satoshi, ed., *Kindai buraku-shi shiryō shūsei* (Tokyo: San-ichi shobō, 1984), esp. vol. 1 and 2. The text of the decree is published in Hirota, *Sabetsu no shosō*, 76–77.

13. Frank Upham, *Law and Social Change in Postwar Japan* (Cambridge, Mass.: Harvard University Press, 1987), 114.

14. Shimazaki Tōson, *The Broken Commandment*, trans. Kenneth Strong (Tokyo: University of Tokyo Press, 1974), 78. Japanese references are from Shimazaki Tōson, "Hakai," in *Shimazaki Tōson-shū* 1 (Tokyo: Kadokawa shoten, 1970), 132.

15. Tōson, *The Broken Commandment*, 114, 147; Tōson, *Hakai*, 217.

16. Ibid.

17. Ibid.

18. Tōson, *The Broken Commandment*, 229; Tōson, *Hakai*, 321.

19. Tōson, *Hakai*, 321; omitted in English.

20. Sugiura Jūgo and Fukumoto Nichinan, *Hankai yume monogatari ichimei shinheimin kaiten-dan*, Kindai Digital Library of the National Diet Library, http://kindai .ndl.go.jp/BIImgFrame.php?JP_NUM=40031423&VOL_NUM=00000&KOMA =1&ITYPE=0.

21. Massimiliano Tomasi, *Rhetoric in Modern Japan: Western Influences on the Development of Narrative and Oratorical Style* (Honolulu: University of Hawai'i Press, 2004), 2.

22. Upham, *Law and Social Change*, 103.

23. This phrase about poesis is drawn from Marx's eleventh thesis on Feuerbach, written just before the *Communist Manifesto*.

24. Upham, *Law and Social Change*, 78. See also Buraku kaihō jinken kenkyūjo, *Buraku mondai jinken jiten* (Osaka: Buraku kaihō jinken kenkyūjo, 2001), 149–50.

25. Ian Neary, *Political Protest and Social Control in Prewar Japan: The Origins of Buraku Liberation* (Atlantic Highlands, N.J.: Humanities Press International, 1989), 85.

26. Noma Hiroshi and Yasuoka Shōtarō, *Sabetsu, sono kongen o tou*, vol. 1 (Tokyo: Asahi shinbunsha, 1984), 205.

27. My account comes from Upham, *Law and Social Change*; Noma Hiroshi, Kokubun Ichitarō, and Hijikata Tetsu, "Buraku sabetsu hihan—Yata kyōiku sabetsu jiken o megutte," in *Buraku kaihō to bunka undō* (Tokyo: Orijin shuppan sentā, 1977), 172–205; and Inoue Kiyoshi's *Buraku no rekishi to kaihō riron* (Tokyo: Tabata shoten, 1969).

28. Noma Hiroshi, Kokubun Ichitarō, and Hijikata Tetsu, "Buraku sabetsu hihan—Yata kyōiku sabetsu jiken o megutte," 172–205.

29. Inoue, *Buraku no rekishi to kaihō riron*, 388.

30. Upham, *Law and Social Change*, 102.

31. Kita Sadakichi, in *Tokushu buraku kenkyū*, Buraku mondai shiryō bunken 5 (Tokyo: Sekai bunko, 1968).

32. Harada, *Hisabetsu buraku no rekishi*, 261.

33. Kita, *Tokushu buraku kenkyū*, 1, 2.

34. See Kita Sadakichi, *Yūwa sokushin* (Tokyo: Chūō yūwa jigyō kyōkai, 1926); and Kita Sadakichi, *Yūwa mondai ni kansuru rekishi-teki kōsatsu* (Tokyo: Chūō yūwa jigyō kyōkai, 1933).

35. For extensive treatment of Kita's work as a colonial bureaucrat in Korea, see Oguma Eiji, *Tan'itsu minzoku shinwa no kigen: "Nihonjin" no jigazō no keifu* (Tokyo: Shin'yōsha, 1995).

36. See Germaine A. Hoston, *Marxism and the Crisis of Development in Prewar Japan* (Princeton, N.J.: Princeton University Press, 1986).

37. Okiura Kazuteru, *Tennō no kuni, senmin no kuni: ryōkyoku no tabū* (Tokyo: Kōbundō, 1990), 219–22.

38. Takahashi, *Hisabetsu buraku issennen-shi*, 26; 39–40.

39. Ibid., 114–53.

40. Ibid., 37.

41. Ibid., 7; 6.

42. Ibid., 5–6.

43. Ibid., 182.

44. Ibid.

45. Ibid., 183.

46. Ibid.

47. Ibid.

48. Kimura, *Bungei tōzai nanboku*, 50 and 52.

49. Ibid., 51.

50. Ibid., 55.

51. Ibid., 56.

52. See Watanabe Katei, *Sōfuren*, Buraku mondai bungei sakuhin senshū 4 (Tokyo: Sekai bunko, 1973); Ōkura Tōrō, *Biwa-uta*, Buraku mondai bungei sakuhin senshū 23–24 (Tokyo: Sekai bunko, 1975).

53. Kimura, *Bungei tōzai nanboku*. 71.

54. Ibid., 64.

55. Dai ikkai Matsumoto Ji'ichirō-shō jūshō—Noma Hiroshi-shi—Kyōto de no kisha kaiken kara, *Buraku kaihô* 100 (1977): 99.

56. The total novel is based on a realistic aesthetic and an existentialist philosophy that connects large panoramas of characters to social issues and anchors the works' style in mimetic realism. See Noma Hiroshi, *Zentai shōsetsu to sōzōryoku* (Tokyo: Kawade shobō shinsha, 1969).

57. Kitahara Taisaku, "Nihon kindai bungaku ni arawareta buraku mondai," *Bungaku* 11, no. 2 (1959): 144–45.

58. See Noma Hiroshi, *Kurai e, Hōkai kankaku* (Tokyo: Iwanami shoten, 1987).

59. Noma Hiroshi, *Kaihō no bungaku sono kongen: Noma Hiroshi hyōron, kōen, taiwa-shū*, Kaihō bungaku sōsho 1 (Osaka: Kaihō shuppansha, 1988), 5–6.

60. Ibid., 23.

61. Hijikata Tetsu, *Chikakei* (Tokyo: San-ichi shobō, 1963), 333.

62. "Hon no shokai: Buraku kaihō to bunka undō—Hijikata Tetsu esseishū," *Buraku kaihô* 112 (1977): 102.

63. Hijikata, *Chikakei*, 325.

64. Ibid., 5.

65. Ibid., 327.

66. Ibid., 55, 56.

67. Ibid., 16.

2. Confession and the Crisis of *Buraku* Writing in the 1970s

1. Watanabe Naomi, *Nihon kindai bungaku to "sabetsu"* (Tokyo: Ōta shuppan, 1994), 32–40.

2. Michael Bourdaghs, *The Dawn that Never Comes: Shimazaki Tōson and Japanese Nationalism* (New York: Columbia University Press, 2003), 33–34.

3. Kitahara Taisaku, "Nihon kindai bungaku ni arawareta buraku mondai," *Bungaku* 11, no. 2 (1959): 133–34. Kitahara was a member of the BLL Central Committee. He was committed to seeing discrimination as irrational and maintains that because race (*jinshu*) and tribe (*shuzoku*) came "late" into Japan via natural and social sciences, the meanings are vague and imprecise. In Kitahara's opinion, *buraku* issues have nothing to do with racial or ethnic issues but make sense purely in the scheme of Japanese feudal remnants (133). However, he makes comparative use of literature to illustrate his theories of liberation. In his treatment of Mulk Raj Anand's 1953 novel *The*

Untouchable and its three theories of liberation—Christianity, Gandhi's nonviolence, and modern technology (in the form of the flush toilet)—he faults the book for failing to critique imperialism, which he sees as the most significant enemy.

4. Umezawa Toshihiko, Yamagishi Takashi, and Hirano Hidehisa, *Bungaku no naka no hisabetsu buraku zō: senzen-hen* (Tokyo: Akashi shoten, 1980), 8.

5. Koga Tadaaki, "E-tta," *Gendai shi techō* 20, no. 11 (1977): 40–44; Usui Yoshimi, "Jiko no tenmatsu," *Tenbō* 221 (1977): 102–95.

6. Hijikata Tetsu, *Sabetsu saiban: gendai no majō gari "Sayama jiken"* (Tokyo: Shakai shinpōsha, 1970), 17.

7. Noma Hiroshi and Yasuoka Shōtarō, "Sabetsu ishiki koso waga ishiki—Sayama saiban o jijuku toshite," *Asahi jānaru* 18, no. 43 (1976): 31.

8. Hijikata, *Sabetsu saiban*, 89–90.

9. Higashi Eizō, *"Hakai" no hyōka to buraku mondai* (Tokyo: Meiji tosho shuppan, 1977), 19.

10. Nakagami Kenji and Karatani Kōjin, *Kobayashi Hideo o koete: taidan hyōron* (Tokyo: Kawade shobō, 1979), 142–43.

11. Bourdaghs, *The Dawn That Never Comes*, 22.

12. See Karatani Kōjin, *The Origins of Modern Japanese Literature* (Durham, N.C.: Duke University Press, 1993).

13. Ibid., 79.

14. Ibid., 79.

15. Noguchi Michihiko, "Nakagami Kenji no roji to buraku mondai," *RIRIANS: kenkyū kiyō* 11 (2001): 85.

16. Moriyasu Toshiji, *Nakagami Kenji-ron: Kumano, roji, gensō* (Osaka: Kaihō shuppansha, 2003), 3.

17. Noguchi Michihiko sees this roundtable as his "coming out" in the literary establishment, where his "coming out" in point of fact (*honkaku*) was his 1977–78 series of reportage essays, *Kishū: ki no kuni, ne no kuni monogatari*. See Noguchi, "Nakagami Kenji no roji to buraku mondai," 83 and 85. The phrase "coming out" became detached from queer identity politics in the 1980s but retained the Foucauldian connection between confession, interface, and identity.

18. Karatani Kōjin and Nakagami Kenji, "Taidan: roji no shōshitsu to ryūbō," *Kokubungaku* 36, no. 14 (1991): 21.

19. Jacques Derrida, *A Derrida Reader: Between the Blinds*, trans. Peggy Kamuf (New York: Columbia University Press, 1991), 40.

20. See Noguchi, "Nakagami Kenji no roji to buraku mondai," 89. His interviewee, Miyazaki Manabu, remarks that he found Nakagami's perspective too close to "universal" cultural partisanship and not close enough to the daily life and struggles of *buraku* residents.

21. Nakagami Kenji, Yasuoka Shōtarō, and Noma Hiroshi, "Noma Hiroshi-Yasuoka Shōtarō no 'sabetsu' teidan—Sayama saiban o kijuku toshite—Nakagami Kenji-shi o mukaete—shimin ni hisomu sabetsu shinri—ge," *Asahi jānaru* 19, no. 12 (1977): 57.

22. Nakagami, Yasuoka, and Noma, "Noma Hiroshi-Yasuoka Shōtarō no 'sabetsu' teidan," 58. The comment is repeated by Senbon in *Kishū: ki no kuni, ne no kuni monogatari,* 333.

23. Nakagami, Yasuoka, and Noma, "Noma Hiroshi-Yasuoka Shōtarō no 'sabetsu' teidan," 58.

24. Ibid.

25. Ibid.

26. Miyako Inoue, *Vicarious Language: Gender and Linguistic Modernity in Japan* (Berkeley: University of California Press, 2006), 125.

27. See David A. Harris and the American Civil Liberties Union, *Driving While Black: Racial Profiling on Our Nation's Highways* (New York: American Civil Liberties Union, 1999).

28. Noma Hiroshi and Yasuoka Shōtarō, "Sabetsu ishiki koso waga ishiki—Sayama saiban o kijuku toshite," *Asahi jānaru* 18, no 43 (1976): 31.

29. Ishikawa Ichirō, *Sayama genchi hōkoku* (Tokyo: San-ichi shobō, 1978), 17.

30. Noma and Yasuoka, "Noma Hiroshi-Yasuoka Shōtarō no 'sabetsu' taidan," 55.

31. See, for instance, Kitahara, "Nihon kindai bungaku ni arawareta buraku mondai," 133–34. and Takahashi Sadaki, *Hisabetsu buraku issennen-shi,* ed. Okiura Kazuteru (Tokyo: Iwanami shoten, 1992), 114. In both cases, irrational means something like counter to scientific or historical materialism.

32. Noguchi, "Nakagami Kenji no roji to buraku mondai," 84.

33. Nakagami Kenji, "Jūkyūsai no chizu," in *Jūkyūsai no chizu* (Tokyo: Kawade bunko bungei, 1974), 79–138.

34. Ibid., 89.

35. Ibid., 98.

36. "Chimei sōkan ichi-nen yūhan—kyūdan no arasoi no katei," *Buraku kaihō* 104 (1977): 37.

37. Ibid., 31.

38. "'Sōkan' kyūdan ni sō-kaiki shiyō—'buraku chimei sōkan' sabetsu jiken kyūdan kokumin sōketsuki-kai kichō teian," *Buraku kaihō* 104 (1977): 16.

39. *Zoku: sabetsu yōgo,* ed. Yōgo to sabetsu o kangaeru shinpoziamu jikō iin-kai (Tokyo: Chōbunsha, 1978), 284.

40. *Sabetsu kyūdan gyōsei tōsō,* ed. Buraku kaihō kenkyū-jo (Tokyo: Buraku kaihō dōmei chūō honbu, 1981), 380–81.

41. "Dai ikkai kaihō buraku bungaku-shō nyūsen happyō," *Buraku kaihō* 53 (1975): 88–89.

42. "Dai ikkai kaihō buraku bungaku-shō nyūsen happyō," 132.

43. See Noma Hiroshi and the Sayama saiban kankō iinkai, *Kanpon Sayama saiban* (Tokyo: Iwanami shoten, 1976).

44. Noma and the Sayama saiban kankō iinkai, *Kanpon Sayama saiban: jō,* 1.

45. Kyōko Inoue, *MacArthur's Japanese Constitution: A Linguistic and Cultural Study of Its Making* (Chicago: University of Chicago Press, 1991), 281 and 283.

46. See Noma Hiroshi, *Kaihō no bungaku sono kongen: Noma Hiroshi hyōron, kōen, taiwa-shū,* Kaihō bungaku sōsho 1 (Osaka: Kaihō shuppansha, 1988).

47. Koga, "E-tta," 40.

48. Ibid., 43.

49. Ibid., 40 and 41.

50. Ibid., 42.

51. Ibid., 40.

52. Koga, "E-tta," 44.

53. *Zoku: sabetsu yōgo,* 78.

54. Usui, *A Complete Account of the Accident,* 183–85.

55. Takeda Katsuhiko and Nagasawa Yoshiaki, *Shōgen "Jiko no tenmatsu"* (Tokyo: Kōdansha, 1978), 23–28.

56. *Zoku: sabetsu yōgo,* 79.

57. Takeda and Nagasawa, *Shōgen "Jiko no tenmatsu,"* 201–2.

58. Usui, *A Complete Account of the Accident,* 103.

59. Ibid., 103.

60. Ibid., 105.

61. Ibid., 131.

62. Ibid., 137.

63. Ishida Rokurō, *Hatsu-koibito no tamashii otta Takuboku no shōgai* (Tokyo: Yōyōsha, 1978), i.

64. Usui, *A Complete Account of the Accident,* 164.

65. Ishida, *Hatsu-koibito no tamashii otta Takuboku no shōgai,* 16; 415.

66. Usui, *A Complete Account of the Accident,* 144.

67. Ibid., 185–86.

68. Ibid.

69. Ibid., 137.

70. Ibid., 145.

71. Ibid., 184.

72. Ibid., 142–43.

73. Ibid., 114 and 152; 123.

74. Ibid., 130; 106.

75. Ibid., 180.

76. Ibid., 130.

77. Nakagami Kenji, *Karekinada* (Tokyo: Kawade shobō shinsha, 1977), 144.

78. See Nina Cornyetz, *Dangerous Women, Deadly Words: Phallic Fantasy and Modernity in Three Japanese Writers* (Stanford, Calif.: Stanford University Press, 1999); Yomota Inuhiko, *Kishu to tensei: Nakagami Kenji* (Tokyo: Shinchōsha, 1996); and Eve Zimmerman, *Out of the Alleyway: Nakagami Kenji and the Poetics of Outcaste Fiction* (Cambridge, Mass.: Harvard University Asia Center, 2007), 107–21.

3. Constituents of National Literature

1. William Faulkner, Frederick L. Gwynn, and Joseph Leo Blotner, *Faulkner in the University: Class Conferences at the University of Virginia, 1957–1958* (Charlottesville: University of Virginia Press, 1959), 89.

2. Owada Eiko, *Faulkner, Haiti and Questions of Imperialism* (Tokyo: Sairyūsha, 2002), 10.

3. Ōhashi Kenzaburō, "Amerika nanbu no hiai to eikō," *ATG (Art Theater Guild)* 39 (1966): 11.

4. Nakagami Kenji, *Kishū: ki no kuni, ne no kuni monogatari*, ed. Senbon Ken'ichirō (Tokyo: Asahi shinbunsha, 1978).

5. Nakagami, *Kishū: ki no kuni, ne no kuni monogatari*, 216.

6. See Taki Kōji, *Tennō no shōzō* (Tokyo: Iwanami shoten, 1988) and Inose Naoki, *Mikado no shōzō* (Tokyo: Shōgakkan, 1986).

7. Takazawa Shūji, *Nakagami Kenji jiten: ronkō to shuzai nichiroku* (Tokyo: Kōbunsha 21, 2002), 326.

8. Noguchi Michihiko, "Nakagami Kenji no roji to buraku mondai," *RIRIANS: kenkyū kiyō* 11 (2001), 85.

9. Hasumi Shigehiko translated numerous works by Deleuze, Derrida, and Barthes in journals *Umi* and *Episutēme*, furnishing an entrée into poststructural contexts for some of Nakagami's key concepts. These include Foucault's idea of an archive constructed around a discourse, rather than specific words, and the structures of tree and rhizome from a Deleuziam idiom. See Hasumi Shigehiko, *Fūkō, Dorūzu, Derida* (Tokyo: Asahi shuppansha, 1978); and "Un nouvel archiviste," in Hasumi Shigehiko, *Fūko soshite/aruiwa Dorūzu* (Tokyo: Ozawa shoten, 1984). Derrida's concept of the supplement is introduced in the 1978 work, *Fūkō, Dorūzu, Derida*. See also Hasumi Shigehiko, *Hihyō, arui wa kashi no shukusai* (Tokyo: Serika shobō, 1974).

10. Mark C. Funke, "Hitachi no Kuni Fudoki," *Monumenta Nipponica* 49, no. 1 (1994): 3.

11. See Miyake Hitoshi, *Kumano shinkō*, Minshū shūkyōshi sosho 21 (Tokyo: Yuzankaku shuppan, 1990). Max Moerman notes in *Localizing Paradise: Kumano Pilgrimage and the Religious Landscape of Premodern Japan* (Cambridge, Mass.: Harvard University Asia Center, 2005) that Kumano mandala offer "a point in time beyond the quotidian ... a past and a future to be experienced in the present"

(26). Other classical texts featuring Kumano include the *Nihon ryōiki* and *Heike monogatari*. See Yomota Inuhiko, "Ikai no hen'yō—gensō shōsetsu wa doko e itta ka?" *Shinchō* 82, no. 3 (March 1985): 224–53, for argument of pre-modern *monogatari*'s fantastic connections to present-day stories.

12. Nakagami, *Kishū: ki no kuni, ne no kuni monogatari,* 323.

13. For a historical semantics, see Richard Koebner and Helmut Dan Schmidt, *Imperialism: The Story and Significance of a Political Word, 1840–1960* (Cambridge: Cambridge University Press, 1964).

14. Nakagami, *Kishū: ki no kuni, ne no kuni monogatari,* 12.

15. Jacques Derrida, *Of Grammatology*. trans. Gayatri Spivak (Baltimore: The Johns Hopkins University Press, 1976).

16. Nakagami, *Kishū: ki no kuni, ne no kuni monogatari,* 13.

17. Nakagami, *Kishū: ki no kuni, ne no kuni monogatari,* 20–21.

18. Ibid., 33.

19. Ibid., 216.

20. Senbon Ken'ichirō, "Itōshisa o ou tabi," in *Kishū: ki no kuni, ne no kuni monogatari* (Tokyo: Asahi shinbunsha, 1978), 334.

21. Ibid.

22. Ibid.

23. Ibid., 332.

24. Ōe Kenzaburō, *The Silent Cry*, trans. John Nathan (Tokyo: Kōdansha International, 1981), 80.

25. "Rūtsu ni kandō no nami," *Asahi shinbun*, October 11, 1977, Yūkan ed., 22.

26. "Beikoku de ninki o yobu 'Rūtsu' no gensaku-sha Arekkusu Hēri-shi," *Asahi shinbun* February 10, 1977, Chōkan ed., 7.

27. "Furusato-rūtsu būmu: hakubutsukan, monzoku shiryōkan nado zoku-zoku nana-nen de san wari chō," *Asahi shinbun* July 28 1977, Yūkan ed., 7.

28. Jacob Gruber, "Ethnographic Salvage and the Shaping of Anthropology," *American Anthropologist* 72, no. 6 (1970): 1290.

29. Marilyn Ivy, *Discourses of the Vanishing: Modernity, Phantasm, Japan* (Chicago: University of Chicago Press, 1995), 104.

30. "'Rūtsu' o tadoro Fukuda-sōri Rondon kaigi kara." *Asahi shinbun* May 7, 1977, Yūkan ed., 2.

31. Morikawa Masamichi, "Arekkusu heirī-cho 'Rūtsu' o yonde," *Buraku kaihō* 112 (1977): 115–20.

32. Ian Neary, "Matsumoto Ji'ichiro and the Making of Democracy in Postwar Japan," *Japan Forum* 19, no. 2 (2007): 217–38.

33. Nakagami, *Kishū: ki no kuni, ne no kuni monogatari,* 12.

34. The genre reentered the leftist field of vision in the 1970s because of the efforts of journalist Honda Katsuichi (1932–). Honda went on special assignment for the *Asahi shinbun* reporting the Vietnam War, pioneering "eyewitness"

reporting from the front, and "broke" the news on the Nanjing Massacre in a 1971 series in the *Asahi shinbun*. Honda names Yokoyama Gen'nosuke's 1899 *Nihon no kasō shakai* (Japan's Stratified Society) as the first work of reportage. See Honda Katsuichi, *Ruporutaju no hōhō* (Tokyo: Suzusawa shoten, 1980).

35. Umezawa Toshihiko, Yamagishi Takashi, and Hirano Hidehisa, *Bungaku no naka no hisabetsu buraku zō: senzen-hen*, 133. Both works are anthologized in vol. 39 of the Buraku mondai bungei•sakuhin senshū series (Tokyo: Sekai bunko, 1977).

36. Nakagami, *Kishū: ki no kuni, ne no kuni monogatari*, 12–13.

37. Maeda Ai, "Utopia of the Prison House: A Reading of *In Darkest Tokyo*," in *Text and the City: Essays on Japanese Modernity*, trans. Seiji M. Lippit and James A. Fujii (Durham, N.C.: Duke University Press, 2004), 47.

38. William Booth, *In Darkest England: And the Way Out* (New York: Funk and Wagnall's, 1890), 12 and 16.

39. Booth, *In Darkest England*, 6.

40. *Kojiki*, trans. Donald L Philippi (Princeton, N.J.: Princeton University Press, 1969), 163.

41. Funke, "Hitachi no Kuni Fudoki," 1. See also Akimoto Kichirō, *Fudoki no kenkyū* (Osaka: Osaka keizai daigaku, 1963).

42. Michiko Yamaguchi Aoki, *Records of Wind and Earth: A Translation of "Fudoki," with Introduction and Commentaries* (Ann Arbor, Mich.: Association for Asian Studies, 1997), 37.

43. Aoki, *Records of Wind and Earth*, 37–38.

44. Nakagami Kenji and Ōe Kenzaburō, "Tayō-ka suru gendai bungaku—sen-kyū-hyaku hachi-jū nendai e mukete," *Gendai shi techō* 77, no. 1 (1980): 228.

45. Umezawa Toshihiko, Hidehisa Hirano, and Takashi Yamagishi, *Bungaku no naka no hisabetsu buraku-zō: sengo-hen* (Tokyo: Akashi shoten, 1982), 5. See, for example, Okiura Kazuteru, *Nihon minshū bunka no genkyō: hisabetsu buraku no minzoku to geinō* (Osaka: Kaihō shuppansha, 1984).

46. Claude Lévi-Strauss, *Tristes tropiques*, trans. John and Doreen Weightman (New York: Penguin Books, 1992), 296.

47. Ibid., 299.

48. Nakagami, *Kishū: ki no kuni, ne no kuni monogatari*, 36.

49. Ibid., 38.

50. Ibid., 56.

51. Ibid., 276.

52. Ibid., 29.

53. Fred Notehelfer's *Kōtoku Shūsui: Portrait of a Japanese Radical* (Cambridge, England: Cambridge University Press, 1971) presents Kōtoku's anti-imperial political philosophy and his relation to anarchism.

54. Notehelfer, *Kōtoku Shūsui*, 192.

55. Kōtoku's execution was also the subject of Yosano Tekkan's poem "Ōishi Seinosuke no shi," Okino Iwasaburō's "Shukumei," Mori Ōgai's "Chinmoku no tō," "Gyakutō" by Kōtoku's defense lawyer Hiraide Shū, and Ishikawa Takuboku's unpublished but circulated essay "Jidai hensoku no genjō" and numerous prison diaries. See Moriyama Shigeo, *Taigyaku jiken bungaku sakka-ron* (Tokyo: San'ichi shobō, 1980); and Watanabe Naomi, *Fukei bungaku-ron josetsu* (Tokyo: Ōta shuppan, 1999).

56. The line breaks and punctuation follow Nakagami's quote of the poem in full in the essay. Nakagami Kenji, "Monogatari no keifu—Satō Haruo," in *Fūkei no mukō e/Monogatari no keifu* (Tokyo: Tōjusha, 1983), 93–94.

57. Nakagami, "Monogatari no keifu—Satō Haruo," 95.

58. Ibid.

59. Ibid.

60. Ibid., 97.

61. Ibid.

62. Nakagami Kenji, "Watashi no naka no Nihonjin—Ōishi Seinosuke," *Nakagami Kenji zenshū* 14, ed. Karatani Kōjin et al. (Tokyo: Shūeisha, 1996), 370 (italics mine).

63. Ibid.

64. Nakagami, *Kishū: ki no kuni, ne no kuni monogatari*, 144–45.

65. Nakagami, "Tsuchi no kōdo," in *Tori no yō ni, kemono no yō ni* (Tokyo: Kōdansha bungei bunko, 1981), 43.

66. Nakagami, *Kishū: ki no kuni, ne no kuni monogatari*, 66.

67. Ibid., 67.

68. Karatani Kōjin, "Fōkunā, Nakagami Kenji, Ōhashi Kenzaburō," in *Sakaguchi Ango to Nakagami Kenji* (Tokyo: Ōta shuppan, 1995), 231.

69. "Mohaya sengo de wa nai," in *Keizai hakushō* (Tokyo: Keizai kikaku-chō, 1956).

70. Karatani Kōjin, "Fōkunā, Nakagami Kenji, Ōhashi Kenzaburō," 231.

71. C. Vann Woodward, "Haiku," *Southern Cultures* 4, no. 4 (1998): 19.

72. Woodward, *Origins of the New South, 1877–1913* (Baton Rouge: Louisiana State University Press, 1951), ix.

73. Ibid., 14.

74. Owada, *Faulkner, Haiti and Questions of Imperialism*, 10; Ōhashi, "Amerika nanbu no hiai to eikō," 11 (italics mine).

75. William Faulkner, *Essays, Speeches & Public Letters: Updated, with Material Never Before Collected in One Volume*, ed. James B. Meriwether (New York: Modern Library, 2004), 83–84.

76. Faulkner, *Essays, Speeches & Public Letters*, 79–80.

77. See Samir Amin, *Unequal Development: An Essay on the Social Formations of Peripheral Capitalism* (New York: Monthly Review Press, 1976).

78. Nakagami Kenji, "Monogatari no keifu—hachi-nin no sakka—5—Orikuchi Shinobu: jō," *Kokubungaku kaishaku to kyōzai no kenkyū* 24, no. 9 (1979): 160.

79. Ibid., 161.

80. Nishimura Tōru, ed. *Orikuchi Shinobu jiten* (Tokyo: Taishūkan shoten, 1988), 158–68.

81. Nakagami, "Monogatari no keifu—hachi-nin no sakka—5—Orikuchi Shinobu: jō," 163.

82. Ibid., 162–63.

83. Roland Barthes, *Monogatari no kōzō bunseki*, trans. Hanawa Hikaru (Tokyo: Misuzu shobō, 1979), 1.

84. Nakagami Kenji and Hasumi Shigehiko, "Seido toshite no monogatari," in *Nakagami Kenji zen-hatsugen 1978–1980* (Tokyo: Shūeisha, 1980), 175–212; Nakagami Kenji and Fujii Sadakazu, "Katari to wa nani-ka?—ikkai kagiri no kami-goroshi," *Kokubungaku kaishaku to kyōzai no kenkyū* 30, no. 8 (1985): 20–37.

85. Karatani Kōjin, "Shōsetsu no isō," in *Keshō* (Tokyo: Kōdansha bungei bunko, 1993), 256.

86. Ibid., 263.

87. Karatani Kôjin, *The Origins of Modern Japanese Literature* (Durham, N.C.: Duke University Press, 1993), 185–86.

88. Karatani, "Shōsetsu no isō," 263.

89. Haruo Shirane, *The Bridge of Dreams: A Poetics of the Tale of Genji* (Stanford, Calif.: Stanford University Press, 1987), 1.

90. Nihon koten bungaku daijiten henshū iinkai, ed., *Nihon koten bungaku daijiten* (Tokyo: Iwanami shoten, 1983), 1819–21.

91. Nina Cornyetz, *Dangerous Women and Deadly Words: Phallic Fantasy and Modernity in Three Japanese Writers* (Stanford, Calif.: Stanford University Press, 1999), 171.

92. Edward Fowler, *The Rhetoric of Confession: Shishōsetsu in Early Twentieth-Century Japanese Fiction* (Berkeley: University of California Press, 1988), xxi.

93. Tomiko Yoda, *Gender and National Literature: Heian Texts in the Construction of Japanese Modernity* (Durham, N.C.: Duke University Press, 2004), 152.

94. See Komori Yōichi, *Yukari no monogatari: "Yoshino kuzu" no retorikku* (Tokyo: Shintensha, 1992); and Margherita Long, "Nakagami and the Denial of Lineage: On Maternity, Abjection, and the Japanese Outcast Class," *differences* 17, no. 2 (2006): 1–32.

95. Yoda, *Gender and National Literature*, 159.

96. Karatani's readings of alienation draw heavily on Hiromatsu Wataru's *sogai-ron* (writings on alienation) interpretations of Marx.

97. Kamei Hideo, *Transformations of Sensibility: The Phenomenology of Meiji Literature*, trans. Michael Bourdaghs (Ann Arbor, Mich: Center for Japanese Studies, University of Michigan, 2002), 1–42.

98. See Gayle Rubin, "Traffic in Women: Notes on the Political Economy of 'Sex,'" in *Toward an Anthropology of Women*, ed. Rayna R. Reiter (New York: Monthly Review Press, 1975), 157–210.

99. Masuda Yoneji, *The Information Society as Post-Industrial Society* (Tokyo: Tokyo Institute for the Information Society, 1980).

100. Karatani Kōjin and Watanabe Naomi, ed., *Nakagami Kenji to Kumano* (Tokyo: Ōta shuppan, 2000), 152.

101. Ishikawa Hiroyuki, "'Chi no hate, shijō no toki' no rekishi-sei to gyaku-setsu," *Goō* 3 (2006): 304–5.

102. Karl Marx and Frederick Engels, *The German Ideology*, trans. C. J. Arthur (New York: International Publishers, 1999), 55.

103. Nakagami and Karatani, *Kobayashi Hideo o koete: taidan hyōron* (Tokyo: Kawade shobō, 1979), 19–20.

104. Alan Tansman, "History, Repetition and Freedom in the Narratives of Nakagami Kenji," *Journal of Japanese Studies* 24, no. 2 (1998): 257–90. Tansman is also, to my knowledge, the only writer in English to note the property of *kōtsū* (272).

105. Nakagami Kenji, *Misaki* (Tokyo: Bungei shunjū, 1976), 185.

106. Nakagami Kenji, *The Cape and other Stories from the Japanese Ghetto*, trans. Eve Zimmerman (Berkeley: Stone Bridge Press, 1999), 23 (my edits).

107. Watanabe, *Nakagami Kenji-ron*, 45–92.

108. Nakagami Kenji and Yoshimoto Takaaki, "Bungaku to genzai," in *Nakagami Kenji mishūroku tairon shūsei*, ed. Takazawa Shūji (Tokyo, 1983), 53.

109. Nakagami, *The Cape*, 104.

4. Inaudible Man

1. Nakagami Kenji, "Nihongo ni tsuite," in *Hatodomo no ie* (Tokyo: Shūeisha, 1968), 5-105.

2. For a more typically lyrical novel, see Mita Masahiro, *Boku-tte nani?* (Tokyo: Kawade shobō, 1977). For a more militant assessment of "barricade" novels that dramatize students pitted against establishment forces and institutions, see Nosaka Rokusuke, *Fukuin bungaku-ron* (Tokyo: Impakuto shuppan-kai, 1997).

3. Bruce Suttmeier, "Ethnography as Consumption: Travel and National Identity in Oda Makoto's 'Nan de mo mite yarō,'" *Journal of Japanese Studies* 35, no. 1 (2009): 66.

4. Andrew Jones and Nikhil Pal Singh, "Guest Editors' Introduction," *positions: east asia cultures critique* 11, no. 1 (2003): 1–9.

5. Adekeye Adebajo, "From Bandung to Durban, Whither the Afro-Asian Coalition?" in *Bandung Revisited: The Legacy of the 1955 Asian-African Conference for International Order*, ed. See Seng Tan and Amitav Acharya (Singapore: NUS Press, 2008), 105.

6. See, for example, Abe Tomoji, "A Negro in Cinema," trans. Ayanna B. Hobbs, in *Modanizumu: Modernist Fiction from Japan, 1913–1938*, ed. William

Jefferson Tyler (Honolulu: University of Hawai'i Press, 2008), 255–69; and Ōe Kenzaburō, "Shiiku," in *Ōe Kenzaburō zensakuhin* 1 (Tokyo: Shinchōsha, 1966), 46–89. Another 1958 story of Ōe's has a G.I. named Peterson, but he vanishes just as the story begins. Ōe Kenzaburō, "Kurai kawa, omoi kai," in *Ōe Kenzaburō zensakuhin* 2 (Tokyo: Shinchōsha, 1966), 7–22.

7. See Ian Neary, *The Buraku Issue and Modern Japan: The Career of Matsumoto Ji'ichirō* (London; New York: Routledge, 2010), 194–97.

8. Yukiyama Yoshimasa, "Niguro kaihō undō no rekishi II," in *Kokujin bungaku zenshū—bekkan*, ed. Kokujin kenkyūkai and Hashimoto Fukuo (Tokyo: Hayakawa shobō, 1969), 291.

9. Noma Hiroshi, Asada Zen'nosuke, and Yukiyama Yoshimasa, "Kome sōdō to Burakku Pawā: buraku kaihō•kokujin kaihō undō to bunka," *Asahi jānaru* 10, no. 48 (1968): 85.

10. Noma, Asada, and Yukiyama, "Kome sōdō to Burakku Pawā," 84.

11. Noma Hiroshi, "Bōrudoin to 'Mō hitotsu no kuni," in *Sōzō to hihyō* (Tokyo: Chikuma shobō, 1969), 183.

12. Noma, Asada, and Yukiyama, "Kome sōdō to Burakku Pawā," 88.

13. Nakagami himself participated in the demos, sometimes as a "fake student." He recounts this outsider role in *Geki-ron zenkyōtō: oretachi no genten* (Tokyo: Kōdansha, 1984).

14. Shalini Puri, *The Caribbean Postcolonial: Social Equality, Post-nationalism, and Cultural Hybridity* (New York: Palgrave Macmillan, 2004), 84.

15. Noma, Asada, and Yukiyama, "Kome sōdō to Burakku Pawā," 82–89; Martin Luther King, Jr. "Beyond Vietnam," in *A Call to Conscience: The Landmark Speeches of Martin Luther King, Jr.*, ed. Clayborne Carson and Kris Shepard (New York: IPM/Warner Books, 2001), 142. Translated as "Betonamu o koete," *Sekai*, no. 263 (1967): 127–36.

16. King, "Beyond Vietnam," 141. The reference is to Luke 24:32.

17. Okiura Kazuteru, ed., "Hakkan no ji," in *Suihei=hito no yo ni hikari* are (Tokyo: Shakai hyōronsha, 1981), 225.

18. Ellison's novel was first translated and published in Japan in 1958 as *Mienai ningen*. Criticism of *Invisible Man* commenced in 1954 when Ōhashi Kenzaburō, the dean of American studies in Japan, published an essay in a leading literary journal, *Kindai bungaku* (Modern literature). Ellison's Japanese title emphasizes that it is the viewer who is unable to perceive and differs from the postwar series of films that derived from H. G. Wells's *Invisible Man*, whose translation indicates that the character himself is not visible (透明な人間). For analysis of the film series and regimes of visibility vis-à-vis the trauma-bearing technology of the bombs, see Akira Mizuta Lippit, *Atomic Light (Shadow Optics)* (Minneapolis: University of Minnesota Press, 2005).

19. See Nakagami Kenji, *Hakai seyo, to Airā wa itta* (Tokyo: Shūeisha, 1979); Ono Yoshie, *Jazu saishū-sho*, ed. Kawamoto Saburō (Tokyo: Shinya sōshosha, 1998), for an elder statesman's cultural history of Japanese jazz; and Michael Molasky, *Sengo Nihon no jazu bunka: eiga, bungaku, angura* (Tokyo: Seidosha, 2005). See especially Tayama Katai, "Rokotsu naru byōsha," in *Kindai bungaku hyōron taikei: Meiji-ki 2*, ed. Inagaki Tatsurō (Tokyo: Kadokawa shoten, 1972), 360–62. For debates on the many motives of description in Meiji-era naturalism, see Wada Kingo, *Byōsha no jidai: hitotsu no shizenshugi bungakuron* (Sapporo-shi: Hokkaidō daigaku tosho kankōkai, 1975).

20. Ralph Ellison, *Invisible Man* (New York: Random House, 1982), 581.

21. See Alan Nadel, *Invisible Criticism: Ralph Ellison and the American Canon* (Iowa City: University of Iowa Press, 1988).

22. Ellison, *Invisible Man*, 3.

23. Abé Markus Nornes, *Forest of Pressure: Ogawa Shinsuke and Postwar Japanese Documentary* (Minneapolis: University of Minnesota Press, 2007), 60.

24. James C. Scott, *Domination and the Arts of Resistance: Hidden Transcripts* (New Haven, Conn.: Yale University Press, 1990), xii.

25. The use of coded communications has been noted in many works on African American music, speech, and writing. See, for instance, Arthur Jones's treatment of signal songs and map songs in *Wade in the Water: The Wisdom of the Spirituals* (Boulder, Colo.: Leave a Little Room, 2005).

26. Henry Louis Gates Jr., *Figures in Black: Words, Signs, and the "Racial" Self* (New York: Oxford University Press, 1987), 247–48.

27. Scott, *Domination and the Arts of Resistance*, 4, 17.

28. Kobayashi Hideo, "Discourse on Fiction of the Self," in *Literature of the Lost Home: Kobayashi Hideo—Literary Criticism, 1924–1939*, trans. Paul Anderer (Stanford, Calif.: Stanford University Press), 92.

29. Tomi Suzuki, *Narrating the Self: Fictions of Japanese Modernity* (Stanford, Calif.: Stanford University Press, 1996), 6.

30. Nakagami Kenji and Karatani Kōjin, *Kobayashi Hideo o koete: taidan hyōron* (Tokyo: Kawade shobō, 1979), 20.

31. André Gide, *The Counterfeiters, with the Journal of "The Counterfeiters,"* trans. Dorothy Bussy and Justin O'Brien (New York: Vintage, 1973),189.

32. Nakagami, *On the Japanese Language*, 54.

33. Ibid., 14; 13.

34. Ibid., 17.

35. Nakagami Kenji, "Kokujin-hei to Nihon no wakamono," in *Nakagami Kenji zenshū 14* (Tokyo: Shūeisha, 1996), 67.

36. Ibid.

37. Ibid.

38. Nakagami Kenji and Murakami Ryū, *Jazu to bakudan* (Tokyo: Kawade shobō, 1983), 32.

39. Takayama Fumihiko, *Erekutora: Nakagami Kenji no shōgai* (Tokyo: Bungei shunjū, 2007), 135.

40. Ibid., 138.

41. In English translations of the similar idea outlined by members of the Frankfurt School, the term appears as "administered society."

42. Takayama, *Erekutora.* 137.

43. Ryan Holmberg, "Hear No, Speak No: Sasaki Maki Manga and *Nansensu,* circa 1970," *Japan Forum* 21, no. 1 (2009): 115–41. At the time, a substantial network of antiwar activists did exist between the United States and Japan. This includes the programs mounted by the largest antiwar group, Beheiren, and its offshoot, JATEC (Japan Technical Committee for Assistance to U.S. War Deserters), or the tours by U.S. leftists such as Howard Zinn and Ralph Featherstone who explicitly compared Okinawa's situation to the situation of black U.S. residents in terms of sovereignty and self-determination. Part of the movement was devoted to convincing soldiers to desert. See Tsurumi Shunsuke, Kaikō Takeshi, and Oda Makoto, *Heiwa o yobu koe: Betonamu hansen, Nihonjin no negai* (Tokyo: Banchō shobō, 1967); *Oda Makoto, ed., Beheiren to wa nani ka?* (Tokyo: Tokuma shoten, 1969); Yoshikawa Yūichi, *Shimin undō no shukudai: Betonamu hansen kara mirai e* (Tokyo: Shisō no kagakusha, 1991); Anai Fumihiko, *Beheiren to dassō beihei* (Tokyo: Bungei shinjū, 2000); and Tsurumi Yoshiyuki, "Dassō beihei to mumei no shimin: Nihon-ban Ani no nikki," in *Tsurumi Yoshiyuki chosaku-shū 2,* ed. Yoshikawa Yūichi (Tokyo: Misuzu shobō, 2002), 286–88.

44. Takayama, *Erekutora.* 136.

45. Nakagami, *On the Japanese Language,* 88. The phrase is "boku jishin mo kikoenai ningen ni natteiru kamoshirenai."

46. Gerald Graff and Steven Mailloux have both written incisive synoptic histories about the discipline of English studies within the American university. See Gerald Graff, *Professing Literature: An Institutional History* (Chicago: University of Chicago Press, 1987); and Steven Mailloux, *Disciplinary Identities: Rhetorical Paths of English, Speech, and Composition* (New York: Modern Language Association of America, 2006).

47. See Lewis Mumford, *The Golden Day: A Study in American Literature and Culture* (New York: Boni and Liveright, 1926); and F. O. Matthiessen, *American Renaissance: Art and Expression in the Age of Emerson and Whitman* (London: Oxford University Press, 1941).

48. Nakagami, *On the Japanese Language,* 7.

49. For discussions of how modernist texts and graphics interlace each other in modern 1920s and 1930s Japan, see William Gardner's *Advertising Tower: Japanese Modernism and Modernity in the 1920's* and William Tyler's *Modanizumu: Modernist Fiction from Japan, 1913–1938.*

50. Nakagami, *On the Japanese Language,* 22 and 24.

51. Jennifer DeVere Brody, "The Blackness of Blackness . . . Reading the Typography of 'Invisible Man,'" *Theatre Journal* 57, no. 4 (2005): 680.

52. Philip Rosen, *Change Mummified: Cinema, Historicity, Theory* (Minneapolis: University of Minnesota Press, 2001), 18.

53. Nakagami, *On the Japanese Language*, 7.

54. The Ellison literature too is far from closed on this score. For a survey of readings of the last line, see Thomas Whitaker, "Spokesman for Invisibility," in *Speaking for You*, ed. Kimberly Benston (Washington, D.C.: Howard University Press, 1987), 386–403.

55. Yanagita Kunio, *Legends of Tōno*, trans. Ronald Morse (Tokyo: Japan Foundation, 1975), 5.

56. See, for example, Sako Jun'ichirō, "'Hakai'-ron josetsu," *Buraku* 15, no. 1 (1963): 63.

57. Ono Kenji, "Sakka Iwano Hōmei to buraku no mondai—sono 'Buraku no musume' o megutte." *Buraku* 15, no. 1 (1963): 72.

58. Umezawa Toshihiko, Yamagishi Takashi, and Hirano Hidehisa, *Bungaku no naka no hi-sabetsu buraku zō: senzen hen* (Tokyo: Akashi shoten, 1980), 14.

59. Nakagami, *On the Japanese Language*, 27.

60. Ibid., 18, 19, 20, 27, 32, 56, 78, and 83.

61. Ibid., 60.

62. See James Baldwin, *Nobody Knows My Name; More Notes of a Native Son* (New York: Dial Press, 1961).

63. Nakagami, *On the Japanese Language*, 54.

64. Ibid., 86.

65. Ibid., 32.

66. Ibid., 58.

67. Ibid., 81.

68. Ibid., 105.

69. Watanabe Naomi, *Nakagami Kenji-ron: itōshisa ni tsuite* (Tokyo: Kawade shobō shinsha, 1996), 39–92.

70. Janet Lyon, *Manifestoes: Provocations of the Modern* (Ithaca, N.Y.: Cornell University Press, 1999), 11.

71. Sumii Sue and Fukuda Makiko, *Suiheisha sengen o yomu* (Osaka: Kaihō shuppan, 1989), 140; Satō Takumi, *"Kingu" no jidai: kokumin taishū zasshi no kokyosei* (Tokyo: Iwanami shoten, 2002), 206–8.

72. Lyon, *Manifestoes*, 15.

73. Frank Upham, *Law and Social Change in Postwar Japan* (Cambridge, Mass.: Harvard University Press, 1987), 103.

74. Ibid., 103.

75. Ibid., 103.

76. See *Sengo buraku mondai no kenkyū 4*, ed. Buraku mondai kenkyūjo (Kyoto: Buraku mondai kenkyūjo shuppanbu, 1979).

77. Upham, *Law and Social Change in Postwar Japan*, 84.

78. Ibid., 86.

79. See also Alain Badiou et al., *1968-nen no sekai-shi*, trans. and ed. Fujiwara shoten henshūbu (Tokyo: Fujiwara shoten, 2009).

80. After Seibu anchored the Shibuya neighborhood, other chains entered, including stores and a performance hall owned by Saison. Later, in 1983, Seibu would introduce the first department store credit card.

81. Yamada Munemutsu, "Hanpaku no shisō to kōdō: mumei-jin no ishi o tsunagu kanōsei," in *Beheiren to wa nani ka: ningen no genri ni tatte hansen no kōdō*, ed. Oda Makoto (Tokyo: Tokuma shoten, 1969), 12–18; Sadakane Hideyuki, "Sōshitsu suru banpaku•shōhi sareru tōi—1970, Ōsaka banpaku ni tsuite," in *Karucharu•poritikusu—1960/70*, ed. Kitada Akihiro et al. (Tokyo: Serika shobō, 2005), 156–72.

82. Thomas R. H. Havens, *Fire Across the Sea: The Vietnam War and Japan, 1965–1975* (Princeton, N.J.: Princeton University Press, 1987), 84.

83. Havens, *Fire Across the Sea*, 84.

84. See Honda Katsuichi, *Ruporutāju no hōhō* (Tokyo: Suzusawa shoten, 1980). for a history of reportage. On the journalist and fiction writer Kaikō Takeshi, who was also one of the initial founders of the Beheiren movement, see Bruce Suttmeier's "Seeing Past Destruction: Trauma and History in Kaikō Takeshi," *positions: east asia cultures critique* 15, no. 3 (2007): 457–89.

85. Kawamura Minato, *Sengo bungaku o tou: sono taiken to rinen* (Tokyo: Iwanami shoten, 1995), 85.

86. Kaikō, *Into a Black Sun*, 8; Suttmeier, "Seeing Past Destruction," 460.

87. Kawamura, *Sengo bungaku o tō, 89.*

88. See Yasutaka Tsutsui, *Betonamu kankō kōsha* (Tokyo: Chūō kōronsha, 1979).

89. Ibid., 205.

90. Ibid.

91. Ibid., 207.

92. Ibid., 204.

93. Ibid., 215.

94. See Isoda Kōichi, *Sayoku ga sayoku ni naru toki: aru jidai no seishinshi* (Tokyo: Shūeisha, 1986), 160.

95. Tsutsui, *Vietnam Travel Agency*, 166.

96. Ibid., 159.

97. See Daniel J. Boorstin, *Imēji no jidai: masu-komi ga seizō suru jijitsu*, trans. Gotō Kazuhiko and Hoshino Ikumi (Tokyo: Tokyo sōgen shinsha, 1964).

98. Tatsumi Takayuki, *Nihon henryū bungaku* (Tokyo: Shinchōsha, 1998), 225.

99. Daniel J. Boorstin, *The Image: A Guide to Pseudo-Events in America* (New York: Harper Colophon, 1961), 11–12.

100. Nakagami, *On the Japanese Language*, 80.

101. See, for example, Suga Hidemi, *Kakumeiteki na amari ni kakumeiteki na: "1968-nen no kakumei" shiron* (Tokyo: Sakuhinsha, 2004).

5. The 38th Parallax

1. Nakagami Kenji, "Fūkei no mukō e," in *Fūkei no mukō e/Monogatari no keifu* (Tokyo: Kōdansha bungei bunko, 2004), 45.

2. Nakagami Kenji, "Rinbu suru, Seoul," in *Nakagami Kenji zenshū* 8, ed. Karatani et al (Tokyo: Shūeisha, 1996), 183.

3. Ibid., 173 and 182.

4. Ibid., 161.

5. The works consist of Kim Ji-shō's poetry collection *Ikaino shishū* at number 54 and, at 88 to 94, two works by Kim Chi-ha, the novel *Minami* and his autobiography *Kugyō: gokuchū ni okeru waga tatakai*; Yun Hŭng-gil's *Nagaame*; the roundtable Nakagami did with Yun, *Tōyō ni itchi suru*; Ko Sokei's book of translations from classical Korean, *Shunkoden*; *Shufukanbetsukyoku*; *Kokitsudoden*; a 1973 collection of contemporary translations, Kim Tong-ni 's *Gendai Kankoku bungaku senshū*; and Sŏ Chŏngchu's poetry collection, *Midō jo teichū shisen: chōsen tanpopo no uta*. An Ushoku writes that Nakagami spent most of his time with writers roughly five years older than he who corresponded to the Third Generation of Ōe and Ishihara in Japan and who placed the Korean War and the June 25, 1950, outbreak of war that inaugurated a literature of division at the center of their writings. See An Ushoku, "Gendai Kankoku bungaku to Nakagami Kenji," *Kokubungaku* 36, no. 14 (1992): 87.

6. Nakagami Kenji, ed., *Kankoku gendai tanpen shōsetsu*, (Tokyo: Shinchōsha, 1985), 292.

7. Ibid., 297.

8. Ibid., 293.

9. Ibid., 293.

10. Ibid., 293; 292.

11. Ibid., 293.

12. See Ōtsuka Eiji's interpretation in light of subculture, in *"Otaku" no seishin-shi: 1980-nendai-ron* (Tokyo: Kōdansha, 2004), 57–83.

13. Nakagami, *Kankoku gendai tanpen shōsetsu*, 293.

14. See especially Yomota Inuhiko, "Ikai no hen'yō gensō shōsetsu wa doko e itta ka?" *Shinchō* 82, no. 3 (March 1985): 224–53, for an argument of premodern *monogatari*'s fantastic connections to present-day stories.

15. Nakagami Kenji and Han U-san, "Nikkan kōryū no shin-jidai," in *Nakagami Kenji mishūroku tairon shūsei*, 445–48; Nakagami Kenji and Kim Yan-ki, "Bunka no kitei ni aru mono: Kankoku no shāmanizumu," in *Nakagami Kenji mishūroku tairon shūsei*, 465–72. Nakagami Kenji and Sakamoto Ryūichi, "Oto wa

kami, soshite ima yomigaeru aratana ishin—Kankoku hōrō-gei samurunori no kirameki," *Asahi Journal* 26, no. 41 (1984): 88–93.

16. Nakagami, "Karatani Kōjin e no tegami," in *Fūkei no mukō e/Monogatari no keifu*, 98.

17. Karatani Kōjin et al., "Kaidai," *Nakagami Kenji zenshū* 8, 728.

18. Michael Robinson, *Korea's Twentieth-Century Odyssey: A Short History* (Honolulu: University of Hawai'i Press, 2007), 130.

19. Kim Hyung-A, "Minjung Socioeconomic Responses to State-led Industrialization," in *South Korea's Minjung Movement: The Culture and Politics of Dissidence*, ed. Kenneth M. Wells (Honolulu: University of Hawai'i Press, 1995), 43.

20. James Clifford, *Routes: Travel and Translation in the Late Twentieth Century* (Cambridge, Mass.: Harvard University Press, 1997), 359.

21. Nakagami, "Rinbu suru, Seoul," 163.

22. Ibid., 206.

23. Ibid., 206–7.

24. "Nikkan bunka kōryū ni nozomu: Yon Ta-ku, Kankoku bunka-in inchō (watashi no ii-bun)," *Asahi shinbun* October 29, 1984, Yūkan ed., 5.

25. Nakagami Kenji, "Shashin no monogatari ryoku," in *Shiruku rōdo・Kankoku*, ed. Shinoyama Kishin (Tokyo: Shūeisha, 1982), 162; Ōba Kazuyuki, "Nakagami Kenji 'Kankoku'-ron josetsu: aratana 'Nikkan jōyaku' taisei to bunka-jin," *Shin nihon bungaku* 40, no. 3 (1985): 6. The phrase "Korean boom" is Ōba's.

26. Studies on Bakhtin flourished in 1980s academic Japan and extended into the world of writers and popular intellectuals, notably Nakagami and Ōe. For a sample in English, see Jeffrey Johnson, *Bakhtinian Theory in Japanese Studies* (Lewiston, N.Y.: Edwin Mellen Press, 2001).

27. Nakagami, "Fūkei no mukō e," 45.

28. Ibid., 20.

29. Nakagami, "Rinbu suru, Seoul," 186; Nakagami, "Fūkei no mukō e," 73.

30. Nakagami Kenji and Ri Saburō, "Naze pansori ka?" in *Nakagami Kenji mishūroku tairon shūsei*, 439.

31. Eve Zimmerman, *Out of the Alleyway: Nakagami Kenji and the Poetics of Outcaste Fiction* (Cambridge, Mass.: Harvard University Asia Center, 2007), 33. Eve Zimmerman points to the unspoken obsession with imposter identity that the story's narrator describes between himself and the Korean boy.

32. See Nakagami Kenji, *Ten no uta: shōsetsu Miyako Harumi* (Tokyo: Mainichi shinbunsha, 1987).

33. Nakagami, "Fūkei no mukō e," 77.

34. Nakagami and Ri, "Naze pansori ka?" 436.

35. Ibid., 436.

36. See Davinder L. Bhowmik, *Writing Okinawa: Narrative Acts of Identity and Resistance* (London: Routledge, 2008).

37. Nakagami, "Fūkei no mukō e," 78. Shimao's accounts depicted Amami as a place outside of history to the extent that, in one essay, he wrote that living in Amami was seamless with reading the eighth-century *Kojiki*. The ahistorical sense that he affirms in the comparison is diametrically opposed to Nakagami's conception of the *Kojiki* as the text that marks the beginning of a history, Kumano's history of subjugation. See Shimao Toshio, *Naze dayori*, Ningen sensho (Tokyo: Nōsan-gyōson bunka kyōkai, 1977), 9.

38. Nakagami Kenji, Ōe Kenzaburō, Yamaguchi Masao, and Kusano Taeko, "Pansori no kosumorojii," in *Nakagami Kenji hatsugen shūsei 6* (Tokyo: Daisan bunmeisha, 1999), 65.

39. Certainly Shimao is committed to aligning his sense of literature to forms that are not visible to the *bundan* literary establishment from places outside its vision. In essays on provincial (*chihō*) literature and Tohoku writings, he looks to decenter the metropolitan cultural imaginary. His model is very nation based at a time when Nakagami is starting to accept different scales. Shimao is always interested in the Japanese metropole; and, when he excludes other influences (China, India), it is on the basis of their national cultural production and its histories of relation with Japan.

40. For descriptions of these debates on stagnation (*teitairon*), see E. Taylor Atkins, "The Dual Career of 'Arirang': The Korean Resistance Anthem that Became a Japanese Pop Hit," *The Journal of Asian Studies* 66, no. 3 (2007): 645–87; Kim Brandt, *Kingdom of Beauty: Mingei and the Politics of Folk Art in Imperial Japan* (Durham, N.C.: Duke University Press, 2007), esp. chapter 1; and Hatada Takashi, *Chōsen to Nihonjin* (Tokyo: Keisō shobō, 1983), 66–92.

41. Ōba, "Nakagami Kenji 'Kankoku'-ron josetsu," 6.

42. Ibid.

43. Nakagami Kenji, "Chosha no ikyo suru Yangban-teki tachiba ga mondai," *Asahi jānaru* 1343 (1984): 68; Ōba, "Nakagami Kenji 'kankoku'-ron hihan," 9.

44. Chongmoo Choi, "The Minjung Culture Movement and the Construction of Popular Culture in Korea," in *South Korea's Minjung Movement*, 109.

45. Kim Chi-ha, "Aratamete Nihon o miru," trans. Takasaki Sōji, *Sekai* 471 (February 1985): 173–84; Ōba, "Nakagami Kenji 'kankoku'-ron hihan," 11.

46. "Būmu no gyojitsu (Seoul gorin-kaimaku made 101–nichi: 4)," *Asahi shinbun* June 6, 1988, Chōkan ed., 1.

47. "Nikkan bunka kōryū ni nozomu," 5.

48. Robinson, *Korea's Twentieth-Century Odyssey*, 93.

49. Nakagami and Ri, "Naze pansori ka?" 437.

50. Ibid.

51. Nakagami, "Karatani Kōjin e no tegami," 90.

52. Suzuki Sadami, *Taishō seimei-shugi to gendai* (Tokyo: Kawade shobō shinsha, 1995), 3.

53. Philip Auslander, *Liveness: Performance in a Mediatized Culture* (London: Routledge, 2008), 8 and 183.

54. Nakagami, "Rinbu suru, Seoul," 192 and 210; Nakagami and Ri, "Naze pansori ka?" 436.

55. Nakagami and Han U-san, "Nikkan kōryū no shin-jidai," in *Nakagami Kenji mishūroku tairon shūsei*, 447.

56. Nakagami, "Fūkei no mukō e," 35.

57. Ibid.

58. Nakagami, "Bunka no kitei ni aru mono," 465.

59. Nakagami, "Chosha no ikyo suru," 68.

60. Nakagami's use of *senmin* to indicate all outcasts through the various kinds of governance and classification from the Kamakura era to the present is probably anachronistic. It condenses many precipitates of outcast into one metonymic structure. Work by Amino Yoshihiko that began to appear in the late 1970s emphasized the shifting nature of status categories as well as the flexible nature of the state that created them. See Amino Yoshihiko, *Muen kugai raku: nihon chūsei no jiyū to heiwa* (Tokyo: Heibonsha Iaiburarī, 1996).

61. Marshall R. Pihl, *The Korean Singer of Tales* (Cambridge, Mass.: Council on East Asian Studies, Harvard University Press, 1994), 8.

62. Ibid., 3.

63. David Eason, "Tracing the Path of 'Medieval Travelers': A Few Words on Amino Yoshihiko's Historical Approach and Legacy," *Review of Japanese Society and Culture* 19 (2007): 8.

64. Nakagami, "Rinbu suru, Seoul," 192.

65. Nakagami, "Fūkei no mukō e," 63.

66. Ibid., 70.

67. Ibid.

68. Nakagami, "Fūkei no mukō e," 59.

69. Ibid., 58.

70. Ibid., 58.

71. Nakagami, "Chosha no ikyo suru," 68; Nakagami, "Fūkei no mukō e," 53 and 56.

72. Nakagami Kenji, "Monogatari wa rinbu suru," in *Fūkei no mukō e/Monogatari no keifu*, 85.

73. Nakagami, "Rinbu suru, Seoul," 164.

74. Ibid., 170.

75. The authors are referring to Friedman's 2005 collection of essays that celebrate globalization. See Thomas L. Friedman, *The World Is Flat: A Brief History of the Twenty-First Century* (New York: Farrar, Straus and Giroux, 2005).

76. Alfred J. López and Ashok K. Mohapatra, "India in a Global Age; or, The Neoliberal Epiphany," *Global South* 2, no. 1 (2008): 2.

77. Ibid.

78. Ibid., 1.

79. Lafcadio Hearn, "Insect Musicians," in *Exotics and Retrospectives* (Upper Saddle River, N.J.: Literature House, 1969), 39–80.

80. Nakagami, "Rinbu suru, Seoul," 161.

81. An Ushoku, "Gendai kankoku bungaku to Nakagami Kenji," *Kokubungaku* 36, no. 14 (1992): 86.

82. Okakura Kakuzō, *The Ideals of the East, with Special Reference to the Art of Japan* (London: J. Murray, 1905), 5.

83. See Yanagi Muneyoshi and Bernard Leach, *The Unknown Craftsman: A Japanese Insight into Beauty* (Tokyo: Kodansha International, 1972).

84. Yanagi Muneyoshi and Bernard Leach, "The Way of Craftsmanship" (1927), in *The Unknown Craftsman*, 198. Folk crafts are different than individual, industrial, and aristocratic crafts. For a history of *mingei* as imagined by Yanagi and other artist-collectors, see Brandt, *Kingdom of Beauty*.

85. Nakagami and Han, "Nikkan kōryū no shin-jidai," 447.

86. On Kadokawa's revamp of film production, see Alexander Zahlten, *The Role of Genre in Film from Japan* (PhD diss., Vols. 1 and 2, University of Mainz, 2009).

87. Nakagami, "Monogatari wa rinbu suru," 81.

88. See Hikmet L. A. Aghanigian, *Cinerama: Its History and Development* (Los Angeles, University of Southern California, 1965).

89. Cinerama Inc., *Cinerama Plunges You into an Exciting New World* (Los Angeles, 1952), 7.

90. In *Shashin wa sensō da: genba kara no senkyo hōkoku* (Tokyo: Kawade shobō shinsha, 1998), Shinoyama Kishin describes his technique as an extreme form of objectivity in which his point of view, as well as that of a viewer, is effaced. His approach is almost the diametric opposite of the *shi-shashin* (personal photo) technique Araki Nobuyoshi follows, in which the photo is the culmination and record of a long process of seducing his photographic object. See also Iizawa Kōtarō's *Shi-shashin-ron* (Tokyo: Chikuma shobō, 2000). The two photographers discuss their differences in a later roundtable discussion, Araki Nobuyoshi and Shinoyama Kishin, "Kimi to boku to wa konna ni chigau," *Bungei shunjū* 67, no. 11 (1989): 366–76.

91. Kawamura Minato blasts Araki's photos, likening their display of the pleasured female body to *kisaeng* sex tours popular with Japanese men. Nakagami reacts in faux offense by saying that the camera is not a phallus: because it develops film, it is a womb! Nakagami Kenji, "Yi Yang-ji *Koku*: Kankoku to Nihon no genzai," *Shinchō* 82, no. 5 (1985): 312.

92. Nakagami, *Monogatari Seoul*, 6–7.

93. Kim Chi-ha, "Five Bandits," in *Sources of Korean Tradition 2*, ed. Yŏngho Ch'oe, Peter H. Lee, and Wm. Theodore de Bary (New York: Columbia University Press, 2000), 403–5.

94. Nakagami, *Monogatari Seoul*, 23.

95. Ibid.

96. Ibid., 214.

97. Ibid.

98. Ibid.

99. Ibid., 211.

100. Nakagami, "Fūkei no mukō e," 25–26.

101. Van Gessel, *The Sting of Life: Four Contemporary Japanese Novelists* (New York: Columbia University Press, 1989), 6.

102. Nakagami Kenji and Chikushi Tetsuya, "Shōsetsu no kanōsei to Minakata-teki sōzō-ryoku," in *Nakagami Kenji hasshin shūsei 5*, ed. Karatani Kōjin and Suga Hidemi (Tokyo: Daisan bunmeisha, 1996), 110.

6. Subculture and the South

1. For example, Tomiko Yoda and Harry D. Harootunian ed., *Japan after Japan: Social and Cultural Life from the Recessionary 1990s to the Present* (Durham, N.C.: Duke University Press, 2006).

2. See Murakami Takashi, *Sūpa furatto = Super flat* (Tokyo: Madora shuppan, 2000).

3. Douglas McGray, "Japan's Gross National Cool," *Foreign Policy* 130 (May/June 2002): 44.

4. Anne Allison, *Millennial Monsters: Japanese Toys and the Global Imagination* (Berkeley: University of California Press, 2006), 2.

5. Azuma's recent work places light novels at the center of his writing. See Azuma Hiroki, *Gēmu-teki realizumu no tanjō: dōbutsu-ka suru posutomodan* (Tokyo: Kōdansha gendai shinsho, 2007).

6. See Dana Goodyear, "I ♥ Novels—Young Women Develop a Genre for the Cellular Age," *New Yorker*, December 22–29, 2008, 62–68; and special issues on portable worlds (kētai sekai) in *Kokubungaku* (April 2008) and literature as information/information as literature (bungaku toshite no jōhō/jōhō toshite no bungaku) in *Nihon bungaku* (January 2008).

7. See Howard Becker, "The Chicago School, So-called," *Qualitative Sociology* 22, no.1 (1999): 3–12.

8. See Albert K. Cohen, *Delinquent Boys: The Culture of the Gang* (Glencoe, Ill.: Free Press, 1955); and Howard Becker, *Outsiders: Studies in the Sociology of Deviance* (London: Free Press of Glencoe, 1963).

9. Azuma Hiroki. *Otaku: Japan's Database Animals*, trans. Jonathan Abel and Shion Kono (Minneapolis: University of Minnesota Press, 2009), xv.

10. Dick Hebdige, *Subculture, the Meaning of Style* (London: Methuen, 1979), 18.

11. Stuart Hall and Tony Jefferson, *Resistance through Rituals: Youth Subcultures in Post-war Britain* (London: Hutchinson, 1976), 6.

12. Ōtsuka was involved in a long dispute with fiction writer Shōno Yoriko that characterized him as a neoliberal promoter of "literature that sells" but subsequently published several works attempting to introduce modern fiction to "amateurs" (*shoshinsha*). His literary genealogy is quite indebted to Karatani Kōjin's treatment of the *genbun-ichi* ideology of writing that wants to fix a signifier to a specific signified and the confessional novel. It depends heavily on a literary history that begins the history of modern fiction with Tayama Katai's 1906 *The Quilt*, which features what Azuma deems the first appearance of a "character." Azuma, *Gēmu-teki realizumu no tanjō*, 85.

13. His wariness dates to an earlier sense of "crisis." See Ōe Kenzaburō and Ōoka Shōhei, "Jun bungaku no kiki o koete," *Gunzō* 41, no. 10 (1986): 312–33. He later reconciled with Murakami by recommending him for the Yomiuri Prize in 1994.

14. For a broader description of Etō's stance on cultural nationalism, see Ann Sherif, "The Politics of Loss: On Etō Jun," *positions: east asia cultures critique* 10, no. 1 (2002): 111–39.

15. Etō Jun, "Murakami Ryū—Akutagawa-sho jushō no nansensu," Sandē mainichi, July 25, 1976, 136.

16. Murakami Ryū, *Almost Transparent Blue* (Tokyo: Kodansha International, 1981), 7.

17. Karatani Kōjin, "Sōzōryoku no bēsu," in *Ryū Book* (Tokyo: Gendai shi techō shuppan, 1990), 84.

18. Etō Jun, *Zen bungei jihyō 1* (Tokyo: Shinchōsha, 1989), 445.

19. Mabuchi Kōsuke, *"Zoku"tachi no sengo-shi* (Tokyo: Sanseidō, 1989), 13.

20. See Dazai Osamu, *The Setting Sun*, trans. Donald Keene (New York: New Directions, 1968). See also W. David Marx, "The Origin of Zoku," *Néojaponisme*, February 3, 2009, http://neojaponisme.com/2009/02/03/the-origin-of-zoku/.

21. Ibid., 2.

22. Ibid., 3.

23. Ibid., 5.

24. Ōtsuka Eiji, *Teihon monogatari shōhi-ron* (Tokyo: Kadokawa bunko, 2001 [1989]).

25. Ibid., 10

26. Ibid., 10–11.

27. Ōtsuka Eiji, *Sabukaruchā bungaku-ron* (Tokyo: Asahi shinbunsha, 2004), 9.

28. Ōhashi Kenzaburō, "Fōkunā to Nihon no shōsetsu (6): Nakagami Kenji to 'katari,'" *Eigo seinen* 127, no. 6 (1981): 391.

29. Kawamura Minato, *Sengo bungaku o tou: sono taiken to rinen* (Tokyo: Iwanami shoten, 1995), 230–33.

30. Azuma Hiroki and Maeda Rui, "Chichi-goroshi no sōshitsu, haha-moe no kajō—Frattona sekai de Nakagami Kenji o yominaosu," *Yuriika* 40, no. 11 (2008): 66–79.

31. My account of Azuma's intellectual genealogy is taken largely from a lecture he gave at the Association for Asian Studies annual meeting, March 29, 2009. The occasion feted the publication of his book in English; some information is from a personal conversation after the lecture.

32. Azuma, *Gēmu-teki realizumu no tanjō*, 80.

33. Azuma, *Gēmu-teki realizumu no tanjō*, 75.

34. Ōtsuka Eiji, "Nakagami Kenji mikōkan shiryō: *Minami kaiki-sen* daiichiwa gekiga gensaku kyakuhon," *Shin genjitsu* 3 (2004): 182.

35. "Kumano daigaku to wa?" Kumano Daigaku internet, February 2004, http://www.kumanodaigaku.net/what/what.html.

36. Ōtsuka Eiji, *Kanojotachi no rengō sekigun: sabukaruchā to sengo minshū-shugi* (Tokyo: Bungei shunjū, 1996), 236.

37. See Kasahara Chiaki, Reiko Tomii, and Murakami Takashi ed., *Little Boy: The Arts of Japan's Exploding Subculture*, ed. (New Haven, Conn.: Yale University Press, 2005); and Azuma, *Otaku: Japan's Database Animals*.

38. Abe Kazushige, *Indabijuaru purojekushon* (Tokyo: Kōdansha, 1996).

39. Yomota, *Kishu to tensei* (Tokyo: Shinchōsha, 1987), 218.

40. Murakami Rori, "'Minami' e no michi—'Izoku' (Nakagami Kenji) no baai," *Nihon bungaku* 48, no. 1 (1999): 54–63.

41. Nakagami Kenji, "Gekidō suru Firipin," in *Nakagami Kenji zenshū* 8, ed. Karatani Kōjin et al. (Tokyo: Shūeisha, 1996), 635; 636.

42. Thomas Schnellbächer, "Has the Empire Sunk Yet?—The Pacific in Japanese Science Fiction," *Science Fiction Studies* 29, no. 3 (2002): 382–96.

43. Yano Ryūkei, *Yano Ryūkei shū*, Meiji bungaku zenshū 15, ed. Ochi Haruo (Tokyo: Chikuma shobō, 1970), 77–178.

44. Kawamura Minato, "Taishō orientarizumu to Ajia ninshiki," in *Bunka no naka no shokuminchi* 7, Iwanami kōza kindai Nihon to shokuminchi (Tokyo: Iwanami shoten, 2004), 107–36. Thanks to Ben Uchiyama for this reference.

45. Robert Tierney, *Going Native: Imagining Savages in the Japanese Empire* (PhD diss., Stanford University, 2005), 138–39.

46. Kawamura, "Taishō orientarizumu to Ajia ninshiki," 107.

47. Ibid., 108.

48. Ōsawa Nobuaki, "'Minami kaiki-sen' chūshaku nōto," in *Senji-ka no "otaku,"* ed. Sakakibara Gō (Tokyo: Kadokawa shoten, 2006), 94 and 102.

49. As Tierney (*Going Native*, 146) notes, Nakajima published two collections of stories in 1942. Both drew on his experiences in Palau, working for the colonial Japanese government, and were included in *Nantōtan* (Tales of the southern islands). Nakajima Atsushi, *Nantōtan* (Tōkyō: Konnichi no mondaisha, 1942).

50. Minamoto no Yoshitsune was a twelfth-century general who battled a legendary monk, Benkei, and won. Benkei then became Yoshitsune's retainer and right-hand man, and died defending him.

51. Nakagami Kenji and Tanaka Akio, *Minami kaiki-sen*, Vol. 3, Akushon komikkusu (Tokyo: Futabasha, 1990), 95–97.

52. See Noel Rutherford, ed., *Friendly Islands: A History of Tonga* (Melbourne: Oxford University Press, 1977).

53. See Mark R. Peattie, *Nan'yō: The Rise and Fall of the Japanese in Micronesia, 1885–1945* (Honolulu: University of Hawai'i Press, 1988).

54. See Yano Tōru, *Nihon no nan'yō shikan* (Tōkyō: Chūō kōronsha, 1979), for descriptions of *seiji shōsetsu* set in the South Seas.

55. Nakagami Kenji, "Gekidō suru Filipin: Shin-jinmin kanbu intabyū," in *Nakagami Kenji zenshū 15* (Tōkyō: Shūeisha, 1996), 634.

56. See Tsubouchi Shōyō, *Shōsetsu shinzui*, in *Tsubouchi Shōyō shū, Nihon kindai bungaku taikei 3* (Tokyo: Kadokawa shoten, 1974).

57. See Michael Brownstein, "From Kokugaku to Kokubungaku: Canon-Formation in the Meiji Period," *Harvard Journal of Asiatic Studies* 47, no. 2 (1987): 435–60; and Tomiko Yoda, *Gender and National Literature: Heian Texts in the Constructions of Japanese Modernity* (Durham, N.C.: Duke University Press, 2004), esp. chapter 2.

58. See Takizawa Bakin and Shirai Kyoji, *Gendaigo-yaku nansō satomi hakkenden* (Tokyo: Kawade shobō shinsha, 2004).

59. Azuma and Maeda, "Chichi-goroshi no sōshitsu," 66–79.

60. See Richard Siddle, "Ainu Liberation and Welfare Colonialism," in *Race, Resistance and the Ainu of Japan* (London: Routledge, 1996), 147–70.

61. Nakagami Kenji, "Izoku," in *Nakagami Kenji zenshū 8* (Tokyo: Shūeisha, 1996), 705.

62. Yomota sees the motif of the wandering prince, the *kishu ryūri-tan*, as one of the myths that Nakagami's stories commonly reprise. See Yomota, *Kishu to tensei*, 155.

63. See Hiramatsu Hiroshi, *Hīrō no shūjigaku* (Tokyo: Seikyūsha, 1993).

64. Moriyasu Toshiji, *Nakagami Kenji-ron: Kumano, roji, gensō* (Osaka: Kaihō shuppansha, 2003), 247.

65. Etō Jun, "'Roji' to takai: koe to moji to buntai," *Bungei* 22, no. 12 (1983): 32–42; Yoshimoto Takaaki, *Masu imēji-ron* (Tokyo: Fukutake bunko, 1988), 95.

66. Moriyasu, *Nakagami Kenji-ron*, 248.

67. Nakagami Kenji, *Sen'nen no yuraku* (Tokyo: Kawade bungei bunko, 1992), 98–99.

Conclusion

1. Nakagami Kenji, "Hanzai-sha Nagayama Norio kara no hōkoku," in *Tori no yō ni, kemono no yō ni* (Tokyo: Kōdansha bungei bunko, 1994), 130.

Index

ANNE McKNIGHT is assistant professor of East Asian languages and cultures and of comparative literature at the University of Southern California.